MW00620168

"Gregory Beale's work on the tem[............ ... unuer-
standing the whole Bible. This shorter version will enable an even wider readership to grasp the often-forgotten message that the really important thing is not how we get up to God but how God's design is to come and dwell with us."

N. T. Wright, senior research fellow at Wycliffe Hall, Oxford, emeritus professor of New Testament and early Christianity at University of St Andrews

"Beale and Kim show the theme of God's presence among us from Genesis to Revelation. We taste in this book the glory, radiance, comfort, and strength of God's presence. At the same time, we learn how to read the entire Bible as we trace the tabernacle/temple theme throughout the Scriptures. A vital and compelling work for students, pastors, and all who want to delve more deeply into God's Word."

Thomas R. Schreiner, associate dean of the School of Theology at The Southern Baptist Theological Seminary

"The importance of this book lies in . . . its evocative unpacking of the theme of the temple . . .; its modeling of the way biblical theology is to be done; and its capacity to cause readers to perceive fresh and wonderful things in the Scriptures."

D. A. Carson, emeritus professor of New Testament at Trinity Evangelical Divinity School

"God dwelling in the midst of his people: this staggering vision is the heart of God's covenantal purposes from Genesis to Revelation. *God Dwells Among Us* brings decades of scholarship on this topic to a wider audience. More than that, it shows how this major biblical theme is the engine of mission in the world today. This clear and compelling study is a real feast."

Michael Horton, J. Gresham Machen Professor of Systematic Theology and Apologetics at Westminster Seminary California

"In Scripture, God dwells not only up above the world but also among us, with us, and within us. Our hearts long to hear more of God's presence, his promise to be with us. One important way for us to understand God's presence in Scripture is through its teaching about the temple and of Jesus as the true temple. Greg Beale has developed this theme cogently in scholarly writings. In *God Dwells Among Us* he and Mitchell Kim have made these ideas accessible to working pastors. It is a valuable aid to preaching and an excellent antidote to the feeling of loneliness that afflicts many today. I recommend it highly."

John Frame, emeritus professor of systematic theology and philosophy at Reformed Theological Seminary

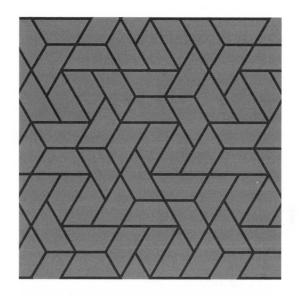

GOD DWELLS AMONG US

A Biblical Theology of the Temple

G. K. BEALE
AND MITCHELL KIM

ivp
Academic

An imprint of InterVarsity Press
Downers Grove, Illinois

InterVarsity Press
P.O. Box 1400, Downers Grove, IL 60515-1426
ivpress.com
email@ivpress.com

First edition ©2014 by G. K. Beale and Mitchell Kim
Published in this format in 2021

*InterVarsity Press® is the book-publishing division of InterVarsity Christian Fellowship/USA®, a
movement of students and faculty active on campus at hundreds of universities, colleges, and schools
of nursing in the United States of America, and a member movement of the International Fellowship
of Evangelical Students. For information about local and regional activities, visit intervarsity.org.*

Cover design and image composite: David Fassett
Interior design: Daniel van Loon
Image: vector pattern: © ilyast / DigitalVision Vectors / Getty Images

ISBN 978-0-8308-5535-3 (print)
ISBN 978-0-8308-5536-0 (digital)

Printed in the United States of America ♾

*InterVarsity Press is committed to ecological stewardship and to the conservation of natural resources
in all our operations. This book was printed using sustainably sourced paper.*

Library of Congress Cataloging-in-Publication Data

Names: Beale, G. K. (Gregory K.), 1949- author. | Kim, Mitchell, author.
Title: God dwells among us : a biblical theology of the temple / G.K. Beale
    and Mitchell Kim.
Description: Downers Grove, IL : IVP Academic, 2021. | Series: Essential
    studies in biblical theology | Includes bibliographical references and
    indexes.
Identifiers: LCCN 2021030790 (print) | LCCN 2021030791 (ebook) | ISBN
    9780830855353 (paperback) | ISBN 9780830855360 (ebook)
Subjects: LCSH: Presence of God. | Temple of God. | Eden. |
    Bible--Theology.
Classification: LCC BT180.P6 B43 2021 (print) | LCC BT180.P6 (ebook) |
    DDC 231.7--dc23
LC record available at https://lccn.loc.gov/2021030790
LC ebook record available at https://lccn.loc.gov/2021030791
A catalog record for this book is available from the Library of Congress.

P   25 24 23 22 21 20 19 18 17 16 15 14 13 12 11 10 9 8 7 6 5 4 3 2

Y   39 38 37 36 35 34 33 32 31 30 29 28 27 26 25 24 23 22

CONTENTS

FOREWORD

MARY DORINDA BEALE

HAVE YOU EVER WONDERED about some of the people described in the Bible? Some of them frankly seem superhuman, not quite real. For example, it seems odd that Paul and Silas sang in prison. Would I sing if I were in prison? Would I have the attitude expressed in Hebrews 10:34, where it portrays Christians as accepting "joyfully" the seizure of their property? Would I be joyful if the authorities came and seized my house? In Acts 5:40-41, it says they flogged the apostles and told them not to speak in the name of Jesus any more. Their response is not what I consider a normal reaction. They went away rejoicing because "they were counted worthy to suffer dishonor for the name."

Would I rejoice if I suffered shame and was beaten? Why is their response so different? How can they act so totally different from most of us? It is as though their reality was different or they were seeing things that the natural eye cannot see. In 2 Kings 6, Elisha prays for his servant. The two men are surrounded by the army of Syria. The servant of Elisha is, naturally,

This foreword originally appeared in G. K. Beale, *The Temple and the Church's Mission: A Biblical Theology of the Dwelling Place of God*, NSBT 17 (Downers Grove, IL: InterVarsity Press, 2004). Republished here with permission.

distressed. Elisha comforts him with these words: "Do not be afraid, for those who are with us are more than those who are with them" (v. 16). I have never been very good at arithmetic, but I do know that a Syrian army outnumbers two men! Elisha then prays that God would open his servant's eyes. We discover that the servant sees "the mountain was full of horses and chariots of fire all around." What happened? He was given eyes to see true reality!

What is this true reality that can so alter all that we say and do? When one becomes a Christian, real truth is seen. True reality is the fact that humanity is drowning in a sea of sin with no way to save itself. The only hope is to cry out to God. Only Jesus, the Messiah, can save. If you cling to him as your Savior, you will not be carried away in the sea of sin because he is the rock of our salvation (Acts 4:10-12).

Second Corinthians 5:17 says, "If anyone is in Christ, he is a new creation. The old has passed away; behold, the new has come." How is this newness of life as a Christian manifested? It seems as though Nicodemus's question to Jesus is understandable: "How can a man be born when he is old? Can he enter a second time into his mother's womb and be born?" (John 3:4). Jesus answers this perplexing question in verse 6, "That which is born of the flesh is flesh, and that which is born of the Spirit is spirit." The significance seems to be that the Spirit is different. It is not at all like the flesh. So, how can we still remain in our fleshly bodies and yet "walk in newness of life" (Rom 6:4)? First Peter 2:11 tells us that we are "sojourners and exiles" on earth, which means earth is not our home. Instead, Ephesians 2:19-22 explains, our home is in heaven, and we are *now* "members of the household of God" (see also 1 Tim 3:15). How can we really be part of God's household *now*? We live on earth. Are we not just in a holding pattern until we actually die or the world ends? Aren't we only looking forward to the future time when we will be part of "the household of God"?

Since Scripture tells us that we are *now* part of God's household and are not just wandering around as sojourners on earth, where is God's household, who is there, and what difference does it make anyway? Hebrews 12:22-24 explains very clearly where we are and who is there with us:

> But you have come to Mount Zion and to the city of the living God, the heavenly Jerusalem, and to innumerable angels in festal gathering, and to the assembly of the firstborn who are enrolled in heaven, and to God, the judge of all, and to the spirits of the righteous made perfect, and to Jesus, the mediator of a new covenant, and to the sprinkled blood that speaks a better word than the blood of Abel.

When we, like Elisha's servant, have our eyes of faith opened, the awesome fact is that we are in the presence of God, and Jesus the mediator of a new covenant. "He has delivered us from the domain of darkness and transferred us to the kingdom of his beloved Son" (Col 1:13). We are there now. Christians are "living stones," "being built up as a spiritual house" (1 Pet 2:5).

When my oldest daughter, Nancy, was three years old, our family lived in England. In the spring of that year, Nancy and I were invited to a picnic at a very large country estate. As we walked around the house and grounds, I realized that she was hardly fazed by the splendor and beauty of this magnificent estate. I pulled her aside and said, "Nancy, I know you are very young, but this is a special place. Try to remember this day."

We, like my daughter, need to be pulled aside and told that we are in the most special place of all—*now*—God's palatial mountain-temple.

This book will explain in detail where we are and the beauty and splendor of the new Jerusalem, the temple of the living God. Israel's physical temple which was seen by the naked eye was a mere shadow of the heavenly reality (Heb 9:24)! May God open our eyes to understand,

> Blessed is the one you choose and bring near,
> to dwell in your courts!
> We shall be satisfied with the goodness of your house,
> the holiness of your temple! (Ps 65:4)

SERIES PREFACE

BENJAMIN L. GLADD

THE ESSENTIAL STUDIES IN BIBLICAL THEOLOGY is patterned after the highly esteemed series New Studies in Biblical Theology, edited by D. A. Carson. Like the NSBT, this series is devoted to unpacking the various strands of biblical theology. The field of biblical theology has grown exponentially in recent years, showing no sign of abating. At the heart of biblical theology is the unfolding nature of God's plan of redemption as set forth in the Bible.

With an influx of so many books on biblical theology, why generate yet another series? A few reasons. The ESBT is dedicated to the fundamental or "essential" broad themes of the grand story line of the Bible. Stated succinctly, the goal of the ESBT series is to explore the *central* biblical-theological themes of the Bible. Several existing series on biblical theology are generally open-ended, whereas the ESBT will be limited to ten or so volumes. By restricting the entire series, the scope of the project is established from the beginning. The ESBT project functions as a whole in that each theme is intentional, and each volume does not stand solely on its own merits. The individual volumes interlock with one another and, taken together, form a complete and cohesive unit.

Another unique dimension of the series is a robust emphasis on biblical theology, spanning the entire sweep of the history of redemption. Each volume traces a particular theme throughout the Bible, from Genesis 1–3 to Revelation 21–22, and is organically connected to the person of Christ and the church in the New Testament. To avoid a flat biblical theology, these projects are mindful of how the New Testament develops their topics in fresh or unexpected ways. For example, the New Testament sheds new light on the nature of the kingdom and messiah. Though these twin themes are rooted and explored in the Old Testament, both flow through the person of Christ in unique ways. Biblical theology should include how Old Testament themes are held in continuity and discontinuity with the New Testament.

The audience of the series includes beginning students of theology, church leaders, and laypeople. The ESBT is intended to be an accessible introduction to core biblical-theological themes of the Bible. This series is not designed to overturn every biblical-theological rock and investigate the finer details of biblical passages. Each volume is intentionally brief, serving as a primer of sorts that introduces the reader to a particular theme. These works also attempt to apply their respective biblical-theological themes to Christian living, ministry, and worldview. Good biblical theology warms the heart and motivates us to grow in our knowledge and adoration of the triune God.

AUTHORS' PREFACE

WHY DID WE WRITE THIS BOOK? We pray that its biblical-theological perspective might fuel the church to fulfill its mission in the world. In writing this book, we see more clearly than ever that the themes of Eden, the temple, God's glorious presence, new creation, and the mission of the church are ultimately facets of the same reality. More specifically, we hope to build a bridge from the world of biblical theology to the needs of the church. The substance and basic thesis of the book is distilled from G. K. Beale, *The Temple and the Church's Mission: A Biblical Theology of the Dwelling Place of God*.[1] The original book spanned from Genesis to Revelation, exploring both the ancient Near Eastern and Second Temple Jewish views of the temple. More extensive argumentation from the biblical text as well as the surrounding world can be found in that original book. However, the basic thesis of this book was then developed into a seven-week sermon series preached by Mitchell Kim at Living Water Alliance Church in Chicagoland, and then condensed into a seminar given at different conferences.

---

[1] *The Temple and the Church's Mission: A Biblical Theology of the Dwelling Place of God*, NSBT (Downers Grove, IL: InterVarsity Press, 2004).

Writing and speaking are two very different mediums. Writing gives liberty to provide in-depth substantiation and explore secondary lines of support for an argument. Preaching demands a laser-like focus on communicating a single point. Adapting the considerable substance of the original temple book to preaching demanded a radical reduction in order to communicate orally. Translating the preached sermons back to a written format allowed a significant amplification and deepening of the preached material while we attempted to maintain the vibrancy and focus of preaching. Some material has been lifted verbatim from the original book; most has been reworked and reworded to communicate more concisely and clearly. Our hope is that the biblical-theological heft of the original will be combined with practical insight to spark a greater zeal and passion for mission by God's people in the world.

There has been somewhat of a hermeneutical shift from the original book to this one. In the original book, G. K. Beale tried to sketch the development of the temple idea through each of the various distinct redemptive-historical epochs (Eden/Noahic/Patriarchal/Israel [Mount Sinai→wilderness tabernacle→Jerusalem temple] /inaugurated latter days/consummated latter days) in order to see how they related to and built on one another. However, because of the condensed nature of this book, we sometimes merge the meaning of the temple in earlier epochs with the developed meaning from later epochs (especially in the earlier chapters). In cases of any ambiguity, the reader should consult the original book.

God has often used our wives to help our theology connect into the realities of daily life. We are both deeply indebted to our wives, Dorinda Beale and Eunsil Kim, who have not only discussed the theology of the temple with us, but also forced us to live out this theology by bringing the presence of God into our homes. They have been crucial in helping us to understand this topic in more depth. In writing this book, we have personally lived out its call to "Be fruitful and multiply and fill the earth" (Gen 1:28), as God has blessed us with children and grandchildren! Greg Beale had a granddaughter, Eden Klamm, and Mitch Kim had a daughter, Eden River Kim. Their names reflect our prayers for these children: that they would abound with life in the presence of God and serve to expand that presence to the ends of the earth.

Too many other people deserve mention in this book. Don Carson made a significant investment in reading and carefully evaluating the original book. His suggestions for revision have definitely made this a better book than it would have been! Brannon Ellis at InterVarsity Press has helped to translate its academic depth to communicate to a broader swath of God's people. His gracious and encouraging input throughout the journey has been invaluable.

Above all, we are thankful to God for the idea for this book and for giving the energy and discipline to write it. We pray that God's glory might be clearly seen through all who read it.

A few comments about some stylistic aspects of the book are in order. English translations follow the English Standard Version or, when different, have been identified as our own translation. With respect to all translations of ancient works, when the translation differs from the standard editions usually referred to, then it is our translation or someone else's (in the latter case we indicate whom).

Dedicated to Eden Kim and Eden Klamm with all our other children (Stephen, Nancy, Hannah, Elise, and Ana) that they might abide as an overflow from God's dwelling place to the ends of the earth.

ABBREVIATIONS

ICC	International Critical Commentary
NICOT	New International Commentary on the Old Testament
NIGTC	New International Greek Testament Commentary
NIVAC	New International Version Application Commentary
NSBT	New Studies in Biblical Theology
WBC	Word Biblical Commentary

INTRODUCTION

BEFORE DEPARTING FOR BURMA AT TWENTY-FOUR, Adoniram Judson's "deep conviction . . . to engage in this [missionary] service" was to be "devoted to this work for life, whenever God in His providence shall open the way."[1] His convictions were tested for thirty-eight years in Burma, through the loss of two wives, seven of thirteen children, and terrible sickness at sea that led to his death. In the face of constant persecution and imprisonment, he not only finished a Burmese-English dictionary and grammar but also translated the entire New Testament into Burmese. After ten years, he had one church of eighteen believers. Nevertheless, this crucible of suffering tempered and strengthened Judson's convictions:

> The path of self-denial is, to carnal eyes, a veiled path, a mystery of the divine kingdom . . . but if thou wilt do what thy hands find to do this hour . . . thou shalt find the path of self-denial open most wonderfully and delightfully before thee; thou shalt find it sweet to follow thy dear Lord and Saviour,

---

[1] Edward Judson, *The Life of Adoniram Judson* (Philadelphia: American Baptist Publication Society, 1883), 22, 24. This work, though dated, provides an in-depth compilation of primary sources from Judson's life, including letters, sermons, and essays that he had written. A popular and more recent biography is Courtney Anderson, *To the Golden Shore: The Life of Adoniram Judson* (Valley Forge, PA: Judson Press, 1987).

bearing the cross, and shalt soon be enabled to say,—"Sweet is the cross, above all sweets, To souls enamored with thy smiles."[2]

Even on his deathbed, he said, "No one has ever left the world with more inviting prospects, with brighter hopes, or warmer feelings—warmer feelings."[3] Deep conviction formed the bedrock of his sacrificial yet joy-filled labor. Today, Burma (known today as Myanmar) has over four million Christians because of that sacrifice.

Is such costly sacrifice an antiquated throwback to a distant past? Today, short-term missions teams can hop on an airplane, care for impoverished orphans in rural China for a week and stop by Starbucks in Beijing before returning to give a missions report in their comfortable church. Even as globalization has eased some of the demands of short-term missions, the challenges for missions today continue to be daunting. More than three thousand unreached and unengaged people groups remain today; they are in some of the hardest to reach places of the world, and they total almost 250 million people.[4] We must go. We must persevere even when we see little fruit.

Even in "Christian America," those with no religious affiliation are the fastest-growing religious group today, growing 28 percent between 2007 and 2012.[5] Both unreached people groups and the increasingly resistant West will only be penetrated by the gospel with great sacrifice and cost.

Will we make the sacrifice that mission demands? Recent studies of American young people are not encouraging. The goal of their faith is primarily "feeling good, happy, secure, at peace" because they desire "subjective well-being, being able to resolve problems, and getting along amiably with other people."[6] If Judson's goal was "subjective well-being," Burma would

---

[2]Adoniram Judson, "The Threefold Cord," quoted in Edward Judson, *Life of Adoniram Judson*, 575.
[3]Edward Judson, *Life of Adoniram Judson*, 518.
[4]"3,050 unreached people groups are not engaged with a church-planting strategy consistent with evangelical faith" (May 2014 Monthly Global Status of Evangelical Christianity report, www.imb.org/research/reports).
[5]Between 2007 and 2012, those in America who profess no religious affiliation grew 28% (from 15.3% of Americans to 19.6%), while Protestants decreased 9% (from 53% to 48%). Based on data from the Pew Forum, accessed at www.pewforum.org/2012/10/09/nones-on-the-rise.
[6]From the American Study of Youth and Religion; see detailed discussion in Christian Smith with Melinda Lundquist Denton, *Soul Searching: The Religious and Spiritual Lives of American Teenagers* (Oxford: Oxford University Press, 2005), 163-64.

remain in darkness today! Given the current challenges of settling into the sacrificial challenges of marriage and career,[7] how much more challenging will it be to embrace the sacrifices of global mission among the least-reached peoples on earth?

Compelling conviction propels us through painful sacrifice. The goal of this book is to strengthen biblical conviction for sacrificial mission. When we are motivated to mission through occasional experiences or isolated Bible verses, the springs of such motivation can run dry in the face of costly challenges. Persevering mission demands full-orbed conviction that is born out of careful and prayerful study of God's Word. Our conviction grows richer and stronger when grounded in God's cosmic mission from Genesis to Revelation. In the next section, we will summarize the purpose and progress of God's mission throughout the Bible that the rest of the book will flesh out.

BIBLICAL CONVICTION FOR SACRIFICIAL MISSION

In military combat, a mission's objectives are articulated through "commander's intent." The US Army has realized that battle plans often became useless ten minutes into the battle because the enemy did not follow the plan. When the opposing force threw off the "script," troops and officers on the ground became paralyzed about what to do next. The commander's intent addresses the problem by distilling the entire battle plan into a simple statement that would give soldiers the freedom and flexibility to improvise without getting off track. This directive helps soldiers adjust fluidly to changing conditions on the battlefield without losing sight of the objective.[8]

Like soldiers on the field, Christians must know their commander's intent. In order to fulfill our commander's intent in the changing and challenging situations of our lives, we must take time to form a compelling biblical picture of it.

---

[7]Young people settle into the commitments of marriage and career later than earlier generations, and many indulge in a "prolonged adolescence" in their late twenties or early thirties (see further in Christian Smith, *Lost in Transition* [Oxford: Oxford University Press, 2011], 149; Jeffery Arnett, *Emerging Adulthood: The Winding Road from the Late Teens Through Twenties* [Oxford: Oxford University Press, 2004]).

[8]Chip Heath and Dan Heath apply this principle to leadership in *Made to Stick* (New York: Random House, 2007), 24-28. We are indebted to David Lee from Harvest Community Church for this reference.

The Bible articulates our commander's intent by painting a picture of our "mission accomplished" in Revelation 21–22. In the closing chapters of Revelation, the new heaven and earth (Rev 21:1) is juxtaposed against a lengthy description of the new Jerusalem (Rev 21:1–22:5). Why does John only briefly mention "a new heaven and a new earth" before extensively describing the new Jerusalem? Probably John looks at the same picture from two different angles so that the resulting images interpret each another. Such juxtaposed images often interpret each another in Revelation (e.g., Rev 5:5-6, 7-13; 21:1- 3).[9] The new heaven and earth remind us of the expansive scope of the new creation, while the new Jerusalem highlights its purpose as a dwelling place for God. In this way, Revelation 21 pictures the entire cosmos and new creation as the dwelling place of God.

This picture in Revelation 21–22 fulfills the mission given in Genesis 1–2, and the progress of this mission can be traced throughout the entire Bible. In Genesis 1–2, Eden is the dwelling place of God, and God commissions Adam and Eve to expand the boundaries of that dwelling place to fill the earth (Gen 1:28). While God's original call seemed to be thwarted by sin in Genesis 3, God continues to establish his dwelling place among the patriarchs until the construction of the tabernacle and temple. After the destruction of Solomon's temple, the prophets anticipate the coming of a new and expanding temple, and these prophecies begin to be fulfilled in Jesus and the church. The church as the dwelling place of God must expand until one day it fills the entire heaven and earth; the entire cosmos becomes the dwelling place of God. Mission does not begin with the Great Commission of Matthew 28:18-20, but mission is God's heartbeat from Genesis 1 until the new heaven and earth become the dwelling place of the Lord God Almighty in Revelation 21–22. This ultimate picture of the whole earth filled with God's presence fulfills God's original intention from the sanctuary of Eden. We begin, therefore, with Eden.

---

[9]For example, the conquering Lion of Judah (Rev 5:5) is interpreted as a slain Lamb (Rev 5:6) because Christ's victory as a Lion is accomplished through his sacrifice as a Lamb. See further G. K. Beale, *The Book of Revelation*, NIGTC (Grand Rapids, MI: Eerdmans, 1999), 350-71 at Rev 5:5-6, 7-13 and 1039-48 at Rev 21:1-3.

Chapter One

EDEN AS A TEMPLE

THE CONTEXT OF GENESIS 1-2

LONGING. We are creatures of longing. When we misdiagnose the object of this longing, then we become frustrated and disappointed. Our longings for relationship often get frustrated in conflict. Our longings for satisfaction get frustrated in discontent. Our longings for significance get frustrated by our own inadequacies. J. R. R. Tolkien diagnoses the roots of our longing: "We all long for [Eden], and we are constantly glimpsing it: our whole nature at its best and least corrupted, its gentlest and most humane, is still soaked with a sense of 'exile.'"[1] The longings of our hearts are frustrated from this exile, but these longings are properly satisfied in the dwelling place of God originally found in Eden. God's presence in his dwelling place satiates our longings for relationship, satisfaction, and significance, and the opening chapters of Genesis show how God intended those longings to be properly satisfied—in Eden. God made us for himself as his images in the Garden-temple in Eden (Gen 1–2). God's presence gives life and purpose in Eden, so

---

[1]J. R. R. Tolkien, *The Letters of J. R. R. Tolkien*, ed. H. Carpenter and C. Tolkien (Boston: Houghton Mifflin, 2000), 110.

we should not wonder that "our hearts are restless until they find their rest in [him]."[2] In this chapter, we will explore how Eden is presented as a temple and dwelling place of God, satisfying our longings for life and purpose.

EDEN AS A DWELLING PLACE OF GOD

Eden is presented as a sanctuary and place where God dwells, as seen in Genesis 1–2 and the wider witness of the Old Testament.[3] Even the seemingly casual mention of God "walking" in the Garden of Eden (Gen 3:8) is rich with connotations that suggest God's presence in the temple. In Leviticus 26, the Lord promises that he will "*walk*" among them and be their God (Lev 26:12). In Deuteronomy 23, the Lord commands the Israelites to keep their camp holy because he "*walks*" in the midst of their camp (Deut 23:14). When David plans to build a temple in 2 Samuel 7, the Lord reminds him that "I have been *walking about* in a tent [the tabernacle!] for my dwelling" (2 Sam 7:6, translation altered). In a similar manner, the Lord is "walking" in Eden (Gen 3:8) because Eden itself was the temple and dwelling place of God.

More explicitly, Ezekiel calls Eden a temple, referring to it as "the garden of God . . . the holy mountain of God" containing "sanctuaries" (Ezek 28:13-14, 16, 18). "Mountain" and "sanctuaries" are both references elsewhere to the temple.[4] Ezekiel also speaks of an Adam-like person in Eden wearing bejeweled clothing like a priest (Ezek 28:13, alluding to Ex 28:17-20) whose sin profanes the sanctuaries and causes him to be cast out (Ezek 28:17-18).[5] Therefore, the Garden of Eden is most explicitly called a temple with an Adam-like figure as its priest in Ezekiel 28:18.

---

[2]Augustine, *Confessions*, trans. J. G. Pilkington (New York: Liveright Publishing, 1943), 1.
[3]A good overview of how a number of recent scholars argue this claim can be found in Richard M. Davidson, *Flame of Yahweh* (Peabody, MA: Hendrickson, 2007), 47-48.
[4]Eden was located on a mountain (Ezek 28:14, 16), just as Israel's temple (e.g., Ex 15:17) and the end-time temple (Ezek 40:2; 43:12; Rev 21:10) were located on mountains. "Sanctuaries" (Ezek 28:18) elsewhere refer to Israel's tabernacle (Lev 21:23) and temple (Ezek 7:24; see also Jer 51:51). Ezekiel probably refers to the one temple in the plural because of the multiple "holy places" within the temple complex (e.g., courtyard, Holy Place, Holy of Holies). There were even smaller sacred areas in the temple complex, e.g., of Solomon's temple (1 Chron 28:11) and of the second temple (1 Macc 10:43). Philo can refer to "the Holy of Holies" as "the Holies of Holies" (*Allegorical Interpretation* 2.56; *On the Change of Names* 192) or "the innermost places of the Holies" (*On Dreams* 1.216).
[5]See n. 10 below for further discussion on this figure as Adam.

A number of other lines of evidence help us see Eden as the first temple. The ark in the Holy of Holies, which contained the Law (which led to wisdom), echoes the tree of the knowledge of good and evil (which also led to wisdom). Both the touching of the ark and the partaking of the tree's fruit resulted in death. The entrance to Eden was from the east (Gen 3:24), just as the entrance to the temple was from the east (e.g., Ezek 40:6). Both Eden and the temple are characterized by the holy presence of God that brings wisdom.

God's presence in Eden is associated with images of life and purpose found in the Garden. The imagery in Eden paints a compelling picture of the satisfaction of basic human desires in God's presence. For example, the desire for life is satisfied by the waters of the river of life and the fruit of the tree of life. The need for purpose is fulfilled in Adam's priestly call to work and keep the Garden-temple (Gen 2:15; see Num 18:5). Parallels between Eden and the tabernacle/temple further demonstrate that our desire for life and purpose are properly satisfied in God's presence.

EDEN AND THE LONGING FOR SATISFACTION: THE TREE AND RIVER OF LIFE

In the concise narrative of Genesis 2, six verses describe the tree of life and the river flowing out of Eden (Gen 2:9-14). Is sacred Scripture "wasting" precious space here? In actuality such seemingly trivial details, easily skipped by a hasty reader, brim with the significance of life found in the presence of God. The verdant imagery of Eden, especially its trees and rivers, reflects abundant life in God's presence, and this verdant imagery is mirrored in the later tabernacle and temple.

The tree of life. Gen 2:9: "And out of the ground the LORD God made to spring up every tree that is pleasant to the sight and good for food. The tree of life was in the midst of the garden, and the tree of the knowledge of good and evil." The "tree of life" stood in the middle of the Garden, and the fruit of this tree would give life forever (Gen 3:22). Why? Proverbs 3 shows us that God's wisdom is compared to the "tree of life" and that his wisdom shines light on the paths of life and peace for God's people (Prov 3:16-18). Similarly, in the tabernacle and temple this "tree of life" served as the model for the lampstand outside the Holy of Holies, since the presence of God would shine light on the paths of life for his people. This lampstand looked like a small tree trunk with seven protruding branches with flowering almond blossoms (Ex 25:31-40; 37:17-24), a picture of the life-giving fruitfulness that is found in God's presence.[6]

Abundant life is seen not only in the tree itself but also in the verdant imagery of the Garden, since "out of the ground the Lord God made to spring up every tree that is pleasant to the sight and good for food" (Gen 2:9). Solomon's temple also abounds with such verdant imagery (1 Kings 6:18, 29, 32, 35; 7:18-20).[7] The end-time temple overflows with life, as trees of life grow on the banks of the river of life to bring healing for the nations (Ezek 47:12; Rev 22:2; see discussion below). The abundance of life found in the Garden paints a picture of the abundance found in the tabernacling presence of God. God's presence overflows with life.

The river of life.

Gen 2:10-14: A river flowed out of Eden to water the garden, and there it divided and became four rivers. The name of the first is the Pishon. It is the one that flowed around the whole land of Havilah, where there is gold. And the gold of that land is good; bdellium and onyx stone are there. The name of the second river is the Gihon. It is the one that flowed around the whole land of Cush. And the name of the third river is the Tigris, which flows east of Assyria. And the fourth river is the Euphrates.

A seemingly incidental reference to a river flowing out of Eden also reminds us of the abundant life flowing from the presence of God. This river in Eden gives life to the many trees growing on its banks, including the tree of the knowledge of good and evil and the tree of life (Gen 2:10, 17; 3:24). This water flows out of Eden to water the Garden before flowing outward to give

---

[6]This imagery is common in temples of the ancient Near East. See further discussion in Carol Meyers, "Lampstand," in *Anchor Bible Dictionary*, ed. D. N. Freedman (New York: Doubleday, 1992), 4:141-43; Howard N. Wallace, "Tree of Knowledge and Tree of Life," in *Anchor Bible Dictionary*, 6:656-60.

[7]E.g., this temple was filled with "cedar . . . carved in the form of gourds and open flowers" (1 Kings 6:18), "carved engraved figures of cherubim and palm trees and open flowers" (1 Kings 6:29; see vv. 32, 35), and "pomegranates" beneath the heads of the two pillars placed at the entrance of the Holy Place (1 Kings 7:18-20).

life to the rest of the earth and places where nations would reside (Gen 2:10-14). Similarly, in later depictions of the temple, a river flows with trees of life on its banks. In Ezekiel 47, a river flows from below the threshold of the temple with trees on the banks of both sides. The waters of this river make seawater fresh (Ezek 47:8), give life to creatures (Ezek 47:9), and cause leaves of healing to blossom on the trees of its banks (Ezek 47:12). In Revelation, a river flows in the new Jerusalem, with "the tree of life with its twelve kinds of fruit, yielding its fruit each month," and "the leaves of the tree were for the healing of the nations" (Rev 22:1-2). This river flows from the presence of God ("from the throne of God and of the Lamb") outward to bring life to the surrounding nations.

This river of life abounding with God's presence flows from the inmost place of God's presence outward into the nations. In the temple, God's holiness is supremely manifest in the Holy of Holies and spreads outward to the Holy Place and then the outer court, where all Israel could assemble for worship, and which symbolized, as we will see, the whole world. In the eschatological temple, the river flows from the Holy of Holies into the temple courts and then the nations outside (Ezek 47:1; Rev 22:1). In Eden, the river flows from God's presence in Eden into the Garden and then the rest of the earth, where nations would eventually reside (Gen 2:10-14). A gradation of holiness is seen in Eden and the temple as the presence of God increases from the innermost place of Eden/Holy of Holies outward to the earth and the lands where nations would live.

As a result, this gradation of holiness is evident in the parallels between Eden and the temple. Just as the Holy Place contained the lampstand, shaped like the tree of life, and the bread of the presence to sustain the priests, so the Garden of Eden is the place of the tree of life (Gen 2:8-9) and provides food to sustain Adam (Gen 2:16). Just as the outer court of Israel's second temple provided a place for the nations to come, so the land and seas to be subdued by Adam outside the Garden are the nations of Cush and Assyria (Gen 2:13-14); though, of course, these lands were not yet populated with peoples.[8] The parallels can be seen in figure 1.1.

---

[8]Discussion of the distinction between Eden and its Garden is based on John Walton, *Genesis*, NIVAC (Grand Rapids, MI: Zondervan, 2001), 167-68, 182-83.

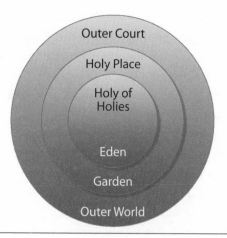

Figure 1.1

Since the river of life flows from God's presence into the lands of nations, so our mission to the nations must flow from the life found in God's presence. When the source of our commitment to mission is located only in the backwaters of our idealism, then we can burn out and become bitter. Many idealistically plunge headlong into a sacrificial commitment to the poor or unreached or hurting, compelled by brokenness over their plight, but the resources of that idealism run dry when tested by the challenges of costly obedience. However, when our resources run dry, we drink more fully and deeply from the abundance of life found in God's presence. Our God gives joy and strength to endure! The life that we find in God's presence is more than enough to overcome every challenge for the mission God has placed before us. However, life must clearly flow from God's presence into the needs of the nations, and the needs of the nations must drive us to drink more fully from the life found in God's presence.

Just outside the Garden, the river is surrounded with land that abounds with good gold, bdellium, and onyx stone (Gen 2:12). Each of these marks life in the presence of God. "Pure gold, like clear glass" covers the temple (Rev 21:18, 21), just as the sacred furniture in the tabernacle was made of gold. Polished gold reflects light, just as we will reflect God's light when we live in the presence of God. Bdellium is a fragrant substance, with the appearance of manna (Num 11:7), which was kept in the ark of the covenant in the Holy of Holies. Indeed, God's presence sustains and strengthens us, as the manna did for Israel in the wilderness (Ps 78:24-25; Jn 6:58). Onyx stones are prevalent in the temple, especially on the breastpiece of the high priest where the names of the sons of Israel were engraved (Ex 25:7; 28:9), reflecting their identity and preciousness before God. In this way, this abundant imagery reminds us how God's presence brings life so that our hearts may not corrode with sin, our lives are sustained with strength and our identities might be properly grounded in our preciousness before him.

Psalm 36 interprets the river from God's presence in Eden as a picture of the abundant life found there:

> How precious is your steadfast love, O God!
>   The children of mankind take refuge in the shadow of your wings.
> They feast on the abundance of your house [temple],
>   and you give them drink from the river of your delights
>   [literally "Edens"].
> For with you is the fountain of life;
>   in your light do we see light. (Ps 36:7-9)

In God's presence and in the temple, the river of Eden flows to bring the fountain of life. God's presence brings life and light. Since true life and sustenance are found in the presence of God, we must regularly drink deeply from the river of his delights. In our weariness, though, we often seek life from entertainment, empty friendships, and ceaseless activity, which all fail to bring life. So many of our recreational activities fail to re-create the inner resources of our soul to face the challenges of each day. Like the Israelites before us, we forsake the river of God's presence and hew out empty cisterns that do not hold water to satisfy our thirsts (Jer 2:13). Will we satisfy our soul at the fountain of living waters? Or will we hew out cisterns of putrid water that do not satisfy? The rivers of life flowing from the presence of God in Eden beckon us to the satisfaction and re-creation of these refreshing waters that are only found in the presence of God.

We sacrifice for what satisfies. The soul-satisfying riches in the presence of God propel us out of our comfort zones, calling us out of the warm confines of our beds to our knees in early-morning prayer and meditation on God's

Word. Only these soul-satisfying riches can sustain us in the rigors of God's calling on our lives as we move out to proclaim his name to the nations across the street and across the globe. A heart for mission grows out of a soul that finds satisfaction in God's presence, the riches of which can be seen in the imagery of Eden.

EDEN AND THE LONGING FOR PURPOSE

God placed Adam in Eden to work it and keep it (Gen 2:15), a priestly work in the Garden-temple of Eden. His work is not only working the soil (Gen 2:5) but serving God (e.g., Deut 4:19), and he keeps the Garden (Gen 2:15) as he keeps God's commands (see Lev 18:5) and guards it from pollution and corruption (see Num 1:53). The verbs *to work* and *to keep* are sometimes used together outside Genesis 2:15 in a priestly context:

> And *you shall keep guard over* the sanctuary and *over* the altar, that there may never again be wrath on the people of Israel. And behold, I have taken your brothers the Levites from among the people of Israel. They are a gift to you, given to the LORD, *to do the work* of the tent of meeting.[9] (Num 18:5-6, translation altered)

In this passage, the priests are to keep the sanctuary from corruption and defilement and do the work of service in the tabernacle. In the same way, Adam serves God in the temple as a priest and keeps the Garden-temple from corruption. Similarly, Ezekiel 28:13 shows Adam in Eden, clothed like a priest with "every precious stone," stones that correspond to the precious stones on the ephod of Israel's high priest (Ex 28:17-21).[10]

---

[9]To be more precise, these two words occur together in the Old Testament (within an approximately fifteen-word range) in reference either to Israelites "serving" God and "guarding [keeping]" his word (approximately ten times) or to priests who "keep" the "service" (or "charge") of the tabernacle (Num 3:7-8; 8:25-26; 18:5-6; 1 Chron 23:32; Ezek 44:14). See further discussion in Walton, *Genesis*, 172-74. And even if the Hebrew word for "to keep" in Gen 2:15 refers to Adam as "keeping" or "cultivating" the garden (as it does in Gen 2:5 and 3:23), it would still have reference to a priestly duty of keeping the garden in an ordered and clean state, which was also a duty of priests in temple-gardens in Egypt (on which see G. K. Beale, *The Temple and the Church's Mission*, NSBT 17 [Downers Grove, IL: InterVarsity Press, 2004], 84-89). Generally, as we will see, part of the priest's duty in Israel was to keep the temple in an ordered and pure condition.

[10]The Ezekiel list either alludes to the human priest's bejeweled clothing in Ex 28, or both Ezek 28 and Ex 28 have roots in a common tradition about Adam's apparel. Though some see the figure in Ezek 28 to refer to Satan, the Greek Old Testament (Septuagint) and Aramaic

This understanding of Adam's work is confirmed by observing the next verses in Genesis 2. After being commanded to work and keep the Garden, Adam is told: "And the LORD God *commanded* the man, saying, 'You may surely eat of every tree of the garden, but of the tree of the knowledge of good and evil you shall not eat, for in the day that you eat of it you shall surely die'" (Gen 2:16-17). After Adam is commanded to keep the Garden, he is also instructed to keep God's commands. Just as the priests were to keep guard over the temple (Num 18:5) by obeying God's commands, so Adam as a priest guards the Garden-temple of Eden by keeping God's commands. Adam works out God's priestly purposes through obedience to his word.

Adam failed in his service as the first priest to guard God's temple, which included guarding the Garden-temple from the intrusion of the serpent who was outside.[11] The serpent slithered into the Garden with deceptive words: "Did God actually say, 'You shall not eat of any tree in the garden'?" (Gen 3:1). Through doubt, the serpent undermined God's word. Eve's reply to the serpent shows that the serpent succeeded in his plot. Notice the subtle differences between God's word in Genesis 2:16-17 and the woman's reply in Genesis 3:2-3.

Targum clearly identify this figure as Adam, following the lead of the Hebrew text (see further, e.g., D. Callender, *Adam in Myth and History*, Harvard Semitic Museum Publications [Winona Lake, IN: Eisenbrauns, 2000], 87-135, 179-89). Though some point to Ezek 28:14a ("you were an anointed guardian cherub") as evidence for a reference to Satan, this phrase could be understood as a metaphor, which is a suppressed simile: "You were [like] the anointed cherub who covers," similar to such metaphorical statements as "the LORD is [like] my shepherd" (Ps 23:1). What further points to this figure being Adam in Eden is that Ezek 28:18 says that the sin of the glorious figure in Eden "profaned" Eden. The only account that we have that Eden became unclean because of sin is the narrative about Adam in Gen 2–3. Furthermore, since the sinful being in Ezek 28 is seen to be standing behind the sin of the human king of Tyre (Ezek 28:1-12), it would appear more suitable that this figure in Eden be a human representative. See also D. I. Block, *The Book of Ezekiel, Chapters 25–48*, NICOT (Grand Rapids, MI: Eerdmans, 1998), 115; M. Hutter, "Adam als Gärtner und König (Gen 2, 8, 15)," *Biblische Zeitschrift* 30 (1986): 258-62.

[11]This serpent is identified in different ways throughout history. Some think it may be a transformation of a mythical motif for evil. The snake is the archetypal unclean animal (Lev 11; Deut 14). The serpent is an archetypal enemy of God as well, as seen in the portrayal of the serpent Leviathan (Job 26:13; Is 27:1). See further discussion in Gordon Wenham, *Genesis*, WBC (Waco, TX: Word, 1987), 1:73. The best identification of the serpent is Satan. This interpretation is clarified by later Scripture, which identifies the Genesis serpent with Satan (e.g., see Rom 16:18-20; Rev 12:3-4, 7-17). We see the narrative in Gen 2–3 about Adam, Eve, and Satan to be historical and not mythological.

Table 1.1

GENESIS 2:16-17	GENESIS 3:2-3
And *the* LORD God commanded the man, saying, "You may surely eat of *every* tree of the garden, but of the tree of the knowledge of good and evil you shall not eat, for in the day that you eat of it *you shall surely die* [literally, "*dying you shall die*"]."	And the woman said to the serpent, "We may eat of the fruit of the trees in the garden, but *God* said, 'You shall not eat of the fruit of the tree that is in the midst of the garden, *neither shall you touch it*, lest you die.'"

First, *the name of God is changed* from "the LORD [Yahweh] God" to "God." While this does not sound like much in English, "the LORD God" is the personal name of God that signifies an intimate and covenantal relationship, while "God" is the God of power who created all things (*Elohim*). While Genesis 2 presents the Lord God issuing commands in covenant relationship to his special people, Eve appears to look at this personal God from a distance in Genesis 3. Next, *God's permission is minimized.* While God lavishly allows to "eat of *every* tree of the garden," Eve reduces this gracious invitation to "the fruit of the trees of the garden" and minimizes God's generous invitation. Also, *God's prohibition is maximized.* God commanded that they could not eat only from one tree, but Eve adds, "neither shall you touch it." She becomes the first legalist and makes God's commands seem more strict than they actually are. Finally, the *consequences of sin are minimized.* God says, "you shall surely die" (literally, "dying you shall die") but Eve only says, "lest you die."[12]

Adam and Eve failed to guard the Garden of God through obedience to God's word. The serpent undermined confidence in God's word, and consequently undermined confidence in God himself. John Calvin rightly says,

> And surely, once we hold God's Word in contempt, we shake off all reverence for him! . . . For Adam would never have dared oppose God's authority unless he had disbelieved in God's Word. Here, indeed, was the best bridle to control all passions: the thought that nothing is better than to practice righteousness by obeying God's commandments; then, that the ultimate goal of the happy life is to be loved by him. Therefore Adam, carried away

---

[12]For further defense of these points, see Beale, *Temple and the Church's Mission*, 66-69, 87, 264; Meredith G. Kline, *Kingdom Prologue: Genesis Foundations for a Covenantal Worldview* (Eugene, OR: Wipf and Stock, 2006), 54-55, 66-67.

by the devil's blasphemies, as far as he was able extinguished the whole glory of God.[13]

When the protection of God's word is removed, the temptations of this world grow far stronger. In Genesis 3:6, Eve is overwhelmed with temptation as she "saw that the tree was good for food, and that it was a delight to her eyes, and that the tree was to be desired to make one wise." The desire for food, the delight of the eyes, and the craving for wisdom are all strong and, in their proper context, legitimate desires. The desires of our flesh may be legitimate, but Eve sought to satisfy them in illegitimate ways. However, the bridle of God's word protects the wild horses of our desires from destroying us.

Adam and Eve failed in their purpose and priestly calling to guard the Garden-temple from intruders by not keeping God's word. Eden is a place where purpose is given to humanity (Gen 2:15; see Gen 1:28). We will see later that as God's presence is restored through the sacrifice of Jesus, our purpose is also restored as a kingdom of priests and a holy nation, serving in God's true end-time temple (1 Pet 2:4-9). The longing for purpose found in the human heart is satisfied when life works according to its purpose, which is life lived in the presence of God. Just as Adam and Eve were to submit to God's word to fulfill their mission in guarding God's dwelling place, so we must submit to God's Word to fulfill our mission in guarding and expanding God's dwelling place to fill the earth.

CONCLUSION

In this chapter, we see Eden as the first temple and place of God's presence. As a result, Eden is a place of satisfaction of life. However, sin closed off the way back to God's presence in Eden. Because Adam and Eve fail to guard the temple by sinning and letting in an unclean serpent to defile the temple, they lose their priestly role, and the two cherubim take over the responsibility to "guard" the Garden-temple (Gen 3:24).[14]

---

[13]John Calvin, *Institutes of the Christian Religion*, Loeb Classical Library 21 (London: SCM Press, 1960), 2.1.4.

[14]The cherubim's role became memorialized in Israel's later temple when God commanded Moses to make two statues of angelic figures and station them on either side of the ark of the covenant in the Holy of Holies in the temple. Like the cherubim, Israel's priests "kept the charge of their

Who will open the way back into God's tabernacling presence? Are we endlessly condemned to our lives east of Eden? Jesus opens up the way back into God's presence by the sacrifice of his body (Heb 10:19-20). As a result, the life-giving waters that flowed in Eden now flow in and through those who believe in Jesus, becoming "a spring of water welling up to eternal life" (Jn 4:13-14). Just as the river "flowed out of Eden" to the lands of the later surrounding nations of Assyria and Cush (Gen 2:10), so those who believe in Jesus not only drink of living waters, but a spring of living water overflows into the nations around them (Jn 7:37-39), as we will see more fully later.

We have established in this chapter that Eden was the first place of worship, since it was where God's presence dwelt and the only place where satisfaction in God could be found. God's plan was not static, but Adam was to expand Eden until it filled the whole earth. How? In the next chapter, we will explore how God's purpose for worship in Eden would overflow in mission to the ends of the earth.

God" (JPS; same word as "guard" in Gen 2:15) over the temple (Neh 12:45) as "gatekeepers" (2 Chron 23:19; Neh 12:45). In the same way, cherubim guard the ark of the covenant in the Holy of Holies (Ex 25:18, 22), symbolically preventing entry into the presence of God.

Chapter Two

EXPANDING EDEN

THE CALL IN GENESIS 1:26-28

EDEN IS A PLACE of God's presence, and the place of God's presence is a place of worship. The expansion of Eden, therefore, is an expansion of worship. Worship fuels mission in Eden—bearers of the image of God reflect his presence in worship and are propelled forward in their mission to "fill the earth" with reflections of God's glory (Gen 1:28). Worship is in fact the goal of mission in Eden, filling the earth by multiplying image bearers in the temple of God's presence who would worship and reflect God's glory to the ends of the earth. Indeed, John Piper rightly reminds us that "worship is the fuel and goal of missions."[1]

While the previous chapter explored Adam's role as a priest in the Garden-temple of Eden to "serve" and "guard" Eden from corruption (Gen 2:15, our translation), this chapter will explore the meaning of Adam being in the image of God, as well as his call to multiply and fill the earth with images of God (Gen 1:26-28). Genesis 1:26-28 reminds us that worship is the fuel of mission, for worshipers bear and reflect the image of God, and worship is

---

[1]John Piper, *Let the Nations Be Glad*, 3rd ed. (Grand Rapids, MI: Baker Academic, 2010), 15.

the goal of mission, as those images are multiplied to fill the earth with divine glory.[2]

WORSHIP FUELS MISSION: THE SIGNIFICANCE OF THE IMAGE OF GOD

We look like what we look at.[3] Pets often resemble their owners, and married people sometimes uncannily resemble their spouses. We are not created to resemble pets or spouses physically, however. We are created to resemble and represent the triune God spiritually, for we are created in his image. In this section, we will explore how images of God represent his tabernacling presence in the world, and how worship helps us grow to reflect and represent that image more clearly. As we grow in worship to reflect his image, then our mission is fueled to subdue the destructive forces of the enemy in the world.

What does it mean to be in the image of God? Images reflect a greater reality. Genesis 1:26-27 says that God made Adam in his "image" or "likeness" four times, and Genesis 2 says that God placed him in a Garden-like sanctuary. In the sanctuary of Eden, Adam and Eve reflect and represent God as his image. In the ancient Near East, gods frequently established kings as their images in a land to express their authority (even though these kings were images of false gods).[4] Adam was created in the image of the triune God to indicate his presence and rule over the earth.[5] As God's image, Adam and Eve were to reign with God as kings and representatives of God.

---

[2]The previous chapter explored how Gen 2:15 develops Gen 1:28 and the priestly calling of Adam in the temple of Eden.

[3]For a book-length exploration of this theme in idolatry, see G. K. Beale, *We Become What We Worship: A Biblical Theology of Idolatry* (Downers Grove, IL: InterVarsity Press, 2008). While the focus is how this theme is worked out in idolatry, Beale also explores the reversal of idolatry in worship.

[4]After conquering a new territory, the Assyrian king Shalmanesar "fashioned a mighty image of my majesty" that was equated with "the glory of Assur" his god (Henri Frankfort, *The Art and Architecture of the Ancient Orient*, 4th ed. [Harmondsworth, UK: Penguin, 1969], p. 90 and plate 93). Similarly, at Tell Fekheriyeh, a statue of King Adad-iti was found that was set up to represent the rule of the god Adad over the geographical province of Guzan (A. R. Millard and P. Bordreuil, "A Statue from Assyria," *Biblical Archaeology* 45 [1982]: 137).

[5]G. von Rad, *Old Testament Theology*, trans. D. M. G. Stalker (New York: Harper & Row, 1962), 1:146-47.

What does it mean to reign as a representative? The Greek translation of "image" is "icon." On a computer screen, an icon is a small picture file that, when clicked, ushers in the megabytes of the computer program that it represents. Metaphorically, humanity is a small picture file in the terabytes of God's glory in creation. Although we often feel small in light of the overwhelming brokenness in the world, God has created us as icons of his powerful presence. Icons do not point to themselves, but icons usher in a far greater reality. Similarly, we represent God so that our presence ushers in the presence of the Almighty God wherever we go.

However, the image of God was distorted by the entrance of sin in the world, and so we do not represent God's authority and glory as we should. This is clearly seen in Genesis 3, when Adam fails to subdue the serpent (see further discussion below on this point). However, God's image in us is restored through worship. Through Jesus Christ, the perfect image of God (Col 1:15), we worship him and "are being transformed into the same image [*eikon*], from one degree of glory to another" (2 Cor 3:18). Worship transforms us increasingly to reflect and represent God's presence more clearly as his image and icon.

As we are transformed to reflect God's presence as his image through worship, then this worship fuels our mission to represent God's authority and "subdue the earth" (Gen 1:27-28). God created humanity in his image, and this image is expressed through humanity's work in having dominion and subduing all the earth (Gen 1:26, 28).[6] Just as God subdued the chaos, ruled over creation and then filled the earth with all kinds of animate life, so Adam and Eve were to "subdue," "have dominion . . . over all the earth" and then "be fruitful and multiply and fill the earth" with images of God (Gen 1:26, 28).[7] More specifically, Adam rules over creation by speaking and naming the animals (Gen 2:19), just as God ruled over creation by speaking and naming parts of creation (e.g., Gen 1:5, 8, 10).[8]

---

[6]The image of God in Adam is not limited to this function but also has ontological aspects (see further Jeremy Cohen, *Be Fertile and Increase, Fill the Earth and Master It* [Ithaca, NY: Cornell University Press, 1989], 22-23; John Walton, *Genesis*, NIVAC [Grand Rapids, MI: Zondervan, 2001], 130-31).

[7]Following W. Austin Gage, *The Gospel of Genesis* (Winona Lake, IN: Eisenbrauns, 1984), 27-36.

[8]Gage, *Gospel of Genesis*, 31.

Adam, however, failed in his mission and allowed an unclean creature to enter the Garden; he did not "subdue" this serpent but was subdued by its deception. As a result, Adam and Eve did not extend the divine presence of the Garden sanctuary but were expelled from it.

Daniel 7 looks forward to a time when a Son of Adam would succeed where the original Adam had failed. Daniel 7:13-14 says,

> I saw in the night visions,
> and behold, with the clouds of heaven
>   there came one like a son of man [Adam!]. . . .
> And to him was given dominion
>   and glory and a kingdom,
> that all peoples, nations, and languages
>   should serve him;
> his dominion is an everlasting dominion,
>   which shall not pass away,
> and his kingdom one
>   that shall not be destroyed.

This "one like a son of man" is, literally, a "one like a son of Adam."[9] This "one like a son of Adam" subdues the beasts (Dan 7:1-8), just as the original Adam was to subdue the beasts of the earth and the sea. These beasts represent forces of destruction that oppose God's purposes in the world (Dan 7:17, 25). The son of Adam in Daniel 7 rises up and accomplishes what the original Adam had failed to accomplish.[10]

Where the original Adam had failed, the second Adam, Jesus, is faithful. Jesus fulfills the son of man prophecies of Daniel 7. Jesus overcomes in temptation with the devil where the original Adam failed (Lk 3:38–4:13). Jesus

---

[9]The Aramaic "son of man" is *bar enosh*, which can be a synonym for the Hebrew *ben adam* (son of Adam). E.g., see the interchangeable use of *enosh* with *adam* in Targum Ongelos of Gen 1:26, 28.

[10]The connection between the Son of Man and the original Adam can be further established by noticing that Dan 7:13-14 grows out of Ps 8:4-8, where the Lord crowns the "son of man . . . with glory and honor," gives him "dominion over the works of [the Lord's] hands" and all things are "put . . . under his feet." This expansive description of the glory and authority of the Son of Man is widely recognized to be an extended commentary on Gen 1:26-28, where Adam, in the image of God, is called to have dominion over the earth. In this way, God's call to Adam in Gen 1:26-28 is developed in Ps 8:4-8 and expanded on in Dan 7:13-14.

subdues and is not subdued by the wild animals (Mk 1:13). At Jesus' ascension to heaven, he embodies the authority over all nations that was to be given to the son of man in Dan 7:13-14, since "all authority in heaven and on earth has been given to me" (Mt 28:17; see further discussion on this point in chap. 6).

While the first Adam failed to subdue the serpent, the second Adam subdued the serpent, and "that ancient serpent, who is called the devil and Satan, the deceiver of the whole world . . . was thrown down to the earth" (Rev 12:9). However, that serpent continues "to make war on . . . those who keep the commandments of God and hold to the testimony of Jesus" (Rev 12:17), but our victory is assured:

> Now the salvation and the power and the kingdom of our God and the au-
> thority of his Christ have come, for the accuser of our brothers has been
> thrown down, who accuses them day and night before our God. And they
> have conquered him by the blood of the Lamb and by the word of their
> testimony, for they loved not their lives even unto death. (Rev 12:10-11)

This ancient serpent is now conquered by the "blood of the Lamb and by the word of their testimony." In this manner, Adam's priestly calling in the Garden to guard against unclean influence[11] can be fulfilled through us because of the work of Christ.

We can only accomplish our mission as we recognize our identity as icons of God. Often the demands of ministering to people expose our inadequacies, and we become depressed since their needs exceed our resources. However, these excessive demands remind us that we are only icons. We are not the answer! We are created as icons through which the glories of God's presence shine. Jesus Christ is the perfect image and icon of God (Col 1:15) who has subdued our enemy (Rev 12:9). In his image (cf. Col 3:9-10), we continue to conquer our enemy "by the blood of the Lamb and by the word of their testimony" (Rev 12:11). Only by the presence of Jesus with us and the power of his word in us can we accomplish his work through our lives. We are icons who conquer through his presence in us.

Recently my (Mitch) daughters got a small glow-in-the-dark lizard. Glow-in-the-dark toys do not always glow in the dark, however; if they are kept in

---

[11]This priestly task of Adam in the Garden-temple of Eden is developed in chap. 1.

a desk drawer all day, then they will not glow. They only glow in the dark after they have been "charged" in the light. So before the lights were turned out for bed, my daughters placed the lizard next to the lamp, "charging" it with light so that it would glow in the dark long after the lights were turned off.

Like that lizard, we are created to glow in the dark. Our mission is to glow with the light of Christ in the darkness of the world. We will only fulfill that mission if we "charge" our souls in the light through worship, drawing near to God. Such worship in God's very presence fuels our mission. We worship in the temple of God's presence as we enter "by the blood of the Lamb" and hold to the word of God, and this worship fuels us so that we can conquer our enemy, the ancient serpent (Rev 12:11), whom the first Adam failed to conquer.

WORSHIP AS THE GOAL OF MISSION: MULTIPLYING IMAGES OF GOD

In worship, we represent God's image more and more clearly, not only to subdue forces of evil but also to multiply these images of God to fill the earth: "And God blessed them. And God said to them, 'Be fruitful and multiply and fill the earth and subdue it, and have dominion over the fish of the sea and over the birds of the heavens and over every living thing that moves on the earth'" (Gen 1:28). The command to "fill the earth" implies that the earth is not yet filled with images that reflect God's glory. While the boundaries of the Garden are clearly delineated (Gen 2:10-14), the call to multiply images of God would expand the boundaries of that Garden sanctuary until it filled the whole earth.[12] Our mission is to be used in God's hand to bring about more worshipers in the image of God who might multiply and fill the earth with even more worshipers.

Outside of the Garden-sanctuary of Eden lay a chaotic inhospitable area. God calls Adam not only to "work and to keep" the Garden of Eden (see Gen 2:15) but also to expand that Garden and "fill the earth" (Gen 1:28). Bible scholar John Walton notes that "people were gradually supposed to extend the Garden as they went about subduing and ruling" in order to "extend the

---

[12]See further Meredith G. Kline, *Kingdom Prologue: Genesis Foundations for a Covenantal Worldview* (Eugene, OR: Wipf and Stock, 2006), 55-56.

food supply as well as extend sacred space (since that is what the Garden represented)."[13] God wanted to expand that sacred space and dwelling place from the limited confines of the Garden-temple of Eden to fill the entire earth. As Adam multiplied children in his image, then they would expand God's dwelling place of his presence into the chaos outside of Eden until it filled the earth, and the whole earth reflected God's order and his glorious presence.

We are created to fill the whole earth with God's glory. God

> formed the earth and made it . . .
> [and] did not create it empty,
>> he formed it *to be inhabited*! (Is 45:18, emphasis added;
>>> see Ps 115:16)

God's ultimate goal in creation was to magnify his glory throughout the earth by means of his faithful image bearers. Psalm 8 begins and ends with the goal of glorifying God:

> O LORD, our Lord,
>> how majestic is your name in all the earth! (Ps 8:1, 9)

This majesty of the Lord is his "glory" (Ps 8:1), a glory reflected in humanity who is "crowned . . . with glory and honor" and given "dominion over the works of your hands" (Ps 8:5-6).[14] God's glory is to be spread "in all the earth" through humanity crowned "with glory and honor" and properly expressing their dominion in creation. We are created to glorify God by filling the earth with image bearers crowned with that glory.

What does it mean to glorify God? The Westminster Catechism reminds us that "the chief end of man is to glorify God and enjoy him forever." If we are created to glorify God, then we should know what that means. We glorify God by multiplying images of him who are crowned with his glory; we glorify God by multiplying disciples. Jesus himself glorified God in this way. Near the end of his life, he declared, "I glorified you on earth, having accomplished the work that you gave me to do. . . . I have manifested your name to the

---

[13]Walton, *Genesis*, 186.
[14]While the phrase *image of God* is not used here, the related term *glory* is used, which is sometimes synonymous with *image of God* (e.g., Ps 8:5; 106:20; see 1 Cor 11:7).

people whom you gave me out of the world. Yours they were, and you gave them to me, and they have kept your word" (Jn 17:4, 6). Jesus glorified God by making disciples who kept God's word. The mark of these disciples was obedience. Similarly, we glorify God by our mission in making disciples who keep God's word.

How then do we multiply disciples? Disciples multiply only as the word of God bears fruit in and through our lives. In Acts, the Genesis 1:28 language of "be fruitful and multiply" marks the growth of the church:

> And the word of God continued to *be fruitful* and the number of the disciples *multiplied* greatly in Jerusalem. (Acts 6:7; our translation)

> But the word of God *bore fruit* and *multiplied*. (Acts 12:24; our translation)

> So the word of the Lord continued to *bear fruit* and prevail mightily. (Acts 19:20; our literal translation)

Unlike Genesis 1:28, the word of God, not people, bears fruit and multiplies in Acts.[15] Similarly, in Colossae the gospel "has come to you, as indeed in the whole world it is bearing fruit [*karpophoreō*] and growing [*auxanō*]" (Col 1:6, our translation; see 1:10). Just as Adam and Eve were to "be fruitful and multiply and fill the earth" (Gen 1:28), so now the gospel is "bearing fruit and growing" and filling the earth (Col 1:6, 10).[16] Spiritual progeny are multiplying to fill the earth through the gospel.

However, why does the word of God increase and multiply in Acts and Colossians through spiritual progeny instead of physical progeny, as in Genesis 1:28? In fact, Genesis 1:28 likely does not have in mind only physical children, but children who also were to be spiritual image bearers of God. We must recall that even in Genesis 1:28, the word of God is essential, since Adam and

---

[15]In Acts, the word of God progresses in stages, from Jerusalem, to Judea and Samaria, and then to the ends of the earth. The progress of the gospel in each of these stages is marked by this "be fruitful and multiply" language, marking the growth of the church in Jerusalem (Acts 6:7), Judea and Samaria (12:24), and Ephesus, the center of the gospel's progress to the ends of the earth (19:20). Interestingly, Luke paints a picture of the expansion of the gospel for worldwide mission in Acts from the palette of Gen 1:28.

[16]See more detailed discussion on this point in G. K. Beale, "Colossians," in *Commentary on the New Testament Use of the Old Testament* (Grand Rapids, MI: Baker, 2007), 842-46; and N. T. Wright, *Colossians and Philemon*, Tyndale New Testament Commentaries 12 (Grand Rapids, MI: Eerdmans, 1986), 53.

Eve were to subdue the earth through obedience to God's word (see Gen 2:16-17). Adam and Eve fail to subdue the serpent because they do not remember and obey God's word properly (Gen 3:1-7).[17] The genealogy of Genesis 5 traces the initial stage of the proper fulfillment of Genesis 1:28, and the "likeness of God" in Adam is passed down to Seth, who is in Adam's "likeness, after his image" (Gen 5:1, 3). Here, the image of God in Adam is passed down through Seth, who keeps God's word, unlike the murderer Cain. Images of God multiply as a vanguard movement, beginning to spread out over the earth with the goal of filling it with divine glory bearers. Acts and Colossians focus now on the spiritual children of Christ, the Last Adam (see Col 1:15-18), who are multiplied (e.g., see Acts 6:7, "And the number of the disciples *multiplied* greatly in Jerusalem," emphasis added).

Therefore, gospel growth is the key to true church growth. Church leaders can often seek programs and marketing processes to accelerate church growth, and such programs and processes may have a place. However, lasting church growth is essentially gospel growth. If church growth is based on programs that do not root people in the "living word" (see Acts 7:38) of God, then they will "in time of testing fall away" (Lk 8:13). We must get people to come to church, but we must also get the word of God to come to people. The only way to integrate people into the body of Christ is by the word of God growing in them.[18] Our mission is to multiply disciples, image bearers of God who know and use God's word to subdue the deceptive work of our enemy in the world. If Jesus Christ himself rides out in victory against the evil one with a "sharp sword" of God's word coming "from his mouth" (Rev 19:15), so we must equip God's people with this sharp sword of God's word to come from their mouths, since we are in union with Jesus, and what is true of him in this respect is true of us.[19]

---

[17]This connection between subduing the serpent and failing to remember the word of God is explored in chap. 1.

[18]Colin Marshall and Tony Payne provide an excellent and practical framework of church growth as gospel growth in *The Trellis and the Vine* (Kingsford, Australia: Matthias Media, 2009). They explore how the "trellis" work of structure and programming must support and not squelch the "vine" work of growing healthy disciples of Jesus Christ.

[19]In this respect, note that the career of the two witnesses in Rev 11, who represent the witnessing church, is modeled after the career of Jesus (on which see G. K. Beale, *The Book of Revelation*, NIGTC [Grand Rapids, MI: Eerdmans, 1999], 567-68).

CONCLUSION

Our mission grows out of Adam and Eve's commission to multiply image bearers who expand the boundaries of God's glorious presence in Eden until it fills the whole earth. Our mission is fueled by our worship as God's image bearers in God's tabernacling presence (which is now in Christ, who is the temple), reflecting and representing God's presence in the earth (Gen 1:26-27). Our mission expresses our worship, as the Lord's name fills the earth through people "crowned . . . with glory and honor" (Ps 8:1, 5-9). Our goal in mission is worship, that we might multiply more and more image bearers who worship the King (Gen 1:28). However, sin threatens this mission. Although we are created as image bearers in God's tabernacling presence who are to multiply and fill the earth, Adam failed in this commission. How will Adam's progeny work out their calling to "be fruitful and multiply and fill the earth" (Gen 1:28)? In Genesis 3, sin enters the world, but nevertheless God's call to Adam is passed on to his followers, as we will see in the next chapter.

Chapter Three

EDEN LOST?

THE CALL TO THE PATRIARCHS
AFTER THE FALL

THE MISSION OF GOD given to Adam continues even as sin spreads to fill the earth. Adam's mission in Eden was to "be fruitful and multiply and fill the earth" (Gen 1:28), and sin does not undermine this mission. Adam's commission is passed down to the patriarchs in the context of the building of small sanctuaries, just as Adam's commission was originally given in the context of the sanctuary of Eden. God's presence guarantees the fulfillment of this mission in the face of the spread of sin. In this chapter, we will explore how the commission to Adam is passed down to his descendants after the entrance of sin in the world.

After a general discussion of how Noah and the patriarchs receive this commission, we will focus on one example of how this commission is worked out in the life of Jacob at Bethel in Genesis 28. Finally, we will explore the purpose of the small sanctuaries built by the patriarchs and connect them to the later tabernacle and temple. In this manner, God continues his purpose begun through Adam to expand his dwelling place to fill the earth through the patriarchs.

THE CALL TO MULTIPLY AFTER THE FALL:
AN OVERVIEW

Adam's commission to fill the earth with images of God is passed to Noah despite the fact that sin spreads to fill the earth. In Genesis 3, Adam and Eve disobey God's command to subdue the beasts and are subdued by a serpent. In Genesis 4, Cain murders Abel. In Genesis 6–9, the earth is filled not with faithful images of God but the wickedness of humanity (Gen 6:5, 11), in whom the image of God is distorted. As a result, God brings a flood, and this flood provides the context for the giving of Adam's commission to Noah. Just as God originally created the heavens and earth through waters (Gen 1:1-2) and blessed and commissioned Adam to be "fruitful and multiply and fill the earth" (Gen 1:28), so God re-creates the world through the waters of the flood[1] and blesses and commissions Noah to "be fruitful and multiply and fill the earth" (Gen 9:1, 7). The commission to Adam is passed down to Noah in the context of a new creation.

However, just as Adam and Eve sinned in a Garden, so Noah sins in a vineyard (Gen 9:20-21). Instead of Noah as a second Adam expanding the sanctuary of God's presence by filling the earth with images of God, the earth is filled with a people so rebellious that they are dispersed "over the face of all the earth" (Gen 11:9). The unabated spread of sin after the flood raises a question: How will the commission of Adam ever be fulfilled in light of the prevalence and power of sin? God passes down the commission of Adam to the patriarchs, and he himself promises and guarantees its fulfillment. In Genesis 12, the focus shifts from "all the earth" to one man—Abraham. From this one man comes offspring in whom "all the families of the earth shall be blessed" (Gen 12:3). While the wide-angle lens of Genesis 11 pictures rebellious humanity scattered over the face of the earth, Genesis 12 zooms in on a promise that the offspring of Abraham might become a blessing to all the families of the earth. The cosmic scope of God's purposes through

---

[1]See, e.g., Gordon Wenham, *Genesis*, WBC (Waco, TX: Word, 1987), 1:206-8.

Abraham and his children can be seen in the repeated promises to bless and multiply their offspring to fill the earth. These promises to the patriarchs grow out of God's original commission given to Adam in Genesis 1:28, as we will see. Adam's commission begins to be passed down to Abram in Genesis 12:1-3:

> Now the Lord said to Abram, "Go from your country and your kindred and your father's house to the land that I will show you. And I will make of you a great nation, and I will bless you and make your name great, so that you will be a blessing. I will bless those who bless you, and him who dishonors you I will curse, and in you all the families of the earth shall be blessed."

God commissioned Adam with his blessing (Gen 1:28), and God reiterates his blessing to Abram to "bless you" and "bless those who bless you." Just as God blessed Adam to fill the earth (Gen 1:28), so God blesses Abram to make him a "great nation" and bless "all . . . the earth." In Genesis 17, the connections to Adam's commission are more explicit, as God blesses Abram and promises to "*multiply* [him] greatly . . . [and] make [him] exceedingly *fruitful*" (Gen 17:2, 6, emphasis added; see 22:17-18), just as Adam was blessed and called to "be *fruitful* and *multiply*" (Gen 1:28, emphasis added). In this way, God's purpose for Abram grows out of God's purpose and commission to Adam.

Just as the commission to Adam was given in God's sanctuary in Eden, this commission to Abram is given in a small sanctuary, where the Lord appears and an altar and tent are built (Gen 12:7-8). The construction of a tent and altar (Gen 12:8) suggests that this area was a smaller form of the sanctuary and tabernacle to be built later.[2] God blessed Adam to fill the earth in the sanctuary of Eden because Adam was to expand that sanctuary to the ends of the earth. Similarly, God blesses Abram to bless the families of the earth (Gen 12:1-3) in the context of God's presence in a small sanctuary at the oak of Moreh.

After Abraham dies, Isaac also receives Adam's commission in the context of the building of a small sanctuary:

---

[2]*Tent* is a word that denotes a tabernacle in the Hebrew Old Testament and the LXX (the Greek translation of the Old Testament). "Tent" and "altar" are used together in Exodus and Leviticus only with respect to the tabernacle and the altar (e.g., Lev 4:7, 18).

Sojourn in this land, and I will be with you and will *bless* you, for to you and
to your offspring I will give all these lands, and I will establish the oath that
I swore to Abraham your father. I will *multiply* your offspring as the stars of
heaven and will give to your offspring all these lands. And in your offspring
all the nations of *the earth shall be blessed.* (Gen 26:3-4, emphasis added)

Once again the combination of blessing, multiplication, and "all . . . the earth"
links this promise to the commission to Adam in Genesis 1:28 (see Gen 26:24).
Again, this promise is passed down in the context of the building of a small
sanctuary. The Lord appears to Isaac, and he builds an altar, calling upon the
name of the Lord and pitching his tent there (Gen 26:24-25).

The next patriarch, Jacob, also receives Adam's commission in the context
of sanctuary building. God appears to Jacob and changes his name to Israel
(Gen 35:10), promising: "I am God Almighty: *be fruitful and multiply.* A nation
and a company of nations shall come from you, and kings shall come from
your own body. The land that I gave to Abraham and Isaac I will give to you,
and I will give the land to your offspring after you" (Gen 35:11-12, emphasis
added). The call to "be fruitful and multiply" clearly points back to the commission to Adam in Genesis 1:28. This call is reiterated in the context of God's
appearing (Gen 35:9) and the building of a sanctuary, since Jacob sets up a
pillar as a memorial there (Gen 35:14). The importance of this sanctuary is
confirmed by its name, Bethel, meaning "house of God."

In summary, the patriarchs Abraham, Isaac, and Jacob receive the Adamic
commission in direct connection with the building of small sanctuaries. Just
as the Genesis 1:28 commission was initially to be carried out by Adam in
the sanctuary of Eden, so this commission is passed down to Israel's patriarchs
and begins to be fulfilled in a small sanctuary. Here in these patriarchal
commissions, (1) God appears to them (except in Gen 12:8; 13:3-4), and
(2) they pitch a *tent* (literally a "tabernacle" in the LXX) (3) on a mountain
and (4) build "altars" to worship God (5) at "Bethel"—the "house of God."
The combination of these five elements occurs elsewhere in the Old Testament
only in describing Israel's tabernacle or temple.[3] We will explore the

---

[3]The only case of altar building not containing these elements or linked to the Gen 1 commission
is Gen 33:20. The combination of "tent" (*ōhel*) and "altar" (*mizbakh*) occur in Exodus and Leviticus
only with respect to the tabernacle and associated altar (e.g., Lev 4:7, 18). "Altar" (*mizbakh*) and

significance of these small sanctuaries and connect them to the tabernacle and temple at the end of this chapter, but first we will look more carefully at how God passes on this commission to Jacob at Bethel.

GOD'S PRESENCE AND PROMISE IN THE FACE OF REBELLION: THE EXAMPLE OF JACOB

In the face of our rebellion and sin, God continues his purpose to fill the earth with his presence, and this purpose is clearly seen with Jacob in Genesis 28. The reality of sin is evident from Jacob's birth; his name, Jacob, literally means "he takes by the heel" or "he cheats" (Gen 25:25-26). Jacob lives up to his name, manipulating Esau out of his birthright (Gen 25:29-34) and cheating him out of his blessing (Gen 27). However, against this backdrop of Jacob's sin, God graciously reveals his presence and his promise, continuing the purposes that began with Adam. Jacob receives Adam's commission with these words from his father: "God Almighty *bless* you and make you *fruitful* and *multiply* you, that you may become a company of peoples. May he give the *blessing* of Abraham to you and to your offspring with you, that you may take possession of the land of your sojournings that God gave to Abraham!" (Gen 28:3-4, emphasis added). This combination of blessing, fruitfulness, and multiplying comes uniquely from Genesis 1:28, and Adam's commission is passed through Abraham and Isaac to Jacob.

Just as Adam was commissioned in the sanctuary of Eden, so Jacob is commissioned in the sanctuary of Bethel. How do we know that Bethel is a sanctuary? In Genesis 28:11, Jacob comes to "a certain place." The significance of this place is emphasized by repeated references to "this place" (Gen 28:11 [2×], 16, 18, 19), and the Hebrew word for "place" is often used to refer to the site of a sanctuary, usually of the tabernacle and temple.[4] The

---

"house" (*bayit*) occur twenty-eight times in the Old Testament with reference to the temple and its altar. Rarely do any of the words in these two combinations ever refer to anything other than the tabernacle or temple and its context. The building of these worship sites on a mountain may represent part of a pattern finding its climax in Israel's later temple that was built on Mount Zion (the traditional site of Mount Moriah), which itself becomes a synecdoche referring to the temple. We do not mean to say that "tent" in the patriarchal episodes is equivalent to the later tabernacle, only that it resonates with tabernacle-like associations because of its proximity to the worship site.
[4]See further J. Gamberoni, "*Maqom*," in *Theological Dictionary of the Old Testament*, ed. G. H. Botterweck et al. (Grand Rapids, MI: Eerdmans, 1974), 8:537-43.

importance of "this place" is seen in Genesis 28:16-17: "Then Jacob awoke from his sleep and said, 'Surely the Lord is in this *place*, and I did not know it.' And he was afraid and said, 'How awesome is this *place*! This is none other than the house of God, and this is the gate of heaven'" (emphasis added). Jacob clearly sees "this place" as "the house of God, and . . . the gate of heaven" (Gen 28:17). The terms *house of God* and *gate of heaven* were familiar terms for the temple in that period, and he names it "Bethel," the "house of God" (Gen 28:19). In this place, he dreams of "a ladder set up on the earth" with "angels of God . . . ascending and descending" from God's presence (Gen 28:12-13), a well-known picture of a temple.[5] Jacob treats the place as a sanctuary, setting up a memorial stone, pouring out oil (Gen 28:18), and planning to offer his tithes there (Gen 28:22). This memorial stone is later identified in Judaism as the foundation stone for Solomon's temple and for the temple at Israel's restoration.[6] The pouring of oil dedicates that stone to God, a symbolic act that usually happened in the tabernacle (e.g., Ex 30:22-29). Later, Bethel is called a "sanctuary" or "house of holiness."[7] These lines of evidence suggest that Bethel is a prototypical temple, a legitimate place of worship before God.

The importance of this place in the land was not limited to that locale. God promises,

> The land on which you lie I will give to you and to your offspring. Your offspring shall be like the dust of the earth, and you shall spread abroad to the west and to the east and to the north and to the south, and in you and your offspring shall all the families of the earth be blessed. (Gen 28:13-14)

The offspring would spread throughout all the earth so that "all the families of the earth [would] be blessed." God's purposes are not limited to Bethel, but God promises that Jacob and his offspring would fill the whole earth.

---

[5]Nahum Sarna, *Genesis*, JPS Torah Commentary (Philadelphia: Jewish Publication Society, 1989), 197-200.

[6]*Pirqe Rabbi Eliezer*, ch. 35; *Midrash Tanḥuma* Gen 6:20. The point we want to make here is not to agree with Judaism's *apparently* literal identification of Jacob's stone with the foundation stone of Solomon's temple or Israel's end-time temple but merely to note that Judaism associated these stones with the temple.

[7]The Targums, an Aramaic paraphrase of the Old Testament, explicitly call Bethel a "sanctuary" or "house of holiness" (*Targum Pseudo-Jonathan* Gen 28:11; *Targum Neofiti* 1 Gen 28:22).

Just as God had called Adam to multiply progeny from the Eden sanctuary to fill the whole earth, so God promises Jacob and his offspring to spread throughout the land from the Bethel sanctuary to bless all the families of the earth.

God commissions his servants in a context of temple worship. With each of the patriarchs, we have stressed that the commission of Adam is passed down in a small sanctuary. As God reveals himself to the patriarchs in the sanctuary, they are propelled forward in their mission to the world. The sanctuary of worship is the engine that propels God's people forward to bless the nations. Without worship, mission stumbles, but the fire of worship kindles a persevering passion for mission.

In the face of the prevalence of sin, how can the deceiver Jacob ever fulfill this high calling? God's own presence guarantees the fulfillment of his promise that Jacob's offspring would fill the land. God promises, "Behold, I am with you and will keep you wherever you go, and will bring you back to this land" (Gen 28:15). His promise does not depend on Jacob alone, but on the presence of the God who is with Jacob. The divine assurance, "I am with you," is central to the task of extending the "temple" of God's presence.

God's promise, "I am with you," guarantees the expansion of his tabernacling presence through Isaac (Gen 26:24), Jacob (Gen 28:15), and Moses (Ex 3:12). Similarly, God promises his presence to build Solomon's temple (1 Chron 22:18), and God promises his presence to rebuild the destroyed temple after the exile (Hag 2:4-5; see Hag 1:13). The glory of this rebuilt temple would be greater than Solomon's (Hag 2:3-9), and this prophecy looks forward to the glorious expansion of the temple that begins in Jesus and extends through the church until it fills the entire heavens and earth (Rev 21). The guarantee of God's presence is critical to the expansion of his glory to fill the earth despite the prevalence of sin. The shortcomings of God's servants like Jacob are amply chronicled throughout the Bible and history. However, God's purpose to expand his presence to fill the earth is not based on the adequacy of his servants, but on the promise of God's presence with those servants. Despite the prevalence of sin, God's own plan and presence guarantees the expansion of that temple presence to the ends of the earth.

SANCTUARIES: FROM PATRIARCHS TO TABERNACLE TO TEMPLE

Adam's commission was passed down to the patriarchs in the context of the building of small sanctuaries, which reminds us that the sanctuary of God's presence continues to expand after Eden, despite sin, through the patriarchs. Worship is decentralized throughout the book of Genesis, as the patriarchs build altars to show God's presence in all the land. Though they are not buildings, these altars can be considered sanctuaries along the lines of the first sanctuary in the Garden of Eden; they mark a place as holy, like the later sanctuaries of the tabernacle and temple.[8] (The small sanctuary in Bethel became a larger sanctuary in the northern kingdom of Israel, though it later became idolatrous and was rejected; see, e.g., Amos 7:13.)[9] These informal sanctuaries in Genesis pointed forward to Israel's tabernacle and temple, from which the temple of God's presence was to branch out over all the earth.

What role do these small sanctuaries play? Since Abraham, Isaac, and Jacob built altars throughout the land, the terrain of Israel's future land was dotted with shrines. This pilgrim-like activity "was like planting a flag and claiming the land"[10] for God and Israel's future temple, where God would take up his permanent residence in the capital of that land. As a result, these smaller sanctuaries pointed to the greater one to come in Jerusalem. The first-century Jewish philosopher Philo sees this incipient sanctuary building at Bethel to be fulfilled when all the saints throughout the earth are cleansed by God's word and "become a house of God, a holy temple, a most beauteous abiding-place" (*On Dreams* 1.148-49).

---

[8]Before Moses, "the altar was the only architectural feature marking a place as 'holy,'" and later "altars were incorporated into the larger [structural] sanctuaries, the tabernacle and the temple" (T. Longman, *Immanuel in Our Place: Seeing Christ in the Old Testament* [Phillipsburg, NJ: P&R, 2001], 16).

[9]Amos is told, "Never again prophesy at Bethel, for it is the king's sanctuary" (Amos 7:13; see also H. Gunkel, *Genesis* [Macon, GA: Mercer University Press, 1997], 313; B. Vawter, *On Genesis* [Garden City, NY: Doubleday, 1977], 311; W. S. Towner, *Genesis* [Louisville: Westminster John Knox, 2001], 139). See also 1 Kings 12:28-29 and Hos 10:5.

[10]Longman, *Immanuel in Our Place*, 20 (and, similarly, Augustine Pagalou, *The Religion of the Patriarchs* [Sheffield, UK: Sheffield Academic Press, 1998], 70). The Talmud affirmed of Gen 28:13 that God "rolled up the whole of the land of Israel and put it under . . . Jacob, [to indicate to him] that it would be very easily conquered by his descendants" (*b. Hullin* 91b).

At Mount Sinai, the Lord appears to Israel as he had appeared to the patriarchs, and Mount Sinai anticipates the building of the tabernacle and temple in four ways.

- Sinai is called "the mountain of God" (Ex 3:1; 18:5; 24:13) where Israel worships (Ex 3:12).[11]

- Just as with the tabernacle and temple (and Eden),[12] so Mount Sinai was divided into three sections of increasing holiness: the majority of the Israelites were to remain at the foot of Sinai (Ex 19:12, 23), the priests and seventy elders were allowed to come some distance up the mountain (Ex 19:22; 24:1), but only Moses could ascend to the top and directly experience the presence of God (Ex 24:2).

- Just as an altar was in the outermost section of the temple, so an altar was built at the lowest and least sacred part of Sinai, where Israel offered sacrifices (Ex 24:5-6).[13]

- Only Israel's "high priest," Moses, could enter the top part of Sinai where God's presence dwelt (Ex 24:15-17), just as God's presence dwelt above the tabernacle (Ex 40:35; Num 9:17-18, 22; 10:12) and temple (1 Kings 8:12-13). Furthermore, the "ten commandments" and the "ark" were created at the top of Sinai (Deut 10:1-5) just as later they found their place in the inner sanctum of the temple in God's presence.

In these ways, God's appearance to Israel at Sinai anticipates the building of the tabernacle and temple. But through the building of the tabernacle God's presence is more fully revealed. When Israel leaves the stationary sanctuary of Sinai, the commission is passed on to them to build the mobile tabernacle in order that God's glorious presence would continue to "dwell in their midst" during their wilderness wanderings (Ex 25:8). God reveals "the

---

[11]E.g., see "mountain of the Lord" as a virtual synonym for "house of God" in Is 2:2 and Mic 4:2.
[12]See discussion in chapter one.
[13]Israel "offered burnt offerings and sacrificed peace offerings of oxen to the Lord. And Moses took half of the blood and . . . threw [it] against the altar" (Ex 24:5-6). The temple atmosphere of this text is apparent from observing that the phrase "burnt offering[s]" occurs approximately thirty-eight times together with "peace offerings" in the Old Testament, and the vast majority refer to sacrifices in the tabernacle or temple (though even some of the remaining uses may be linked to a sanctuary setting: e.g., Judg 20:26; 21:4; 1 Sam 10:8; 13:9). Likewise, the majority of the numerous uses of each of the two phrases by themselves refer to the same temple context.

pattern of the tabernacle, and of all its furniture" for its construction on
Mount Sinai (Ex 25:9; see 25:40). The outer courts, Holy Place, and Holy of
Holies in the tabernacle are modeled on the tripartite pattern of Sinai.[14] The
building of the tabernacle would be a step toward the construction of the
immovable temple in Jerusalem.

God continues to reveal his presence through the construction of the temple
in Jerusalem, since here the movable tabernacle is established in one place.
While the parallels between the tabernacle and temple are clear and widely
recognized, David's preparations to build the temple also parallel the small-scale
temple-building activities of the patriarchs. Both begin their preparations on
a mountain (2 Chron 3:1; cf. Gen 22:2, 9, 14) with a theophany (1 Chron 21:16;
see 2 Chron 3:1; cf. Gen 22:15-18), as altars are built to the Lord (1 Chron 21:26;
cf. Gen 12:7, 8; 13:4) for sacrifices to God (1 Chron 21:26; cf. Gen 22:13; 31:54;
46:1) at a place called "the house of God" (1 Chron 22:1; cf. Gen 28:17, 22). These
parallels confirm that the building activities of Abraham, Isaac, and Jacob point
to a sanctuary that is to come. First Chronicles 21 particularly mirrors the
episode with Jacob at Bethel, where God and angels also appear to David and
a link between "earth" and "heaven" is underscored.[15]

The revelation of God's presence at Sinai provides a model not only for
the temple in Jerusalem but also for the eschatological temple at the end of
time. The opening of the heavenly Holy of Holies at the end of history brings
"flashes of lightning, rumblings, peals of thunder, an earthquake, and heavy
hail" (Rev 11:19), echoing the "thunder and the flashes of lightning and the
sound of the trumpet" at God's appearance on Mount Sinai (Ex 20:18).[16] This
eschatological temple fills the new heavens and new earth (Rev 21), even as

---

[14]Similarly, Mary Douglas, *Leviticus as Literature* (Oxford: Oxford University Press, 1999), e.g.,
59-64, has argued this on the basis of many of the same observations made above.

[15]The Aramaic Targum of 1 Chron 21:23-24, together with Targum 2 Chron 3:1, identifies the place
with Jacob's experience in Gen 28 as well as the place where Abraham prepared Isaac for sacrifice.
The former text identifies a heavenly "sanctuary-house" that existed above the place, apparently,
at least since the time of Jacob's small-scale building activities recorded in Gen 28. David and
Solomon were completing a temple-building process begun with the patriarchs, wherein the
earthly temple was to reflect the heavenly (accordingly, Targum 2 Chron 6:2 says that Solomon
"built a sanctuary house . . . corresponding to the throne of the house where you dwell, which
is for ever in the heavens").

[16]For the allusion to Sinai in Rev 11:19, see R. Bauckham, *The Climax of Prophecy* (Edinburgh:
T&T Clark, 1993), 202-4. Similarly, Jewish tradition believed that at the final resurrection, "the

the purpose for the original temple is finally fulfilled with the establishment of this temple.

CONCLUSION

God's original call to Adam is extended to Abraham and the patriarchs even in a world messed up by sin. Even as sin spreads to fill the whole earth in Genesis 11, God plans to bring blessing to the whole world through Abraham in Genesis 12. Just as the images of God were to multiply and fill the earth, so Abraham's offspring would spread to the ends of the earth and establish the land as God's dwelling place. This calling begins to be fulfilled as the patriarchs establish small sanctuaries of God's presence in different parts of the land.

The patriarchs' small sanctuaries are one link in the process of how God's presence expands to fill the earth. As God reveals himself to the patriarchs who build small sanctuaries throughout the land, they begin to show the expansion of God's presence beyond one locale. God's presence continues to move with the tabernacle, but this presence seems to be confined to one locale with the building of the temple. However, this temple is destroyed, and its rebuilding after the Babylonian exile points forward to an even greater end-time temple, whose glory is not confined to any one locale but fills the whole earth. This is the original purpose of God's sanctuary in Eden, and this is fulfilled in the glorious picture of Revelation 21–22.

In the next chapter, we want to explore more fully the revelation of God's presence in the tabernacle and the temple.

---

ark will be the first to be resurrected . . . and be placed on Mount Sinai" (*Lives of the Prophets* 2:15), implying that this author viewed Sinai itself to be a mountain temple.

Chapter Four

EDEN REMIXED

THE TABERNACLE IN A CONTEXT OF SIN

ON MARCH 23, 2009, the song "Do Re Mi" from *The Sound of Music* began playing from the loudspeakers at the Antwerp train station in Belgium. Shocked commuters gaped as people gathered one by one to perform a choreographed dance to music. The event was so disruptive of the norm that most did not even notice that an electronic dance beat was added underneath this song. The song, and indeed the whole experience, was what has come to be called a *remix*—a familiar song or activity refashioned in surprising ways. In this case, the Von Trapp children, who chafed against a harsh father, are replaced by people chafing against the busy demands of a modern life. Like this Belgian flash mob, the biblical tabernacle is something of a remix: in this case, a remix of Eden in a context of sin.[1]

The tabernacle is Eden remixed. The tabernacle shows a number of similarities with Eden, since God

---

[1]"Sound of Music | Central Station Antwerp (Belgium)," YouTube video posted by Matthias De Boeck, March 23, 2009, www.youtube.com/watch?v=7EYAUazLI9k.

built his sanctuary like the high heavens,
like the earth, which he has founded forever. (Ps 78:69)

Just as a remix of "Do Re Mi" sets the frolicking joys of childhood in an urban context, so the tabernacle sets the dwelling place of God in a sinful context. Eden was created before sin entered the world, and the tabernacle is constructed in the midst of sin in the world. Even as God shows his presence through the tabernacle in Exodus, his people reject that presence with the building of the golden calf in idolatry. Provision must be made to deal with sin in the remix of Eden.

The problem of sin must be resolved in order to fulfill our mission in the world. If worship in God's dwelling place is the fuel and goal of mission, and sin separates us from this dwelling place, then this problem must be resolved for God's mission to propel us forward to fill the earth. In this chapter, we will explore how the tripartite structure of the tabernacle reflects the tripartite structure of the sanctuary of Eden. Our discussion of the tabernacle will be woven together with comments on the later temple as well, because the temple is built on the structure of the tabernacle. Within this tripartite structure, we will focus specifically on the provision found in the tabernacle to deal with the problem of sin, since this problem must be overcome to fulfill our mission.

THE TRIPARTITE STRUCTURE OF THE TABERNACLE

The tabernacle was composed of three main parts, and each part represented a major part of the cosmos as first seen in the sanctuary of Eden: (1) the Holy of Holies symbolized the presence of God with his heavenly host in the invisible dimension of the cosmos; (2) the Holy Place in the temple was emblematic of the visible heavens and its light sources; (3) the outer court represented the habitable world where humanity dwelt.[2] We have seen this tripartite structure in Eden in chapter one and Mount Sinai in chapter three. The central difference of the tabernacle from Eden is the means provided for the purification of the sinful people through the altar of burnt offering in the outer court.

---

[2]Similarly, see the early Jewish historian Josephus's observation that the tripartite structure of the tabernacle signifies "the earth [= outer court] and the sea [= inner court] . . . [and] the third portion [the heavens = holy of holies] . . . reserved for God alone, because heaven also is inaccessible to men" (*Jewish Antiquities* 3.181; see 3.123).

The Holy of Holies: The presence of God in the tabernacle. The Holy of Holies represents the heavenly dimension of the cosmos where God dwells, and the ark of the covenant demonstrates God's presence with his people here. In the Holy of Holies, cherubim are woven in the curtain separating the ark of the covenant (e.g., Ex 25:18-22; 26:1, 31-34). Just as the angelic cherubim guarded the way back to God's presence in Eden (Gen 3:24) and God's throne in the heavenly temple (e.g., Rev 4:7-9), so the sculpted cherubim guard the ark of the covenant in the Holy of Holies (1 Kings 6:23-28). They reflect the cherubim in heaven who stand guard around God's throne in the heavenly temple (see 2 Sam 6:2; 2 Kings 19:15; 1 Chron 13:6; Ps 80:1; 99:1). In this manner, the Holy of Holies represents God's unseen heavenly dwelling in his temple amidst ministering angels (Is 6:1-7; Ezek 1; Rev 4:1-11).[3]

The Holy of Holies is part of God's heavenly throne room. Yahweh "sits enthroned above the cherubim" on the "ark of God" (1 Chron 13:6). Since the ark was the footstool of God's heavenly throne (1 Chron 28:2; Ps 99:5; 132:7-8; Is 66:1; Lam 2:1), the Holy of Holies was the bottom part to where the heavenly throne room extended. Since the ark represented the heavenly presence of God, its movement outside the Holy of Holies signaled the movement of God himself breaking into the earthly realm to scatter his enemies (Num 10:35). While the Israelites wrongly attributed magical powers to the ark (1 Sam 4:4, 10-11), God's throne and kingdom are established through his word spoken at the ark. God speaks his commandments to his people "from between the two cherubim that are on the ark of the testimony" (Ex 25:22), which is his revelation breaking into the earthly realm from the heavenly. The centrality of God's word is clear in that the ark contained the tablets of stone, the words of the covenant that God established with his people. God's presence and throne is not found in some magical object but in submission to his living word. We have seen this originally in Eden, as God addressed Adam as a king to his vice regent in the garden sanctuary, speaking and commanding him (Gen 2:15, 18-19).

God's throne and kingdom are established through submission to God's word. Like the Israelites who believed that God's kingdom would automatically be established by the presence of the ark in battle (1 Sam 4:4, 10-11),

---

[3]So also V. Poythress, *The Shadow of Christ in the Law of Moses* (Brentwood, TN: Wolgemuth and Hyatt, 1991), 31, who cites also in this respect 1 Kings 8:30; Job 1:6; and Ps 89:7.

Christians today can think that God's kingdom might automatically be established by involvement in the right cause or group. However, participation in a cause or group alone is not enough. Our urgency for causes like social justice in urban centers or missions to unreached people groups must grow out of deep, prayer-soaked submission to God's word. The history of kingdom breakthrough is a history of faithful submission to God's word over time in difficult places. God's presence and kingdom is manifest as God's people daily submit themselves to God's word. The book of Acts amply attests to this, since the kingdom of God advances through the progress of the word of God, as we will see in chapter seven (Acts 6:7; 12:24; 19:20).

The Holy Place: The visible heavens and the presence of God with his people. Immediately outside the Holy of Holies was the Holy Place with the lampstand, the table of bread, and the altar of incense. Since the earthly tabernacle was patterned after the heavenly tabernacle (Ex 25:8-9; Heb 9:23), the objects of the earthly tabernacle are only properly understood when we discern the heavenly realities behind them. Together, these objects show God's presence with his people, who are a prayerful and witnessing community living out his mission in the world.

The lampstand in the Holy Place symbolized the lights of the visible heavens. The seven lamps on the lampstand were associated with the seven light sources visible to the naked eye in the sky (five planets, sun, and moon). In Genesis 1, the word for "lights" (5×) of the heavens is a unique word, used elsewhere in the Pentateuch (10×) only for the "lights" on the tabernacle lampstand.[4] In addition, John's Apocalypse closely identifies the seven lamps on the lampstand with stars (Rev 1:20).[5]

---

[4]This is the first hint that the cosmos itself was conceived as a huge temple (J. H. Walton, *Genesis*, NIVAC [Grand Rapids, MI: Zondervan, 2001], 148). Among the three other uses elsewhere in the Old Testament, two also refer to the "lights" of the heavens. The only other use is Ps 90:8 ("the light of your presence"), which may suggest that the lampstand "lights" also symbolized the light of God's glorious presence, just as the stars were held to reflect God's glory (Ps 19:1; 148:3-4; see Ps 8:1; 50:6; 57:5). Such an identification may be represented in the Qumran Hymn Scroll (1QH VII, 24): "I [the Teacher of Righteousness] will shine with a *seven-fold li[ght]* in the E[den which] Thou has [m]ade for Thy glory."

[5]G. K. Beale, *The Book of Revelation*, NIGTC (Grand Rapids, MI: Eerdmans, 1999), 211-19. Vern Poythress also contends along similar lines that the lamps signify the seven main lights of the heavens (*Shadow of Christ*, 18-19).

Just as the visible heavens reflected the glory of God (Ps 19:1), so this lampstand reflected the presence of God shining outward from the Holy Place. These lamps would always burn in the presence of God, and the priests were to trim the lamps and keep them filled with oil. This lampstand was a stylized tree of life, looking back to the tree of life in Eden, with branches on both sides with cups shaped like almond blossoms.[6] In the ancient Near East, trees were placed at the center of temples and symbolized huge cosmic trees at the center of the earth, and Israel's temple with its lampstand/tree was "the cosmic center of the universe, at the place where heaven and earth converge and thus from where God's control over the universe is effected."[7]

Later, the tree of life is understood as a witness since

the fruit of the righteous is a tree of life,
    and whoever captures souls is wise. (Prov 11:30)

Similarly, the tree of life in the new Jerusalem yields fruit and leaves "for the healing of the nations" (Rev 22:1-2), and the lampstand pictures the witness of the church (Rev 1:20) in its role of shining light and witness to the nations (Rev 11:4).[8] God's presence in the tabernacle was to blaze forth as a light to the nations.

Another object in the Holy Place was the table of bread, reminding us that God pursues fellowship with his people in his presence. On the table were plates with twelve loaves of fresh bread made daily. Every week, Aaron and his sons would go into the Holy Place to eat this fresh bread in God's presence (Lev 24:5-9). Similarly, at Mount Sinai, Moses and the seventy elders came into the presence of God to eat and drink (Ex 24:11). This occurred at the middle section of the Sinai mountain temple, which corresponds to the middle part of Israel's temple, the Holy Place. When Jesus comes as the emerging new temple (Jn 1:14), God's commitment to fellowship with his people is seen

---

[6]Carol Meyers explores this in "Lampstand," in *Harper's Bible Dictionary*, ed. P. J. Achtemeier (San Francisco: Harper & Row, 1985), 546, which summarizes her dissertation, *The Tabernacle Menorah: A Synthetic Study of a Symbol from the Biblical Cult*, American Schools of Oriental Research 2 (Missoula, MT: Scholars Press, 1976).

[7]Carol Meyers, "Temple, Jerusalem," in *Anchor Bible Dictionary*, ed. D. N. Freedman (New York: Doubleday, 1992), 6:359-60.

[8]See discussion of this theme in Beale, *Revelation*, 234-36.

in Jesus' frequent meals with sinners (e.g., Mt 9:10; 11:19; Mk 2:15; Lk 5:30; 7:34). These meals culminate with the communion table, where Jesus invites sinners to come and take of his body and blood. God not only reconciles us to himself (Eph 2:1-10), but also places us in a temple community with one another (Eph 2:11-22). Like any family that enjoys fellowship around the dinner table, our Heavenly Father invites us to his banqueting table through his Son (e.g., Rev 3:20), even as we wait for the culmination in the wedding feast of the Lamb (Rev 19:6-10). God invites his people to eat in his tabernacling presence.[9] The bread on the table in Israel's tabernacle shows God's commitment to fellowship and relationship with his people.

Also in the Holy Place, the golden altar of incense reminds us of the importance of prayer. On this altar, incense burned with a fragrant aroma, representing the prayers of the saints (Ps 141:2). As we saw earlier, the incense from this altar was taken into the Holy of Holies by the high priest on the Day of Atonement, and God would appear in this incense cloud to the priests (Lev 16:2, 12-13). In the Holy Place, the priests would pray at the altar of incense so that their prayers from this altar would ascend before the presence of God. In our role as priests (1 Pet 2:9), our prayers similarly rise before God's throne as incense (Rev 5:8; 8:4). Just as priests' prayers came before the throne of God's presence in the Holy Place, so now the prayers of all believers as priests ascend before the throne. Since our prayers come before the presence of God, we pray with confidence that "we may receive mercy and find grace to help in time of need" (Heb 4:16).

Together, the images of the lampstand, table of bread, and altar of incense point to God's presence. God draws his servants in community so that his presence might pervade our witness as our priestly prayers ascend before his throne; our witness to the world grows out of the place of worship in God's presence. From God's presence, the fire of our witness burns bright as we are lampstands and reflect the glory of God to the world. In God's presence, the intimacy of community is found as we feast together before him, just as the showbread was placed before the very presence of God, directly in front of the curtain of the Holy of Holies. Because of God's presence,

---

[9]See further discussion in Craig Blomberg, *Contagious Holiness: Jesus' Meals with Sinners*, NSBT (Downers Grove, IL: InterVarsity Press, 2005).

our prayers ascend before his throne. The power of God's presence fuels our witness to the world.

One problem remains. How can a sinful people, even priests, come into the presence of a holy God? If God's presence fuels our witness, then sin has cut off the fuel line. However, provision is made in the outer court for an impure people to come into the presence of a holy God.

The outer court: The presence of God in the midst of an impure people. The outer court of the tabernacle corresponds with the visible earth and sea where humanity dwells. In this outer court, all Israelites could enter, just as the earth is the place where all people live. The altar was to be an "altar of earth" or an "altar of [uncut] stone" (Ex 20:24-25), identifying it with the natural earth. The altar in the tabernacle is the basis for the altar in the temple, called (literally in Hebrew) the "bosom of the earth" (Ezek 43:14)[10] next to a washbasin called the "sea" (1 Kings 7:23-26). Both the "sea" and "altar" were cosmic symbols associated with the seas and the earth,[11] the place where all humanity dwells.

As Eden is remixed, the problem of sin must be remedied to provide access to a holy God, and the outer courtyard is the place where provision was made in Israel's tabernacle for that sin. Specifically, the problem of sin is addressed through the altar of burnt offering and the basin for washing. On the altar of burnt offering, offerings were given to make atonement for sin (Lev 17:11). Instead of the death of the sinner, an animal is offered (Lev 6:25-27; see Heb 6:19-20), and the blood is sprinkled on the lid of the ark of the covenant

---

[10]The ESV translates this phrase as "base on the ground" in Ezek 43:14. The altar also likely was identified with the mountain of God in Ezek 43:12. For why the "altar" in Ezek 43:16 is to be associated with the "mountain of God," see further J. D. Levenson, *Creation and the Persistence of Evil: The Jewish Drama of Divine Omnipotence* (San Francisco: Harper & Row, 1988), 92-93; G. A. Barrois, *Jesus Christ and the Temple* (Crestwood, NY: St. Vladimir's Seminary Press, 1980), 65-66; T. C. Mitchell, "Altar," in *The Illustrated Bible Dictionary*, ed. J. D. Douglas (Leicester: Inter-Varsity Press, 1980), 1:36.

[11]On which see C. Meyers, "Sea, Molten," in Freedman, ed., *Anchor Bible Dictionary*, 5:1060-61. Also, the water imagery is enhanced with ten smaller washbasins in the Holy of Holies (1 Kings 7:38-39), and the earthly imagery is further seen in the twelve bulls "entirely encircling the sea" and the "lily blossom" decorating the brim, a miniature model of land and life surrounding the seas of the earth (2 Chron 4:2-5; so NASB). Twelve bulls also supported the washbasin and were divided into groups of three, facing to the four points of the compass and four quadrants of the earth. That twelve oxen held up the "sea" and designs of lions and oxen were on the washbasin stands points further to an "earthly" identification of the outer courtyard.

in the Holy of Holies. The basin for washing served the practical purpose of allowing priests to wash after the messy process of animal sacrifice. Also, this washing provided a picture of consecration for the priests for service (Ex 29:4). Through the altar of burnt offering and basin for washing in the outer court, sinful priests are cleansed to represent sinful people in the presence of a holy God.

In Christ, the foreshadowing functions of both the altar and the basin are fulfilled. The sacrifice of bulls and goats look forward to "the Lamb of God, who takes away the sin of the world" (Jn 1:29):

> For if the blood of goats and bulls, and the sprinkling of defiled persons with the ashes of a heifer, sanctify for the purification of the flesh, how much more will the blood of Christ, who through the eternal Spirit offered himself without blemish to God, purify our conscience from dead works to serve the living God. (Heb 9:13-14)

Just as the blood of these animals purified the flesh, so the blood of Christ purifies our conscience from dead works to serve the living God. Christ is presented as the high priest of the "greater and more perfect tent" or tabernacle, who entered "into the holy places . . . by means of his own blood" (Heb 9:11-12). As a result, the blood of Christ gives us confidence "to enter the holy places" (that is, the Holy of Holies), the true tabernacle and dwelling place of God (Heb 10:19). No matter how great our sin, provision is made for access into the place of God's presence through the blood of Christ.

Similarly, the washing by water is accomplished by the blood of Jesus Christ. Before the throne of the Lamb, the saints from every nation, tribe, and tongue wear white robes (Rev 7:9). Their robes are washed and white because "they have washed their robes and made them white in the blood of the Lamb" (Rev 7:14). Washing in blood does not stain garments red, but the blood of the Lamb washes the saints to be white as snow (see Is 1:18). Jesus' blood has power to wash our sins white as snow so that we might stand in confidence before the throne of God himself. As a result, the altar of burnt offering and basin for washing point forward to the ultimate sacrifice of Christ, whose blood takes care of our sins so that sinful humanity might stand in the presence of a holy God and "serve him day and night in his [heavenly] temple" (Rev 7:15).

At the cross, Christ the High Priest offered himself as the ultimate sacrifice for sin in the invisible temple of God.[12] The sacrifice of Christ opens access for sinful people into his end-time sanctuary that reestablishes the sanctuary at Eden and escalates it.[13] Christ, the last Adam, finally obeyed, in contrast to the first Adam. Consequently, his death and resurrection launched the temple of the new creation, which Christ expands through bringing believers into that temple. As more believers become part of this temple, the temple expands, and will continue to do so until Christ's final coming. At that time, the temple will be expanded to cover the entire new and consummated cosmos for eternity.

As a result, sin does not undermine the mission that God had originally given to Adam. In the Holy Place, God's presence empowered a prayerful and witnessing community, as represented by the incense, lampstand, and table of bread. However, the outer courts made access to God's presence possible, where the altar for burnt offering and basin for washing cleansed God's people from the stains of sin so that they might be acceptable to worship and so that the high priest could represent them and their sacrifice in the holy God's very presence in the Holy of Holies. The Old Testament sacrifices in Israel's temple foreshadow the sacrifice of Jesus Christ, and washing by his blood cleanses us so that we might have access to the power of God's presence. Only in Jesus' name do we pray, witness, and walk together in community.

THE RELATIONSHIP BETWEEN TABERNACLE AND TEMPLE

Up to this point, our focus has largely been upon the tabernacle as detailed in Exodus. However, the symbolism of the tabernacle is incorporated in Israel's later temple in Jerusalem. The tabernacle was a moving temple, and the subsequent Jerusalem temple was the permanent and immovable temple. Before the Promised Land was subdued, the tabernacle moved about until

---

[12]The "propitiation" that God put forward in Jesus Christ for our justification (Rom 3:25) refers literally to the mercy seat in the Holy of Holies, the place where Christ offers himself as a sacrifice of atonement—he bears the wrath of God for us—so that we can come into the presence of God. See extended discussion in G. K. Beale, *A New Testament Biblical Theology: The Unfolding of the Old Testament in the New* (Grand Rapids, MI: Baker Academic, 2011), 486-92.

[13]See further discussion in chapter seven; also, Rev 2:7 further identifies the sanctuary with Eden in which believers begin to reside in this world (Beale, *Revelation*, 234-36).

that work was completed. When Israel's enemies were subdued, the temple did not move from Jerusalem, and God resided and rested in this more permanent temple.

THE RELATIONSHIP BETWEEN TABERNACLE AND COSMOS

Even though the tabernacle and temple are localized manifestations of God's presence, this presence was never ultimately to be limited to one place; all heaven and earth is to be the temple of the Lord. Isaiah 66:1 says,

> Thus says Yahweh:
>
> "Heaven is my throne,
> > and the earth is my footstool;
> what is the house that you would build for me,
> > and what is the place of my rest?" (Is 66:1, translation altered; see Is
> > 6:1; Jer 23:24)

Likewise, Psalm 78:69 says God

> built his sanctuary like the high heavens,
> [He built it] like the earth, which he has founded forever.

We have seen that the tabernacle is a symbolic microcosm of God's future cosmic temple. Why are the three parts of the tabernacle and temple symbolic of the cosmos? Part of the reason is to show that God's special revelatory presence in the invisible heavenly dimension (= the Holy of Holies) will break out and fill the heavenly (= Holy Place) and earthly (= outer court). Though this old cosmos will be destroyed, God will finally fill with his presence the new cosmos that he will create at the very end of time. Thus, this is why God creates the cosmos and tabernacle in similar ways. Not surprisingly, both are framed with similar language. "And God said" marks the seven days of creation, just as "And the LORD said" marks the seven speeches about the tabernacle.[14] "And it was so" and "God saw that it was good" conclude the

---

[14]Compare "And God said" in Gen 1:3, 6, 9, 14, 20, 24, 26 (see also vv. 11, 28, 29) with "And the LORD said" in Ex 25:1; 30:11, 17, 22, 34; 31:1, 12.

days of creation seven times; similarly, "just as the LORD commanded Moses" appears in two sets of sevenfold occurrences in Exodus 35–40. Just as the seventh day of creation climaxed with the Sabbath (Gen 2:3), so the seventh speech climaxes with instructions about the Sabbath (Ex 31:12-17). The creation of the cosmos and the sanctuary culminate with similar terminology (see table 4.1).[15]

Table 4.1

CREATION OF THE WORLD	CONSTRUCTION OF THE SANCTUARY
Gen 1:31: And God saw everything that he had made, and behold, it was very good. And there was evening and there was morning, the sixth day.	Ex 39:43: And Moses saw all the work, and behold, they had done it.
Gen 2:1: Thus the heavens and the earth were finished, and all the host of them.	Ex 39:32: Thus all the work of the tabernacle of the tent of meeting was finished, and the people of Israel did according to all that the LORD had commanded Moses; so they did.
Gen 2:2: And on the seventh day God finished his work that he had done, and he rested on the seventh day from all his work that he had done.	Ex 40:33: So Moses finished the work. Ex 39:43: And Moses saw all the work, and behold, they had done it; as the LORD had commanded, so had they done it. Then Moses blessed them.

Isaiah 6:3 confirms that the entire cosmos appears to be seen as a temple:

Holy, Holy, Holy, is the LORD of hosts;
    the whole earth is full of his glory.[16]

This glory is the divine radiance by which God manifests his presence in the temple. Just as God's glory filled both the tabernacle and temple at the conclusion of their construction, so God's glory fills the entire cosmos and will consummately fill the coming new heavens and earth.[17]

  While the tabernacle is a small model of the cosmos, a critical difference remains. Although God's glory already fills heaven and earth (Is 6:1, 3; 66:1) in the sense that he is providentially omnipresent, this glory is not yet fully

---

[15]Our analysis here builds on J. Blenkinsopp, "Structure of P," *Catholic Biblical Quarterly* 38 (1976): 280.

[16]Jon D. Levenson, "The Temple and the World," *Journal of Religion* 64 (1984): 289-98.

[17]Levenson, "Temple and the World," 289.

perceived by sinful humanity (see Rom 1:20-23). In the temple, Isaiah himself recognizes that his sin brings judgment and needs atoning (Is 6:5-7). Furthermore, God's special, revelatory, glorious presence remains sequestered in the back room of the temple in the Old Testament epoch. The cosmic design of the temple indicates that this sequestered presence will break out from the heavenly Holy of Holies and fill every nook and cranny of the new cosmos. God's glory in all of the present creation cannot be seen fully even by redeemed humanity. However, in the tabernacle and temple, provision was made for sinful humanity to be forgiven and cleansed and to be represented before God's presence by the high priest on the Day of Atonement. As a result, God intends for the tabernacle to expand and fill the earth with his special, revelatory presence, so that sinful humanity throughout might see and worship before the glory of the triune God in the new creation. God's intentions are seen in the call to expand Eden (see chap. 2) and in the expanding purpose of the patriarchs' small sanctuaries (see chap. 3). God's consistent purpose for his tabernacle was to expand and fill the earth, so that his special, revelatory presence would fill it and so that sinful humanity might be forgiven and cleansed and perceive the full extent of his glory in all the coming new earth.

Therefore, the parallels between the creation of the tabernacle and creation of the heavens and the earth remind us of the ultimate purpose of the tabernacle: to fill the entire heavens and earth with the consummate, end-time glory of God. The tabernacle not only teaches us worship and how sinners can come into the presence of a holy God; the tabernacle reminds us of the mission of that tabernacle to expand and fill the entire earth with the eschatological glory of God. The goal of worship is mission, to expand the dwelling place of God until it fills the entire earth that God will create for all eternity.

CONCLUSION

In the tabernacle, God's dwelling place in Eden is remixed in a context of sin. God's throne is established in the Holy of Holies through submission to God's word, reminding us that God's kingdom is established only through ongoing submission. The priests in the Holy Place reflect the blessings of this presence to others as they represent the rest of Israel, tend the lampstand of witness, gather at the table of bread and pray at the altar of incense. Similarly, worship, community, and prayer fuel our mission and witness to the world. However, sinful Israel and sinful humanity can only stand in the presence of God through the altar of burnt offering and basin for washing in the outer court. This provision for sin marks the major difference between the tabernacle and the temple of the cosmos. The tabernacle is a small model of the entire cosmos and points forward to a huge worldwide sanctuary for God's presence in the new creation. As this tabernacle expands, more and more of sinful humanity would find access to the special revelatory presence of a holy God. In sum, the tabernacle remixes the dwelling place of God in Eden and makes provision for our sin. This tabernacle was not to remain in one place, but to expand and fill the earth so that all humanity might worship the glory of God throughout the cosmos. In this manner, the tabernacle provides not only the means for our worship but the impetus for our mission.

Our mission from the beginning is to see God's localized special presence in Israel and the old, fallen world to spread and to fill the entire new created order. How will this tabernacle spread from an immovable temple in Jerusalem to fill the entire consummated cosmos? To begin to answer this question, we must explore the implications of the destruction of the temple at the time of the exile and the prophecies of its restoration found in the prophets.

Chapter Five

EDEN RESTORED

THE PROMISE OF THE EXPANSION
OF EDEN IN THE PROPHETS

FROM ITS BEGINNINGS in Eden, God designed his dwelling place to expand and fill the earth at the end of time. In the wilderness, God's dwelling place in the tabernacle was always on the move until Israel conquered the Promised Land and set the ark at rest in the temple under Solomon. However, the establishment of the temple did not contain the fullness of God's presence, since "heaven and the highest heaven cannot contain you, how much less this house that I have built!" (2 Chron 6:18). Solomon's prayer at the dedication of the temple was expansive and directed to the nations "in order that all the peoples of the earth may know your name and fear you . . . and that they may know that this house that I have built is called by your name" (2 Chron 6:33).

God's expansive purposes for his dwelling place, though, were not accomplished by Israel, since the temple became an idol for Israel and failed to be a beacon for the nations. Jeremiah castigated Israel for trusting in the temple instead of the living God (Jer 7:1-11). As a result, God would judge and destroy "the house that is called by my name, and in which you trust"

(Jer 7:14). Israel was sent into exile and the temple was destroyed. So are God's purposes for his dwelling place and temple devastated by Israel's rebellion and subsequent exile?

In this chapter, we will explore how the prophets reiterate God's purpose to establish and expand his presence in a new Edenic temple even after the exile. Israel's return from exile is understood as a restoration of Eden (Is 51:3; Ezek 36:35; Joel 2:3). Eden would not only be restored but also expanded (Is 54:2-3) to fill the earth, fulfilling the commission given to Adam as expressed through the promises to Abraham. As Eden is expanded, the nations would come (Is 2:2; Dan 2:28, 35), and God's commission to Adam would be fulfilled (Jer 3:16; see Lev 26:9). God's glorious dwelling place would expand to fill all heaven and earth (Zech 2:4-11; Is 66:1). In this manner, God promises in the prophets to restore and expand the sanctuary of Eden to fill the earth after the exile. In this way, the prophets look forward to the fulfillment of the mission first given to Adam.

RETURN FROM EXILE AS RESTORATION OF EDEN

Although Israel was devastated in exile because of her sin, her restoration from exile is pictured as a restoration to the pristine beauty of Eden. Even as Israel was "barren, exiled and put away" (Is 49:21), barren Israel would multiply and bear fruit again (Is 54:1) like Sarah. This restoration from barrenness is seen in Isaiah 51 as a restoration of Eden on an escalated scale:

> Look to Abraham your father
>   and to Sarah who bore you;
> for he was one when I called him,
>   that I might bless and multiply him.
> For Yahweh comforts Zion;
>   he comforts all her waste places
> and makes her wilderness *like Eden*,
>   her desert *like the garden of the* LORD;
> joy and gladness will be found in her,
>   thanksgiving and the voice of song. (Is 51:2-3, translation altered,
>   emphasis added)

Just as the Lord restored Sarah from barrenness to have children, so the Lord restores Israel in the wilderness back to an Edenic state of flourishing, joy, and gladness. The return from exile is pictured as a restoration of Eden. Similarly, Joel 2:3 compares the restoration of Israel's land after judgment to the "garden of Eden."

Ezekiel also connects the return from exile with the restoration of Eden: "And they will say, 'This land that was desolate has become *like the garden of Eden*, and the waste and desolate and ruined cities are now fortified and abandoned'" (Ezek 36:35, emphasis added). God not only promises to restore Eden, but also to make them "multiply and be fruitful" (Ezek 36:10-11; see Ezek 36:29-30), a fulfillment of the original commission given in Eden to "be fruitful and multiply and fill the earth" (Gen 1:28). This promise of multiplication restores Israel's desolated land to "become like the garden of Eden" in which God will "increase their people like a flock" (Ezek 36:35-38). This restoration of Eden is interpreted as God's dwelling place and sanctuary:

> I will make a covenant of peace with them. It shall be an everlasting covenant with them. And I will set them in their land and multiply them, and will set my sanctuary in their midst forevermore. My dwelling place shall be over them, and I will be their God, and they shall be my people. Then the nations will know that I am the LORD who sanctifies Israel, when my sanctuary is in their midst forevermore. (Ezek 37:26-28, translation modified)

Verse 27 indicates that this tabernacle is not to be like the former physical temple. "My dwelling place shall be *over* them," since God's glory would be over them as it was in the wilderness. The new tabernacle will extend over all of God's people who have "multiplied" and "dwell in the land" of promise, and it will not be limited merely to the Jerusalem temple or to Jerusalem itself. This shows that God's end time dwelling place will expand (on which see Ezek 37:24-28).[1] Verse 28 suggests that the temple's worldwide goal is

---

[1] So M. H. Woudstra, "The Tabernacle in Biblical-Theological Perspective," in *New Perspectives on the Old Testament* (Waco, TX: Word, 1970), 98. See D. I. Block, *The Book of Ezekiel*, NICOT (Grand Rapids, MI: Eerdmans, 1998), 421, who agrees that the preposition '*al* is to be translated "*over* them," but sees this only as a possible reflection of the glory of the Lord that resided over the tent of meeting in the wilderness.

being achieved, since "the nations will know that I am the Lord" (both in judgment and in "blessing" those who believe).

RESTORING EDEN AND HOPE IN SMALL BEGINNINGS

Restoring Eden and hope for the nations. As Eden is restored through the return from exile, a beacon of hope shines forth to all the nations. Isaiah 54 pictures the temple of Eden not only restored (Is 54:1; see Is 51:2-3) but also expanding:

> *Enlarge the place of your tent,*
>   and let the curtains of your habitations be stretched out;
>   do not hold back; lengthen your cords
>   and strengthen your stakes.
> For you will spread abroad to the right and to the left,
>   and your offspring will possess the nations
>   and will people the desolate cities. (Is 54:2-3,
>   emphasis added)

What is this tent that is to be enlarged and expanded? "Place of your tent" (Is 54:2) probably refers to the house of God (e.g., Gen 28:17),[2] a tent that expands to encompass the entire earth as the dwelling place of God (Is 40:22; see Is 66:1). In this manner, "Enlarge the place of your tent" (Is 54:2) can be seen as a call to expand the tent of God's presence.[3]

This call to "enlarge the place of your tent" (Is 54:2) is followed by a promise to "spread abroad to the right and to the left, and . . . possess the nations" (Is 54:3), building on the prophecies to Jacob and Abraham in Gen 28:14 and Gen 22:17, respectively (see table 5.1).

---

[2]We saw in Gen 28:17 that "the place" often refers to a holy place or house of God. "Place" and "tent" occur together only in references to the tabernacle as God's dwelling place (e.g., 1 Chron 15:1 says that David "prepared a place for the ark of God and pitched a tent for it" [see Lev 6:16, 26; 8:31; 2 Sam 6:17]).

[3]Is 54:11-12 confirms that the temple of God's presence is in mind here with walls of sapphires, pinnacles of agate, gates of ruby, and walls of precious stones; such stones are used elsewhere in Scripture only with the temple. E.g., 1 Chron 29:2 identifies onyx and stones for setting, antimony, colored stones, all sorts of precious stones and marble in the temple, while the city-temple vision of Rev 21:19-20 pictures "every kind of jewel . . . sapphire . . . emerald . . . beryl . . . topaz . . . amethyst."

Table 5.1

GENESIS 28:13-14; 22:17	ISAIAH 54:3
And behold, the LORD stood above it and said, "I am the LORD, the God of Abraham your father and the God of Isaac. The land on which you lie I will give to you and to your offspring. Your offspring shall be like the dust of the earth, and you shall spread abroad to the west and to the east and to the north and to the south, and in you and your offspring shall all the families of the earth be blessed."	For you will spread abroad to the right and to the left,
And your offspring shall possess the gate of his enemies	and your offspring will possess the nations and will people the desolate cities.

Just as Jacob would "spread abroad" in every direction from the place of God's presence at Bethel (Gen 28:14), so Israel restored after the exile would spread abroad throughout the nations from the restored tent of God's presence (Is 54:2-3). This call to "spread abroad" for Jacob grows out of the original call to Adam to "fill the earth" with image bearers (see discussion in chap. 2). Similarly, to "possess the nations" (Is 54:3) develops a promise to Abram (Gen 22:17) that grows out of Adam's call to "subdue the earth" (Gen 1:28).[4] In this manner, Isaiah 54:3 looks forward to a fulfillment of the commission first given to Adam.

Isaiah 54:3 adds "and will people the desolate cities" to the quotation from Genesis 22:18. Cities are desolated because of the sin of the exile, but God's people would regain what sin had destroyed to restore the pristine beauty of Eden (Is 51:3). As the desolation of these cities is restored by God's people, the nations would come. This theme runs throughout the book of Isaiah. Earlier, God promised that his word would go out as a light to the peoples

---

[4]Before Adam's disobedience, his dominion would have been expressed by subduing the creatures of the earth, including the serpent (see discussion in chap. 1). After Adam's sin, the commission would be expanded to include renewed humanity's reign over unregenerate human forces arrayed against it. Hence, the language of "possessing the gate of their enemies" is included, which elsewhere is stated as "subduing the land." "All the nations of the earth" are "blessed" by Abraham's "offspring" because a renewed humanity in God's image would "fill the earth" with regenerated progeny in that image to reflect the glory of God to the nations. In this manner, God's presence would not be limited to the place of the Promised Land only. Abraham's offspring would spread out and fill the land, and all the families of the earth would be blessed.

from a restored Eden (Is 51:3-4), and the nations would be drawn to his presence. This hope is most fully spelled out as the nations stream into the "mountain of the house of the LORD," his Edenic temple (Is 2:2-3).

When God restores what sin has destroyed, then a beacon of hope blazes forth to all the nations. Restoring Eden not only brings forgiveness for sins, but also restores the Eden of Israel's Promised Land (on which see Gen 13:10; Joel 2:13; cf. Is 51:3; Ezek 36:35) from devastation (Is 51:2-3) and desolation (Is 54:3).

The history of mission shows how this work of restoration brings hope to the nations. In 2008, Matthew Parris, an atheist, wrote a column in *The Times* of London titled, "As an Atheist, I Truly Believe Africa Needs God." He comments on the good done by Christians through hospitals, schools, and infrastructure in Africa:

> Now a confirmed atheist, I've become convinced of the enormous contribution that Christian evangelism makes in Africa. . . . Education and training alone will not do. In Africa Christianity changes people's hearts. It brings a spiritual transformation. The rebirth is real. The change is good. . . . The [African] Christians were always different. Far from having cowed or confined its converts, their faith appeared to have liberated and relaxed them. There was a liveliness, a curiosity, an engagement with the world—a directness in their dealings with others—that seemed to be missing in traditional African life.[5]

This atheist columnist could not deny that Christian evangelism and mission in Africa brought holistic restoration of brokenness throughout Africa. Just as Israel's return from exile restores God's presence in Eden and rebuilds the devastation of their nation, so Africa's restoration to God's presence through Christ has begun to restore Eden to that part of the world.

Restoring Eden from small beginnings: Daniel 2. Despite the glorious picture of Eden restored (Is 51:1-3) so that the nations stream to God's presence there (Is 2:2-3), this picture often has inauspicious beginnings. Daniel 2 brings clarity to how the mountain of the house of the Lord will be "lifted up above

---

[5]Matthew Parris, "As an Atheist, I Truly Believe Africa Needs God," *The Times* (London), December 27, 2008.

the hills" so that "all the nations shall flow to it" (Is 2:2), occurring "in the latter days" (Dan 2:28; Is 2:2). Despite the glorious power of the kingdoms of the world, represented by a great image of gold, silver, and bronze with feet of iron and clay, a "stone . . . cut out by no human hand . . . struck the image on its feet of iron and clay and broke them in pieces" (Dan 2:34). A small stone destroys this great image.

What does this stone "cut out by no human hand" (Dan 2:34) refer to? Such uncut stones are only used in the Old Testament for altars (Ex 20:25; Deut 27:6; Josh 8:31; see 1 Kings 6:7). Consequently, the New Testament writers draw from the image of the stone "cut out by no human hand" to describe the new, end-time temple (Mk 14:58; Acts 17:24; 2 Cor 5:1; Heb 9:24; see Acts 7:48), seen as "the greater and more perfect tent . . . not made with hands . . . not of this creation" (Heb 9:11). As a result, it seems plausible that the stone cut out without hands refers to some form of the temple.

This small uncut (temple?) stone expands to fill the earth, since "the stone that struck the image became a great mountain and filled the whole earth" (Dan 2:35). Throughout the Old Testament, mountains and hills frequently refer to the temple (e.g., Ps 15:1; 24:3; Is 2:2; Mic 4:1; see Jer 26:18; Is 66:20). This stone not only expands to fill the earth but establishes God's kingdom, "a kingdom that shall never be destroyed . . . [that] shall break in pieces all these kingdoms" (Dan 2:44).

Consequently, Daniel 2 sees that God's kingdom and dominion will permeate the entire earth: the "stone" that became a "great mountain . . . filled the whole earth." The notion of God's kingdom "filling the whole earth" appears to echo Genesis 1:26, 28, where God commissions Adam to "fill the earth" and to "rule . . . over all the earth."[6] The idea is that God will establish his worldwide temple and rule from his throne in that temple.

---

[6]Further evidence of a Dan 2 allusion to Gen 1:28 appears in Dan 2:38, where Daniel says that God has given the Babylonian king rule over "the beasts of the field, and the birds of the heavens," an almost verbatim repetition of the Greek Old Testament of Gen 1:28. A. Lacocque, *The Book of Daniel* (London: SPCK, 1979), 50, notes also the same parallel with the Adamic Ps 8:8. Similarly in line with the Greek Old Testament of Gen 1:28 is the mention that the second kingdom "shall rule over all the earth" (Dan 2:39). The link between Dan 2 and Gen 1 may be pointed to further by recognizing the parallel between the four sections of the statue that are demolished and replaced by God's eternal kingdom and the four beastly kingdoms that are judged and replaced by God's eternal kingdom in Dan 7. In this respect, it has been noticed by more than one commentator

Since a small stone destroys the proud kingdoms of the earth and expands to fill the earth in Daniel 2, we must not despise the day of small beginnings. Jesus himself had inauspicious beginnings in his birth in a manger, yet this birth was the birth of the Savior of the world who would both destroy and rebuild the temple (Jn 2:19-22; see discussion in chap. 6). We must not despise "the day of small beginnings" (Zech 4:10, translation altered), for the expansion of God's dwelling place usually begins in surprising places (note that Zech 4:10 refers to the "small beginnings" of the building of Israel's second temple, which was a foreshadowing of the end-time temple). Adoniram Judson persevered in decades of ministry with little visible fruit to lay a foundation for powerful gospel expansion in Burma (known today as Myanmar). Similarly, we must persevere through the day of small beginnings. God's kingdom and temple often advance and take hold in surprising places.

PROMISES FROM EDEN REVISITED IN LEVITICUS 26 AND JEREMIAH 3

God promises to fulfill the commission given in Eden (Gen 1:28) in Leviticus 26:9 and Jeremiah 3:16. Leviticus 26:6-12 clearly alludes to the commission of Genesis 1:28 in direct connection to the erection of the tabernacle (= Eden) in Israel's midst.[7] If Israel is faithful, they will defeat their enemies in the land, and God promises,

> I will turn to you and *make you fruitful and multiply you* and will confirm my covenant with you. You shall eat old store long kept, and you shall clear out the old to make way for the new. I will make my *dwelling* among you, and my soul shall not abhor you. And I will walk among you and will be your God, and you shall be my people. (Lev 26:9-12, emphasis added)

---

that the portrayal in Dan 7 alludes to the remnant of Israel as God's true humanity, a kind of corporate Adam figure, who has been given dominion over "beasts" that had formerly persecuted them (so, e.g., N. T. Wright, *The Climax of the Covenant: Christ and the Law in Pauline Theology* [Minneapolis: Fortress, 1992], 23; Lacocque, *Daniel*, 128-29, 132-33). In both Dan 2 and Dan 7 God's kingdom replaces the ungodly kingdoms who had abused the rule over creation that God had placed into their hands.

[7]See Jeremy Cohen, *Be Fertile and Increase, Fill the Earth and Master It* (Ithaca, NY: Cornell University Press, 1989), 32-33, for fuller substantiation of the allusion to Lev 26.

The dwelling place of God will be established as God makes the people fruitful and multiply. Just as God had walked in the Garden of Eden (Gen 3:8), so God would walk among his people once again as his dwelling place is established. However, this promise is contingent upon Israel's faithfulness (see Lev 26:14-39).

Though God's promise is predicated on Israel's faithfulness in Leviticus 26:9, God's promise in Jeremiah 3:16 endures despite their faithlessness. Jeremiah 3:16 looks forward to a time "when you have multiplied and been fruitful in the land" (see Gen 1:28; Lev 26:9), so that Israel will finally fulfill the Genesis commission to "be fruitful and multiply" at the time of her latter-day restoration. During that time, "Jerusalem shall be called the throne of the LORD, and all nations shall gather to it" (Jer 3:17). Jeremiah 3 alludes to Genesis 1:28 in the context of a rebuilt temple of God's presence that brings the nations to itself. However, the ark of the covenant will be absent in the renewed Jerusalem (Jer 3:16), even though the ark was God's footstool (1 Chron 28:2; Ps 99:5; 132:7) and was inextricably linked to God's heavenly throne and presence.[8] However, in the future, God's throne room in the Holy of Holies will not be localized to any cultic structure in Jerusalem (i.e., the ark), but Jerusalem itself will be called "the throne of the LORD" (Jer 3:16-17). The reason for this is that the essence of the old temple, God's ruling and special revelatory presence, which was sequestered in the back room of the Holy of Holies, will be expressed in an unfettered way at the end time. A greater temple with a greater glory than a mere physical one will not only encompass all of Jerusalem (thus the point of Jer 3:17) but the entire earth, as other biblical texts will testify. At the consummation of the final form of the new cosmos, God's glorious and special revelatory presence will inhabit every inch of the new creation, all of which will be his cosmic temple and dwelling place.

This fulfillment of Genesis 1:28 in Jeremiah 3:16 is predicated not on Israel's faithfulness but her repentance (Jer 3:11-14). Though she is unfaithful, as she acknowledges her guilt, then the Lord will provide "shepherds after my own heart" (Jer 3:15) and make her multiply and increase (Jer 3:16). Repentance

---

[8]See W. L. Holladay, *Jeremiah I*, Hermeneia (Philadelphia: Fortress, 1986), 121, who says that some Old Testament writers viewed the ark as God's throne itself.

and faithfulness are the conditions for the fulfillment of Genesis 1:28 in Jeremiah 3:16. Although Adam's faithlessness caused him to fail to fulfill Genesis 1:28, Israel's repentance will enable her to fulfill this commission. Similarly, our ongoing faithfulness to the commission of Genesis 1:28 may seem daunting. However, God's faithfulness to fulfill his promise in the face of our faithlessness is strengthening. He will do it. However, we must repent, recognizing that we fall short of his purposes and trusting in the fulfillment of his purposes for us. Though we feel inadequate in the face of the scope and challenge of God's call to be fruitful and multiply, we can find strength in God's promise to fulfill the work, to make us fruitful and multiply and expand his glorious dwelling place to fill the earth.

VISION OF A RESTORED EDEN IN ZECHARIAH 1-2 AND ISAIAH 66

Mission flows from the vision of God's purposes for his restored temple. At great length, Zechariah spells out a vision for Jerusalem as a dwelling place of God's expanded presence. God will have returned "to Jerusalem" and his "house will be built in it . . . and the measuring line will be stretched out over Jerusalem" (Zech 1:16), expanding the temple complex since it "shall be inhabited as villages without walls, because of the multitude of people and livestock in it" (Zech 2:4). Walls are not needed because the Lord "will be to her a wall of fire all around, and . . . be the glory in her midst" (2:5). In this manner, Zechariah speaks not merely about the enlargement of Jerusalem but refers to its entirety as a holy sanctuary in which God's flaming glorious presence will reside. Further, God's holiness is not restricted to the temple but spreads throughout the future new Jerusalem and Judah (Zech 14:20-21); "God's fiery presence fills the eternal city to its unwalled limits. . . . It is in its entirety a temple, hence has no temple within it."[9]

This vision of Jerusalem spurs captive Israel forward in its mission, moving out of captivity (Zech 2:6-7) to return to Zion and "spread . . . abroad as the four winds of the heavens" from there.[10] Just as Israel, as a

---

[9]Meredith G. Kline, *Glory in Our Midst* (Overland Park, KS: Two Age Press, 2001), 76.

[10]On which see Kline, *Glory in Our Midst*, 79, though it is possible that the "spreading out" in v. 6 merely refers to God's past dispersing of Israel into exile, which is the point of v. 6a and v. 7.

corporate Adam, was to spread out to subdue the earth and fill it with his glory, so Israel must spread out as the "four winds of the heavens." This commission to spread out is combined with a promise that God would establish his dwelling in their midst. Israel rejoices because God "will dwell in" Israel's midst when they return (Zech 2:10), and "many nations . . . shall join themselves to the Lord . . . and shall be *my people*" as God "will dwell in your midst" (Zech 2:11, emphasis added), establishing God's dwelling place and tabernacle there.[11] In this manner, Zechariah paints a vision of how the future tabernacle of God's presence encompasses many nations, filling out the picture of the expansion of Jerusalem seen earlier in Zechariah 1:16. God will construct his future temple on a huge scale, and his tabernacling presence will reside with both Jews and Gentiles who trust in him.[12] The last phrase of Zechariah 2 ("For he has roused himself from his holy dwelling") suggests that his coming judgment has begun or is imminent, and his heavenly tabernacling presence will descend once again and fill Israel in a greater way than ever before.

Similarly, a vision of God's heavenly throne extended to earth instigates the mission of prayer for more of God's presence in Isaiah. Isaiah 63:15 pleads for God to see from his heavenly temple,[13] since the earth is the footstool of God's heavenly throne (Is 66:1). The Holy of Holies represented the invisible, heavenly temple and throne of God (= Is 66:1a), where the heavenly dimension extended down to earth as God's footstool.[14] The vision of God's heavenly

---

Since, however, vv. 1-5 focus on an expansion of the temple by means of God's expanding theophanic presence, v. 6 might naturally refer to God's people also spreading out, impelled by that presence.

[11] The repeated Hebrew verb "dwell" is the typical word used for God's "dwelling" in the tabernacle, and the noun form of the verb is rendered "tabernacle" throughout the Old Testament. Also, throughout the Old Testament "my people" is reserved for ethnic Israel, but is now applicable to all who trust in him in the latter days; see also Zech 8:22-23; Hos 1:8–2:1; Rom 9:25-26; 1 Pet 2:10.

[12] For a more in-depth analysis of Zech 1–2 along the lines just given, see Kline, *Glory in Our Midst*, 71-94, who refers to the future Jerusalem as a "cosmic temple-city" that is a renewed "Eden" (76-78).

[13] Is 63:15 asks, "Look down from heaven and see, from your holy and beautiful habitation," which is the temple in heaven (so L. Koehler and W. Baumgartner, *The Hebrew and Aramaic Lexicon of the Old Testament*, rev. W. Baumgartner and J. J. Stamm [New York: Brill, 1994], 263).

[14] The same use of "footstool" occurs also in 1 Chron 28:2; Ps 99:5; 132:7; Lam 2:1. See further Menaham Haran, *Temples and Temple-Service in Ancient Israel: An Inquiry into the Character of Cult Phenomena and the Historical Setting of the Priestly School* (Oxford: Clarendon Press, 1977), 255-57.

temple descending and encompassing the earth instigates the prayer of
Isaiah 64:1-2 (especially in light of Is 63:15):

> Oh that you would rend the heavens and come down,
>   that the mountains might quake at your
>   presence—[see Ex 19:18!] . . .
> to make your name known to your adversaries,
>   and that the nations might tremble at your presence!

Isaiah pleads for God's special, revelatory presence to descend as it did at
Mount Sinai (which we have argued was a mountain temple) and the first
tabernacle to accomplish finally the divine intentions inherent in that initial
exodus.[15] God intended at that time for his special revelatory presence to not
be limited to the tabernacle (and to Moses) but extended to all of God's true
people. As a result, God includes even the Gentiles in the priesthood, and
makes them priests and Levites in the new, expanded temple (Is 66:18-21;
see also Is 56:3-8). Isaiah 66:1 therefore looks to a future new cosmos and
temple that God will create, and in which he will dwell forever as an extension
of the present *heavenly* temple.

CONCLUSION

This chapter has explored God's purposes to expand Eden to fill the earth
even after the painful judgment of the exile. Even in the face of that judgment
because of Israel's sin, God promises to restore Eden and to expand the
dwelling place of his revelatory presence until it fills the earth. At this time,
this renewed Eden would contain escalated blessings that even the original
Eden had not contained. The prophets promise the restoration and expansion
of Eden to fill the earth, but these prophecies and promises are not fulfilled
in the Old Testament period. Nevertheless, God intends for his mission to
be completed.

Unlike Adam's disobedience in Eden that led to exile from God's presence,
Israel must obey in their "Eden" (Gen 13:10; cf. also Is 51:3; Ezek 36:35; 47:12;
Joel 2:3) to fulfill their renewed commission as a corporate Adam. However,

---

[15]So E. J. Kissane, *The Book of Isaiah* (Dublin: Browne and Nolan, 1943), 2:299.

Israel sinned like Adam and was exiled from God's presence and out of the land, and God withdrew his presence from their temple (Ezek 9:3; 10:4, 18-19; 11:22-23). As a result, the prophecies and promises for God's people to be fruitful and multiply and fill the earth, expanding the sanctuary of Eden, are neither fulfilled in the line of Abraham in the Old Testament nor in Israel's temple. How will these promises be realized and our mission fulfilled? We must turn to the work of Jesus, the second Adam and new Israel, to answer this question.

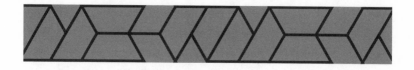

Chapter Six

EDEN REBUILT

JESUS AS THE NEW TEMPLE IN THE GOSPELS

SIN CONTINUALLY SEPARATES US from the presence of God. After sin in Eden, Adam and Eve were exiled from God's presence. Even as typological provision for sin was given in the tabernacle and temple as Eden remixed, Israel's lack of repentance over sin led to exile from the land and destruction of that temple. After the exile, the Israelites longed for the restoration of Eden and the presence of God in the temple. After the destruction of Solomon's temple and the Babylonian exile, the temple was rebuilt and dedicated in 516 BC. Again in 20 BC, Herod undertook a massive expansion project of the temple, but this expansion failed to fulfill prophecies of the future glory of God drawing the nations to Jerusalem (e.g., Is 2:2-3). In Jesus, however, the locus of fulfillment for the prophecies of the temple shifts from the architectural temple to his person. In this chapter, we will explore how the Old Testament hopes for the temple begin to be fulfilled in Jesus. Jesus' sacrifice reunites sinful humanity to a holy God so that we might begin to fulfill our mission in his presence.

FAILURE OF THE JERUSALEM TEMPLE

John 2:13-17: The Passover of the Jews was at hand, and Jesus went up to Jerusalem. In the temple he found those who were selling oxen and sheep and pigeons, and the money-changers sitting there. And making a whip of cords, he drove them all out of the temple, with the sheep and oxen. And he poured out the coins of the money-changers and overturned their tables. And he told those who sold the pigeons, "Take these things away; do not make my Father's house a house of trade." His disciples remembered that it was written, "Zeal for your house will consume me."

The location of the animal sellers and money changers in the temple is problematic. Their presence was inevitable since travel to the temple over long distances made transport of animals difficult. However, the issue is their location. Though they could have easily bought and sold on the Mount of Olives just outside the Temple Mount, business was done in the Court of the Gentiles. Though Israelites could move beyond this raucous outermost court to the Court of Israel to worship, people from other nations could only enter the Court of the Gentiles. Since this Court of the Gentiles was filled with buying and selling, any Gentiles who came to worship the Lord would find themselves disappointed. Even if they might come hungry for God's presence, they would go away hungry.

Jesus is concerned for all people to find satisfaction in the presence of the Lord. As a result, he drives out the oxen sellers, sheep sellers, pigeon sellers, and moneychangers from the courtyard, commanding them, "Do not make my Father's house a house of trade" (Jn 2:16). The issue is that this is "my Father's house." Even more explicitly, "My house shall be called a house of prayer for all the nations" (Mk 11:17). Jesus quotes Isaiah 56:7, a prophecy that the temple would become a rallying place and location of prayer for the Gentiles (Is 56:3-8). The temple "was not fulfilling its God-ordained role as witness to the nations but had become, like the first temple, the premier symbol of a superstitious belief that God would protect and rally his people irrespective of their conformity to his will."[1] The Father's house, a house intended to bless all the nations, prevented the nations from worship.

---

[1] D. A. Carson, "Matthew," in *Expositor's Bible Commentary*, ed. Frank E. Gaebelein, J. D. Douglas, and Walter Kaiser, vol. 8 (Grand Rapids, MI: Zondervan, 1984), 442; see also M. D. Hooker,

As a result, the temple is like a fig tree that had leaves but no fruit. From a distance, the temple looked very beautiful and promised fruit and satisfaction with its "leaves" but failed to satisfy hunger with any fruit. Mark 11 makes this point clear. Jesus inspects the temple (Mk 11:11), curses the fig tree (Mk 11:12-14), cleanses the temple (Mk 11:15-19), and then teaches about the cursing of the fig tree (Mk 11:20-25). The cursing of the fig tree and the cleansing of the temple are intertwined. Jesus explains the cursing of the fig tree: "Truly I say to you, whoever says to this mountain, 'Be taken up and thrown into the sea,' and does not doubt in his heart, but believes that what he says will come to pass, it will be done for him" (Mk 11:23). Though many have tried in vain to move anthills with their "faith," the context of the temple cleansing suggests that "this mountain" refers to the Temple Mount. The command to "speak to this mountain" is not a formula to fix our problems, as some may assert, but Jesus speaks here of the destruction of the temple that had leaves but not fruit (representing unfruitful Israel herself), failing to impart the life that it advertised. Jesus returns to the temple and exposes the ignorance and failure of the temple leaders (Mk 11:27-33). Even as the failures of the temple are exposed, "the stone that the builders rejected has become the cornerstone" of a new temple, built upon Jesus as the chief cornerstone (Mk 12:1-11).

Jesus' cleansing of the temple presumably would have briefly stopped the offering of sacrifices (as possibly suggested by Jn 2:15-16). As a result, Jesus may suggest that the temple's purpose in offering sacrifices for forgiveness was passing away and that the temple itself was awaiting judgment.[2] Although the blind and lame were forbidden to draw near to the tabernacle as priests (Lev 21:18), they are now healed by Jesus in the temple after its cleansing (Mt 21:14). Jesus clears the way for the eschatological temple, where outcasts are gathered and made joyful in God's presence in his house (Is 56:3-8).

The Gospel According to Mark, Black's New Testament Commentaries (Peabody, MA: Hendrickson, 1991), 268.

[2]See N. T. Wright, *Jesus and the Victory of God* (Minneapolis: Fortress, 1992), 423, though Wright's proposal needs further exegetical substantiation, since mention of the shutting down of the sacrifices is omitted in Matthew and the other Synoptic parallels.

DESTROYING AND REPLACING THE TEMPLE

So the Jews said to him, "What sign do you show us for doing these things?" Jesus answered them, "Destroy this temple, and in three days I will raise it up." The Jews then said, "It has taken forty-six years to build this temple, and will you raise it up in three days?" But he was speaking about the temple of his body. When therefore he was raised from the dead, his disciples remembered that he had said this, and they believed the Scripture and the word that Jesus had spoken. (Jn 2:18-22)

The Jews demand a sign, and Jesus declares, "Destroy this temple, and in three days I will raise it up." The Jews cannot understand this statement, since it had taken forty-six years to build the temple. However, John clarifies that "he was speaking about the temple of his body" (Jn 2:22). How does the destruction and rebuilding of the temple relate to the death and resurrection of Jesus? Let us now take a closer look at this passage.

The locus of God's presence: from the temple building to the person of Jesus. The reference to Jesus as a temple in John 2 develops John 1:14: "And the Word became flesh and *tabernacled* among us, and we beheld his glory" (our translation). Just as the glory of God filled the tabernacle (Ex 40:34-35), so the glory of God now tabernacles in Jesus. The presence of God, formerly contained in the Holy of Holies, has begun to burst forth into the world in the form of the incarnate God, Jesus Christ. As a result, Jesus reveals to Nathanael that "you will see heaven opened, and the angels of God ascending and descending on the Son of Man" (Jn 1:51). This statement alludes to God's appearance to Jacob at Bethel (Gen 28:12), leading to the establishment of a temporary altar/sanctuary that brought heaven and earth together, pictured by a ladder to heaven with angels ascending and descending (see discussion in chap. 3). This little temple at Bethel was a precursor of the larger temple to be built in Jerusalem, which became the permanent place (until the exile) where God's presence in heaven was linked to the earth. Jesus identifies himself with the temple stairway of Genesis 28 and claims that he, not the Jerusalem temple, is the primary link between heaven and earth.[3] Therefore, Jacob's

---

[3]We have subsequently found that I. H. Marshall, "Church and Temple in the New Testament," *Tyndale Bulletin* 40 (1989): 211-12, has made the same observation; likewise A. Spatafora, *From the "Temple of God" to God as the Temple* (Rome: Gregorian University Press, 1997), 111-12.

small sanctuary in Genesis 28 pointed forward not only to the temporary Jerusalem temple but ultimately to the permanent temple built by Christ.

The locus of God's presence shifts from the Jerusalem temple to the person of Jesus so that he is the continuation of the true temple. Consequently, Jesus teaches that the time was dawning when true worship would not occur at the Jerusalem temple, but would be directed toward the Father (and, by implication, through the Messiah) in the sphere of the coming eschatological Spirit of Jesus (Jn 4:21-26). The Spirit creates a link with heaven through trust in Christ, and this trust brings them into the sphere of the true temple consisting of Christ and his Spirit. Worship in the true temple would no longer be geographically located in Jerusalem but in Christ.

Similarly, the Synoptic Gospels suggest that the locus of God's presence was changing from the temple to the person of Jesus. Mark suggests that Jesus replaces Israel's old temple ("this temple that is made with hands") with the new temple of his resurrection body (a temple "not made with hands"; Mk 14:58). When Jesus was crucified, the curtain of the temple separating the presence of a holy God from a sinful people was torn in two (Mk 15:38). Jesus himself had begun to represent the new temple during his earthly ministry, and the temple of Jesus' body was destroyed at the cross, so the curtain that separated God from humanity was also destroyed. The destruction of Jesus as the emerging true temple and the destruction of the old idolatrous temple go hand in hand. Accordingly, the crucifixion is the destruction not only of Christ's body but also of the old temple itself, so that God's presence could be released from the old Holy of Holies into the new, unseen Holy of Holies. Even before the formal rebuilding of the new temple at Jesus' resurrection, the crucifixion was the destruction of the old temple, in the midst of which the new Holy of Holies had already begun to emerge. Jesus' death and resurrection are a destruction and raising up of the temple. This is why the writer to the Hebrews says,

> Therefore, brothers, since we have confidence to enter the holy places by the blood of Jesus, by the new and living way that he opened for us through the curtain, that is, through his flesh, and since we have a great priest over the house of God, let us draw near with a true heart in full assurance of faith, with our hearts sprinkled clean from an evil conscience and our bodies washed with pure water. (Heb 10:19-22)

While Jesus' death destroyed the temple curtain, it opened up a "new and living way through the curtain." Furthermore, the embroidery on the temple veil represented the starry heavens of the old cosmos. Consequently, the tearing of the curtain suggests symbolically the tearing and the beginning of the destruction of the old world, as the presence of God breaks out from the Holy of Holies and begins to create a new world.[4] Through the sacrifice of his body, we can enter through the new and living way of Jesus into the very presence of God.

Since Jesus is the new temple, the life of the temple is now found in Christ. A river of life flowed from the presence of God in the sanctuary of Eden (Gen 2:10-14), and the eschatological temple (Ezek 47:1-12; see Joel 3:18; Zech 14:8) will be surrounded by tree(s) of life that bring healing to the nations (Gen 2:9; Ezek 47:12; Rev 22:2). In light of this background, Jesus' offer of living water to the Samaritan woman (Jn 4:14) suggests that Jesus is the beginning form of the new temple from which true life in God's presence proceeds. Notably, Jesus shifts the discussion from a place of worship ("neither on this mountain nor in Jerusalem" [Jn 4:21]) to a manner of worship ("true worshipers will worship the Father in spirit and truth" [Jn 4:23]), where Jesus will give water that "will become in him a spring of water welling up to eternal life" (Jn 4:14).

John 7:37-39 confirms the connection between the rivers of living water found in Jesus and the waters flowing from the temple. Teaching in the temple on the last day of the Feast of Tabernacles, Jesus says:

> If anyone thirsts, let him come to me and drink. Whoever believes in me, as the Scripture has said, "Out of his heart will flow rivers of living water." Now this he said about the Spirit, whom those who believed in him were to receive, for as yet the Spirit had not been given, because Jesus was not yet glorified.

In verse 38 Jesus alludes to the prophecy of water flowing from the temple in Ezekiel, Joel, and Zechariah.[5] The "heart" from which "flow[s] rivers of living water" is Jesus himself as the new "Holy of Holies." In the Old Testament, the waters clearly flowed from the innermost part of the temple (i.e., the Holy

---

[4]See further G. K. Beale, *The Temple and the Church's Mission*, NSBT (Downers Grove, IL: InterVarsity Press, 2004), 300-301; see also 38, 45-47.

[5]Commentators generally acknowledge these Old Testament allusions here, especially that of Ezekiel (recently, see Spatafora, *From the "Temple of God,"* 114, 292).

of Holies) where Yahweh's presence had dwelt in the past and would dwell
again in the latter-day temple. Jesus was that presence on earth. John 7:39
interprets the "living water" to be the Spirit poured out at Pentecost by Jesus
himself to all those who would believe in him (see Acts 2:32-38). John 7:37
tells us that Jesus spoke the words of John 7:37-39 "on the last day of the feast,
the great day" (of tabernacles), the time of a special water-drawing and
pouring ritual in the temple (*m. Sukkah* 4:9-10).[6] The timing of Jesus' pronouncement during the feast of tabernacles may have enhanced further his
identification with the water of the new temple.

Further, Jesus' self-identification with the temple is underscored in
Matthew 12:6, where he says about himself, "Something greater than the
temple is here." Jesus "is greater than Jonah" as a prophet, and his deliverance
is greater than Jonah's because he will *actually* die for three days and rise
(Mt 12:39-41). Jesus is "greater than Solomon" because he is a greater king
and has more wisdom (Mt 12:42). Similarly, Jesus is greater than the temple
now because "God's presence is more manifest in Him than in the Temple.
On him, not on the Temple, rests the 'Shekinah' glory in an even greater way
than previously in the temple."[7] Therefore, Jesus not only takes over the
temple's role in sacrifice, but becomes the unique place for God's special
revelatory presence. God began to manifest his glorious presence in Jesus'
life, death, and resurrection in a greater way than it was ever manifested in
Israel's old, physical temple structure.

Under construction: Jesus as cornerstone. While Jesus identifies himself
with the temple, he hints that this temple is still under construction. In
Matthew 21:42, he identifies himself with the rejected cornerstone of
Psalm 118:22-23:

> The stone that the builders rejected
>   has become the cornerstone.
> This is the LORD's doing;
>   it is marvelous in our eyes.

---

[6]On which see further A. Edersheim, *The Temple* (Peabody, MA: Hendrickson, 1994), 220-27.
[7]A. Cole, *The New Temple* (London: Tyndale Press, 1950), 12; this perhaps echoes the prophecy in
Hag 2:9, "The latter glory of this house shall be greater than the former."

The "cornerstone" in the psalm is likely to be identified with the "corner-stone" of the temple (see the context of Ps 118:19-20 and Ps 118:26-27). Just as the wicked tenant farmers are destroyed because they fail to tend the vineyard and murder the landowner's son, so Israel is destroyed because it fails to tend their vineyard and murder God's Son (Mt 21:33-46). As a result, the temple would be destroyed, and a new temple would be con-structed. Thus, Jesus identifies himself with the "cornerstone" of a new temple that is being laid in their midst: "The stone that the builders rejected has become the cornerstone."

Jesus applies the psalm's temple "cornerstone" image to himself. The context of Matthew 21 is the temple: (1) he cleanses the temple (Mt 21:12-13); (2) the physically handicapped come to him in the temple to be healed (Mt 21:14); (3) he is praised in the temple for his healings (Mt 21:15); (4) he speaks the parable of the tenants after he had "entered the temple" (Mt 21:23, 33-44). This temple context suggests that Jesus is not simply a cornerstone of a generic building, but the cornerstone of a newly constituted temple. Consequently, the rejection of Jesus as the "cornerstone" of the temple ("the stone that the builders rejected") is equivalent to rejection of Jesus as the true temple ("has become the cornerstone") that is being built. Jesus applies the cornerstone metaphor in Psalm 118 to himself, since he is the foundation stone of the new temple.[8]

Furthermore, the stone that crushes in Matthew 21:44 enhances the picture of Jesus as the beginning of a new sanctuary, since "the one who falls on this stone will be broken to pieces; and when it falls on anyone, it will crush him." This stone that crushes comes from Daniel 2:34-35:[9] "A stone was cut out by

---

[8]Further, Paul and Peter confirm Matthew's identification of this cornerstone with this temple, since Jesus is the "cornerstone" upon which the rest of the "temple" of the church is being built and from which it will grow (Eph 2:20-22; 1 Pet 2:4-8, which also quotes Ps 118:22). Outside the New Testament, the Epistle of Barnabas 6:14-15 also appears to identify Christ as the temple, together with his followers, which also plausibly develops earlier references to him as the stone of Psalm 118 (Barnabas 6:3-4). Also, W. D. Davies and D. C. Allison, *The Gospel According to Saint Matthew*, ICC (Edinburgh: T&T Clark, 1991), 2:185-86, identify the "cornerstone" with the new temple in Matt 21:42, citing in partial support *Testament of Solomon* 22-23, which refers to the stone of Ps 118 as the one that completed Solomon's temple.

[9]E.g., J. Nolland, *Luke 18:35–24:53*, WBC 35C (Dallas: Word, 1993), 953, 955; D. L. Bock, *Luke 9:51–24:53*, Baker Evangelical Commentary on the New Testament (Grand Rapids, MI: Baker, 1996), 1604-5; see also C. A. Evans, *Mark 8:27–16:20*, WBC 34 (Nashville: Thomas Nelson, 2001), 445,

no human hand, and it struck the image . . . and broke [it]" and it "became like the chaff of the summer threshing floors; and the wind carried [it] away." In Daniel 2 this stone would destroy evil kingdoms and become "a great mountain [that] filled the whole earth." Earlier, we suggested that this statement in Daniel 2 described the "stone" as a foundation stone of a temple that would expand to fill the entire earth. Consequently, Jesus follows up his reference to the temple "cornerstone" of Psalm 118 with the same temple "stone" of Daniel 2,[10] since the temple images from Psalm 118 and Daniel 2 portray the same victorious act of establishing a new temple brought about in Christ's resurrection.

Accordingly, Jesus says, "The kingdom of God will be taken away from you, and be given to a nation producing the fruit of it" (Mt 21:43, our translation). In the context of the preceding vineyard parable, his pronouncement combines the notions of *kingdom* and *vineyard*.[11] This may also be the reason that the image of the withered "fig tree" precedes the vineyard parable, since it was a common image found in botanical descriptions for Israel's prosperous land throughout the Old Testament,[12] as first seen in Genesis 3:7. In particular, as we have seen, since Israel's land was viewed sometimes as "the Garden of Eden" with connotations of the first primal sanctuary, the fig tree would have been a suitable feature to include together with the vineyard and temple imagery in Matthew 21. The Old Testament temple represented God's presence on earth, and Jesus now represents that presence in the midst of his followers. Jesus makes it abundantly clear in Matthew 24 (and parallels) that Israel's

---

who sees Christ's claim in Mk 14:58 to "build another [temple], not made with hands" to be an allusion to Dan 2:44-45. Some manuscripts omit Mt 21:44, though it is probably original; but even if not, Lk 20:18 includes it without any manuscript variants to the contrary.

[10]See S. Kim, "Jesus—The Son of God, the Stone, the Son of Man, and the Servant: The Role of Zechariah in the Self-Identification of Jesus," in *Tradition and Interpretation in the New Testament: Essays in Honor of E. E. Ellis*, ed. G. F. Hawthorne and O. Betz (Grand Rapids, MI: Eerdmans, 1987), 134-48, who argues that Jesus understood these Old Testament passages, together with others like Zech 4 and 6, to be fulfilled in the temple-building activity of his sacrificial death.

[11]See Joseph Fitzmyer, *The Gospel According to Luke X–XXIV*, AB 28A (New York: Doubleday, 1985), 1282, 1286, who identifies Jesus as "the chief stone of the heavenly sanctuary" in Lk 20:17-18, and sees an allusion to Dan 2:34-35, 44-45 partly behind the stone image.

[12]Such descriptions occur four times in the Old Testament. In addition, the stock phrase "each man sitting under his vine and his fig tree" occurs five times, referring to prosperity in the land (two of which pertain to eschatological conditions: Mic 4:4; Zech 3:10; see Joel 2:22). Conversely, destroying vines and fig trees connote judgment on Israel (approx. eight times).

temple will be destroyed. Nevertheless, another temple would arise instead in the form of Jesus and his followers.

The "stone" texts of Matthew 21 may grow out of Jesus' mention of the "rock" in chapter 16: "And I tell you, you are Peter, and on this rock I will build my church, and the gates of hell shall not prevail against it" (Mt 16:18). While this "rock" may be Jesus,[13] it more likely refers either to Peter's confession that Jesus is "the Christ, the Son of the living God" (Mt 16:16) or to Peter himself.[14] Though Jesus is not here the foundation stone, he is certainly the builder of the new temple.[15] He builds his church on the foundation stone of the apostles' teaching (as Paul later asserts in Eph 2:19-22), which, of course, is about himself. In view of the entire Gospel of Matthew, Jesus builds both on the foundation stone of himself and the disciples.

As Jesus builds this new temple, the locus for the forgiveness of sins shifts here as well. Matthew 16:19 continues, "I will give you the keys of the kingdom of heaven, and whatever you bind on earth shall be bound in heaven, and whatever you loose on earth shall be loosed in heaven." The binding and loosing in this verse describe the forgiveness of sins. God originally instituted Israel's temple to offer sacrifices for the forgiveness of sins, but now Jesus has become the divinely instituted location where forgiveness is to be found (see Lk 7:49-50) since he himself is also the sin offering.[16] The locus for the forgiveness of sins shifts from Israel's old temple to the new temple of the church, centered in Jesus. In Matthew 16:19, Jesus introduces the means of forgiveness in the new age by saying, "I will give you the keys of the kingdom of heaven,"

---

[13]This receives early attestation from the *Odes of Solomon* 22:12 (AD 100), which identifies the "rock" of Mt 16:18 as the foundation of the new temple: "And the foundation of everything is your rock. And upon it you have built your kingdom, and became the dwelling place of the holy ones."

[14]On the debate about the identification of the "rock," see C. C. Caragounis, *Peter and the Rock*, Beihefte zur Zeitschrift für die neutestamentliche Wissenschaft 58 (Berlin: W. de Gruyter, 1990), who himself prefers that Peter's confession about Christ is the "rock." Alternatively, see also Carson, *Matthew*, 367-70, and D. A. Hagner, *Matthew 14–28*, WBC 33B (Dallas: Word, 1995), 470-72, who identify Peter with the "rock."

[15]See Davies and Allison, *The Gospel According to Saint Matthew*, 2:626-27, who also understand the "stone" of Mt 16:18 to be the foundation of a temple.

[16]On which see further Mt 18:15-18, where the church authoritatively proclaims forgiveness or lack thereof based on one's life as a consistent expression of faith in Christ; likewise see Jn 20:23: "If you forgive the sins of any, their sins have been forgiven them; if you retain the sins of any, they have been retained" (our translation).

showing that the authoritative basis for dealing with sins has passed from the old temple to the new temple, the church in Christ.[17] Matthew 9:2-6 (see Mk 2:1-12; Lk 5:18-26) says that "the Son of Man [Adam] has authority on earth to forgive sins," since the pardoning of sins, formerly obtained at the temple, is part of his work as the priestly last Adam. Hence, again, we have the close association of a temple function with the Adamic commission to have authority over the earth.[18] Consequently, Jesus sent out his disciples to announce this new basis of forgiveness of sins (Mt 16:19; Jn 20:23). Thus in the midst of Jesus' ministry the locus of forgiveness was being transferred from the temple sacrifices to himself.

Jesus, the temple, and the new creation. Jesus' death and resurrection inaugurate the new creation, as God's purpose in the original creation and temple of Eden begins to be fulfilled in the new creation and temple of Jesus. This process can be seen most clearly in Matthew 27:50-54, where the death of Jesus is tied to the tearing of the temple veil and shaking of the entire cosmos. The emphasis on the new creation is also to be observed in the allusions to Genesis at the beginning of each of the Gospels, and in the portrayal of Jesus as a new Adam and Israel.[19] Before we explore Jesus' death and

---

[17]See Carson, *Matthew*, 367-74, for fuller elaboration of the meaning of Mt 16:18-19. Furthermore, if Mt 16:19 is an allusion to Is 22, it might enhance the possibility that Jesus is speaking about the temple. Is 22:22 portrays Eliakim, prime minister to King Hezekiah, as having "on his shoulder the key of the house of David" because he controlled who could enter into the king's presence and service. There were priestly connotations associated with Eliakim's kingly administration, since Is 22:21 portrays him clothed with a "robe" and a "sash [bound] on him." The Aramaic translation of Is 22:22 says that God "will place the key of the sanctuary and the authority of the house of David in his hand." And then Is 22:24 (of the Aramaic version) says that even Eliakim's relatives will be "priests wearing the ephod." Like Eliakim, Christ establishes himself as having an authoritative position in the new temple in Mt 16:18, and then extends his priestly authority to his disciples, who also have priestly authority. Mt 16:19, in the light of Mt 18:15-18 and Jn 20:23, says they express what would appear to be their priestly task by declaring who is forgiven and who is not. Rev 3:7 portrays Christ as having the "key" of Is 22:22, and relates this "key" to his followers being able eventually to become "a pillar in the temple of my God" (see Rev 3:8-9 with Rev 3:12). "Keys of the temple" are also said to be in the possession of priests in 1 Chron 9:27 and 2 Baruch 10:18. In both Is 22 and 2 Baruch, the keys are being taken away from unworthy keepers in Israel and transferred elsewhere, which also appears to be the case here in Mt 16:19; could the idea be that the keys to the true temple are being taken from old Israel and transferred to true Israel—Jesus and his followers?

[18]Wright, *Jesus and the Victory of God*, 406-12, has inspired this paragraph.

[19]See further the discussion below in this chapter for examples of Jesus as a new creation, last Adam, and true Israel.

resurrection as a new creation in Matthew 27, we will briefly survey how Jesus is a new Adam restoring a new creation in the Gospel of Matthew.

Matthew's Gospel begins with the Greek expression *biblos geneseōs,* which can be translated the "book of the genealogy" or the "book of beginning" or even the "book of genesis." The only places in the entire Greek Old Testament where this phrase occurs is in Genesis 2:4 ("These are the generations") and Genesis 5:1-2 ("This is the book of the generations of Adam"). Furthermore, just as Genesis 5 continues with a genealogy of the generations of Adam, so Matthew 1 continues with a genealogy of Jesus. Matthew uses this phrase to record the new age and new creation launched by the coming of Jesus Christ. Similarly, Luke's genealogy connects Jesus with the work of a new age and new creation by showing Jesus as "the son of Adam, the son of God" (Lk 3:38).[20] Also, Mark's Gospel begins with "the beginning of the gospel of Jesus Christ," alluding to the "in the beginning" of Genesis 1:1.

Furthermore, Jesus succeeds where Adam and Israel had failed. Jesus' temptation for "forty days and forty nights" in the wilderness echo Israel's forty years in the wilderness. Jesus responds with faith to each temptation with words taken from the account of Israel's failure in the wilderness (Deut 8:3 in Mt 4:4; Deut 6:16 in Mt 4:7; Deut 6:13 in Mt 4:10). Jesus overcomes the temptations to which Israel succumbed. Also, as a new and end-time Adam, Jesus conquered temptations that defeated Adam and Eve. After Jesus' temptations, "he was with the wild animals, and the angels were ministering to him" (Mk 1:13, suggesting that he is the promised one of Ps 91:11-12); he subdues the beasts instead of being subdued by a beast like Adam. Why do Jesus' temptations have in mind both the temptations of Adam and Israel? It is likely because Israel herself was conceived of as a corporate Adam, since the Adamic commission, as we have seen in earlier chapters, was passed on to Israel. Israel, like her forefather Adam, also failed in the temptations that Christ, the Last Adam, overcame.

Consequently, Jesus' victory over temptation appears to have prepared him to conquer the ultimate satanic prince of all wicked nations[21] and to

---

[20]S. C. Glickman, *Knowing Christ* (Chicago: Moody, 1980), 55-58.

[21]This idea may be enhanced by recalling that the devil is elsewhere referred to in the Gospels as "Beelzebul" (Mt 10:25) or "Beelzebub," variant names for deities associated with "Baal" in Canaan

conquer the land in a way that Israel had not been able. His resistance to these satanic allurements was the beginning of his defeat of the devil. This ministry of casting out demons continues this holy warfare of the true Israel, Jesus. Christ's casting out demons was an expression of his beginning, though decisive, defeat of Satan, who had brought creation into captivity through his deception of Adam and Eve. This is the significance of the parable of the binding of the strong man (Mt 12:29). By casting out the devil and his forces, Jesus was accomplishing the latter-day defeat of Satan that Adam should have accomplished in the first Garden.[22] The devil tries to tempt Christ by quoting Scripture:

> If you are the Son of God, throw yourself down [from the pinnacle of the temple], for it is written,
>
> "He will command his angels concerning you,"
>
> and
>
> "On their hands they will bear you up,
>   lest you strike your foot against a stone." (Mt 4:6)

This is a quotation of Psalm 91:11-12. Psalm 91:13, however, goes on to say that this person

> will tread on the lion and the adder;
>   the young lion and the serpent you will trample underfoot.

(e.g., see "Baal-zebub" in 2 Kings 1:2-3, 6, 16, referring to the Philistine god, apparently translated as "lord of the flies"). See further T. J. Lewis, "Beelzebul," in *Anchor Bible Dictionary*, ed. D. N. Freedman (New York: Doubleday, 1992), 1:638-40.

[22]D. J. McCartney, "*Ecce Homo*: The Coming of the Kingdom as the Restoration of Human Vicegerency," *Westminster Theological Journal* 56 (1994): 10. McCartney also mentions that Jesus' proclamations of the kingdom are expressions that the vicegerency lost with the first Adam was now being announced, and that his power over nature was another example of exercising the dominion over the earth as God's vicegerent, which the first Adam should have exercised. See also M. G. Kline, *Kingdom Prologue* (Eugene, OR: Wipf and Stock, 2006), 65-67, who makes the suggestive observation that "the tree of the discernment of good and evil" in Gen 2 refers to Adam's duty to discern between good and evil, so that when the serpent entered the Garden, he was to judge the serpent as an evildoer. Kline supports this partly by adducing other texts that refer to a discerning between "good and evil" as the exercise of "a legal-judicial kind of discrimination" (Is 5:20, 23; Mal 2:17), such as "a king engaged in rendering judicial decisions" (2 Sam 14:17; 1 Kings 3:9, 28).

Psalm 91:13 may allude to the great Genesis 3:15 promise:

> He shall bruise your head,
> and you shall bruise his heel.

Christ's refusal to follow Satan's advice during the wilderness temptations was the beginning of the victory over Satan prophesied in the psalm. Matthew likely intends to some degree that the reader be aware of this broader context of the psalm, which together with the three Deuteronomy contexts above further reveals the theme of Jesus' victory over opposition.

After defeating the devil in the wilderness, Jesus begins to fulfill Isaiah's promises of Israel's restoration (Mt 4:12-16). Consequently, in Matthew 4:18-22 Jesus regathers the tribes of Israel by calling his twelve apostles, a microcosmic true Israel under their leader Jesus, who is identified with Yahweh.[23] This restoration involves various kinds of healings, which were prophesied to occur when Israel would undergo her true end-time restoration to God (Mt 4:23-25; 11:4-6; Is 32:3-4; 35:5-6; 42:7, 16). Such healings also represented the restoration of creation from the fallen condition of the world. The physical (and spiritual) curses of the fall are beginning to be removed by Jesus, as he is reestablishing the new creation, temple, and kingdom that Adam should have established. Seen within the framework of the new creation, Christ's miracles of healing not only inaugurated the end-time kingdom but signaled the beginning of the new creation, reversing the curse of the old fallen world. Those he healed, and especially raised from the dead, foreshadowed his own resurrection. Christ's resurrection was the first fruits of all believers. They, like him, would be raised with perfected, restored bodies at the very end of the age, when the new world would be ushered in. The repeated and dominating notion of the kingdom in the Gospels is one of the main ways by which the Evangelists express ideas about the new creation.

Jesus not only restores Israel but also ushers in the beginning of the new creation and brings the nations to himself, and this can be seen at his death and resurrection. At Jesus' crucifixion, the mockers declare, "You who would destroy the temple and rebuild it in three days, save yourself! If you are the

---

[23]See D. C. Allison, *The New Moses* (Minneapolis: Fortress, 1993).

Son of God, come down from the cross" (Mt 27:40).[24] Subsequently, Jesus dies and the temple veil is torn. Though Jesus is mocked for his promise to tear down and rebuild the temple in three days, Jesus' death immediately results in the tearing of the temple curtain in two (Mt 27:50-51). The tearing of the curtain is a symbolic picture of the destruction of the entire temple and of the entire old creation that the temple symbolized, which begins at the crucifixion.

Jesus' death leads to the breakup of the old creation; after Jesus' death, "the earth shook, and the rocks were split. The tombs also were opened. And many bodies of the saints who had fallen asleep were raised" (Mt 27:51-52). Since the temple veil was embroidered with the starry heavens, its tearing would be an apt symbol of the beginning of the destruction not only of the temple (which itself symbolized the cosmos) but of the very cosmos itself. Consequently, the veil's destruction admirably fits with the earthquake, splitting of rocks, raising of believers (Mt 27:51-53), and the darkness covering the land (Lk 23:44-45).[25] Just as the old temple and even old cosmos began to be destroyed in Jesus' death, so his resurrection was the beginning of a new temple and new cosmos, a new creation.[26]

In this new creation, God's presence breaks out from Israel's temple to bless the nations, as seen in the Gentile centurion's confession: "Truly this was the Son of God" (Mt 27:54). God's ultimate purpose for the temple can be seen here as Yahweh's revelatory presence was extending out beyond the boundaries of ethnic Israel to include Gentiles. The prophetic vision of the nations streaming into the eschatological temple (Is 2:2-3; Mic 4:1-3) led by God himself (Is 56:7) begins to be fulfilled in this Roman centurion's confession.

---

[24]Commentators tend to see these passages affirming Jesus as the builder of the new temple and the temple itself as the new Christian community (see Donald Juel, *Messiah and Temple*, Society of Biblical Literature Dissertation Series 32 [Missoula: Scholars Press, 1977], 145, for a representative list of commentators on the Markan statements).

[25]In the light of Mk 15:30-39, the tearing of the veil happened immediately after Christ's death, and three days later the earthquake at the end of Mt 27:51 occurred together with the event of Christ's and the saints' resurrection (Mt 27:52-53; Mt 27:54 appears to identify the breakup of the earth in Mt 27:51 with the "earthquake" that occurred when Christ rose from the dead).

[26]Since this was not the consummate end of the world and the final new creation, the saints who did come out of their tombs (Mt 27:52-53) presumably, like Lazarus, died again at some subsequent point, only to be raised again at the very end of history.

In this manner, Jesus inaugurates a new creation as a true latter-day Adam, since he is inaugurating and expanding a new eschatological temple, which the first Adam should have done in the beginning of the first creation. Likewise, Jesus does what old Israel failed to do, which included establishing and widening the temple of God's presence to bring in the nations.

Jesus, the Great Commission, and the new creation/temple. Understanding the background of Jesus as a new Adam in a new creation in Matthew sheds light on the Great Commission of Matthew 28:18-20:

> And Jesus came and said to them, "All authority in heaven and on earth has been given to me. Go therefore and make disciples of all nations, baptizing them in the name of the Father and of the Son and of the Holy Spirit, teaching them to observe all that I have commanded you. And behold, I am with you always, to the end of the age."

To this point, we have seen that Jesus reflects both the Old Testament figures of Adam and Israel because the commission to Adam was passed down to Israel and her patriarchs. Consequently, Israel can be seen as a corporate Adam who had failed in their "Garden of Eden,"[27] just as the original Adam had failed in the first Garden. In this section, we will connect the Great Commission to the son of man/Adam in Daniel 7 and the temple-building commission of 2 Chronicles 36:23. As a result, the Great Commission can be seen as a recommission of Genesis 1:28 by Jesus to his disciples.

First, we shall explore the connections with the son of man in Daniel 7:13-14, which highlights the authority and kingdom of the son of man:

> I saw in the night visions,
>
> and behold, with the clouds of heaven
>   there came one like a son of man,
> and he came to the Ancient of Days
>   and was presented before him.
> And to him was given dominion
>   and glory and a kingdom,

---

[27] Note, again, Old Testament texts where Israel's Promised Land is called the "Garden of Eden" (Gen 13:10; Is 51:3; Ezek 36:35; Joel 2:3).

that all peoples, nations, and languages
  should serve him;
his dominion is an everlasting dominion,
  which shall not pass away,
and his kingdom one
  that shall not be destroyed.

In Matthew, Jesus has already been identified as the son of man of Daniel 7:13, coming in glory with his angels (Mt 24:30; 25:31). The expression "son of man" from Daniel 7:13 refers to end-time Israel and her representative king as the son of Adam who is sovereign over beasts (recall that the "son of man" takes over the kingdoms of former evil empires portrayed as beasts). In the Great Commission, Jesus says that "all authority in heaven and on earth has been given to me" (Mt 28:18), looking back to the son of man who is given all "dominion and glory and a kingdom" (Dan 7:14).[28] Consequently, the command to "make disciples of all nations" by "teaching them to observe all that I have commanded you" (Mt 28:19) fulfills the prophecy that "peoples, nations, and languages should serve" the son of man (Dan 7:14).

Daniel 7 itself grows out of the Genesis 1:28 commission (via the Adamic Ps 8), as we have seen in chapter two. Matthew 28:19 also looks back to Genesis 1:28 through the lens of the Abrahamic promise, since "all the nations" (Mt 28:19) echoes the promise to Abraham that "in your offspring shall *all the nations* of the earth be blessed" (Gen 22:18; see Gen 18:18). As a result, "the blessings promised to Abraham and through him to all peoples of the earth (Gen 12:3) are now to be fulfilled in Jesus the Messiah."[29] Also, the divine accompaniment formula ("I am with you"; Mt 28:20) indicates how the disciples will be empowered to carry out the commission, just as the same divine accompaniment formula referred to God's presence that would empower the patriarchs (Gen 26:24; 28:15) and Israel to carry out their commission (1 Chron 22:18; Hag 2:4-5). Our mission is not fulfilled because of the adequacy of our financial and intellectual resources, but our mission is

---

[28]See also R. T. France, *Jesus and the Old Testament* (Grand Rapids, MI: Baker, 1971), 142-43, who also sees the allusion to Daniel 7.

[29]Carson, *Matthew*, 596. Genesis 12:3 (LXX) has "all the tribes of the earth."

guaranteed by the supernatural resources of a God who promises his presence to fulfill that mission.

Strikingly, the Great Commission in Matthew 28:18-20 is not only connected to Daniel 7:13-14, but also to the temple-building commission of 2 Chronicles 36:23:

> Thus says Cyrus king of Persia, "The LORD, the God of heaven, has given me all the kingdoms of the earth, and he has charged me to build him a house at Jerusalem, which is in Judah. Whoever is among you of all his people, may the LORD his God be with him. Let him go up."

The 2 Chronicles passage has three things in common with Matthew 28:18-20: (1) both Cyrus and Jesus assert authority over all the earth, (2) the commission to "go," and (3) the assurance of the divine presence to fulfill the commission. Jesus escalates Cyrus's commission since he has authority over "heaven" as well as "earth," and his own presence will accompany his people. In addition, Jesus' commission is not aimed at old Jerusalem but "nations" throughout the whole earth. Furthermore, if the temple construction of 2 Chronicles is in mind in Matthew 28:18-20, then this is an implicit commission for the disciples to fulfill the Genesis 1:26-28 mandate by building the new temple with worshipers throughout the earth.

By alluding to the last verse of the Hebrew Bible (2 Chron 36:23) at the conclusion of this Gospel, Matthew seems to construct his Gospel on the framework of 1 and 2 Chronicles. Second Chronicles is the last book in the Hebrew Bible, and the commission to rebuild the temple in 2 Chronicles 36:23 is the last verse. This verse provides a canonical transition to an even more escalated commission to build the temple in Matthew 28:18-20. Just as 1 Chronicles begins with an extensive genealogy of the kings of Israel, so Matthew begins with the genealogy of King Jesus, in partial dependence on 1 Chronicles 1–3. Just as 2 Chronicles ends with the temple-building commission of the "messiah" Cyrus (see Is 44:28–45:1), so Matthew ends with the temple-building commission of the Messiah Jesus (Mt 28:19). Thus, the concluding commission is not spoken by a pagan king to Israel, but spoken by the true, divine king Jesus to the beginning remnant of true Israel, "the twelve." In this respect, the 2 Chronicles passage would be viewed as a historical event commissioning a temple that foreshadowed typologically the much greater event of Jesus' Great Commission to build a greater temple.[30]

We have seen in our discussion of Genesis that Adam's commission in Genesis 1 was to be carried out by him serving in the Edenic temple, managing it in an orderly manner and expanding its boundaries. In fact, we have seen that the reapplication of Adam's commission to Noah, the patriarchs, Israel, and end-time Israel was inextricably linked from the beginning to temple building and expansion. Therefore, it should be no surprise that Christ also initiates the building of a new temple and performs the duties that the first Adam and Israel failed to execute. At various points in the Gospels, Christ indicates that the old temple is becoming obsolete and being replaced with a new one. Thus, Christ is the Son of Adam, "the Son of Man," who accomplishes what the first Adam failed to accomplish and begins to inherit what the first Adam should have, including the glory reflected in God's image. Jesus was the perfect image of God, standing in God's invisible new temple. Jesus accomplishes what Adam should have done by establishing the new temple and extending it obediently. In reality, he himself was not only the true image in God's temple but was that temple itself, because he was the beginning of the new creation, especially in his resurrection. To call Christ the "temple" is merely another way of referring to him as the new creation, since the temple was symbolic of creation and especially of the coming new cosmos (see discussion in chap. 4).

CONCLUSION

In this chapter, we have explored the significance of Jesus as the temple. The Jerusalem temple failed since it was like the cursed fig tree, offering the promise of satisfaction but without the fruit. Jesus promises that the temple

---

[30]This discussion of 2 Chron 36:23 is based on A. B. Vance, "The Church as the New Temple in Matthew 16:17-19: A Biblical-Theological Consideration of Jesus' Response to Peter's Confession as Recorded by Matthew" (ThM thesis, Gordon-Conwell Theological Seminary, 1992). In this light, it may be more understandable that later Judaism identified Is 41:25 (Cyrus's efforts to restore Jerusalem and the temple, in view of Is 44:28; 45:1) with the Messiah who would rebuild the temple (so *Midrash Rabba Numbers* 13.2; *Midrash Rabba Leviticus* 9.6; *Midrash Rabba Song of Songs* 4.16, §1). Perhaps not coincidentally, Cyrus elsewhere is referred to as God's "shepherd" and "anointed" one, who commands that the temple "foundation shall be laid" (Is 44:28–45:1).

would be destroyed and raised up in three days. According to his promise, the death of his body led to the destruction of the temple veil, showing the beginning of the dissolution of the old temple. However, Jesus' resurrection from the dead demonstrates the inauguration of a new order, with Jesus as the new temple, from whom flow the rivers of life, and through whom the temple veil is opened so that peoples from all nations might enter in. God's original purpose for the temple in Eden—that it would be a place to expand and fill the whole earth—begins to be fulfilled in Jesus, the new temple, whose death opens the way even for a Roman centurion to believe. In the next chapter, we will explore how this temple expands with the birth of the church.

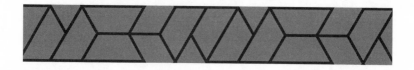

Chapter Seven

EDEN EXPANDING

THE CHURCH AS THE NEW TEMPLE

THE SHOCK AT JESUS' STATEMENT, "Destroy this temple, and in three days I will raise it up" (Jn 2:19) probably paled in comparison to the shock at Paul's question, "Do you not know that you are God's temple and that God's Spirit dwells in you?" (1 Cor 3:16). The outward walls of the temple in those days were covered with so much gold that they were blinding in "fiery splendor" at sunrise (Josephus, *Jewish War* 5.222). Its beauty was so well known that "no one has seen a truly beautiful building unless he has seen the temple" (*m. Sukkah* 51:2). How could God's people be identified with this beautiful architectural structure and temple (1 Cor 3:16; 1 Pet 2:5; Eph 2:22)?

This chapter will explore the church as the true temple of God. If our mission is to expand the temple of Eden to fill the earth, then we must properly understand what this temple of Eden looks like in the new covenant age. Jesus' own resurrection body was the beginning of the end-time temple (Jn 2:21), where God's unique revelatory presence was located and expressed. The special presence of God in the Eden temple has now come to be located in Jesus. Since Christians are now the body of Jesus Christ, Old Testament prophecies of the temple are fulfilled in the church. As a result, God's presence in this true temple enables reconciliation and calls for purity or holiness. Just as Eden was to grow and fill the earth, so the church grows as the beginning fulfillment of the end-time temple in Jesus. Specifically, just as Adam and Eve were to be nourished by God's word, the church grows by means of the word of God in a context of suffering in a fallen world. In this chapter, we will explore reconciliation and purity in the true temple, and how the church grows by means of the word of God in a context of suffering.

RECONCILIATION AND PURITY IN THE TRUE TEMPLE

Numerous passages describe the church as a temple (e.g., Eph 2:21-22; 1 Cor 3:16; 2 Cor 6:16; Heb 8:2), and these passages show how Old Testament prophecies of the temple begin to be fulfilled in the church. The temple is not simply a metaphor for the church, but the church commenced as an actual temple at Pentecost (Acts 2), and it is the initial phase of the building of the final temple that will appear at the end of the age in fulfillment of Old Testament temple prophecies.[1] Some Old Testament prophecies seemed to predict an eschatological architectural temple, while others foresaw God's very glorious presence by itself as the essence of the end-time temple. This apparent tension is clarified in that these prophecies are seen to find fulfillment first in Christ, the epitome of God's special presence, and in the church, which came into union with Christ. In this section, we will focus on the Old Testament background of Ephesians 2:21-22, 2 Corinthians 6:16, and Hebrews 8:2. These passages help us see how reconciliation (Eph 2:14, 17-22) and purity (2 Cor 6:16-18) are made possible by

---

[1] Cf. C. L. Feinberg, "The Rebuilding of the Temple," in *Prophecy in the Making*, ed. C. F. H. Henry (Carol Stream, IL: Creation House, 1971), 99, which sees here only "that the church is presented under the figure of a temple." The irony in this is that Feinberg insists that where the New Testament refers to eschatological prophecies about the temple, they must be taken "literally." If he were aware that Ephesians was referring to an eschatological prophecy about the temple, one wonders if he would change his figurative view of Eph 2. Perhaps he would say that Paul does not have in mind the eschatological-prophetic element of the temple but wants only to take the image of the temple and apply it analogically. The problem with this is that Paul would not be paying attention to the main *prophetic* contextual idea of the Old Testament text, but neutering its redemptive-historical significance. For the beginning of the church as a temple at Pentecost in Acts 2, see G. K. Beale, *The Temple and the Church's Mission*, NSBT (Downers Grove, IL: InterVarsity Press, 2004), 201-16.

Christ in the true tabernacle and dwelling place of God (Heb 8:2; 9:11), the church.

In the presence of God in the eschatological temple, reconciliation is possible (Eph 2:14-22). Animosities between Jew and Gentile ran deep since Jews saw Gentiles as dogs (Mt 15:26-27), and they prohibited interaction with Gentiles lest they compromise their worship.[2] However, the church brought both Jew and Gentile together in worship. Reconciliation to God through the blood of Christ (Eph 2:1-10) makes possible reconciliation with one another (Eph 2:11-22), resulting in peace (Eph 2:14, 17) through access into God's presence (Eph 2:18). Ephesians 2:17 quotes Isaiah 57:19, "Peace, peace, to the far and to the near . . . and I will heal him." The wider context of Isaiah 56–57 pictures Jews and Gentiles reconciled and restored in God's presence at the temple (e.g., Is 56:6-8; 57:14-19; cf. Is 66:18-21). Christ's work inaugurates the fulfillment of this reconciliation of Jew and Gentile in the new temple anticipated by Isaiah 56–57.[3] Since the church is the "dwelling place for God" and "a holy temple in the Lord" (Eph 2:21-22), reconciliation is now possible even between deeply antagonistic groups.

The possibility of reconciliation does not lessen the pain of reconciliation as we are "being joined together" and "built on the foundation of the apostles and prophets" with Christ as the chief cornerstone (Eph 2:20-21). In the

---

[2]The *Letter of Aristeas* 139 (ca. 150–100 BC) said that God has "fenced us round with impregnable ramparts and walls of iron, that we might not mingle at all with any of the other nations, but remain pure in body and soul, free from all vain imaginations, worshiping the one Almighty God above the whole creation." Since even mingling with Gentiles was prohibited, it should not be surprising that intermarriage was also prohibited (Neh 13:23-27).

[3]This identification of Gentiles with Christ to fulfill the prophecies about Israel in the latter-day temple is part of the "mystery of Christ" that was not made known in previous generations but "has now been revealed" (Eph 3:4-5).While the manner in which the Messiah would reconstitute Israel was not clear in the Old Testament, the "mystery" reveals that Jews and Gentiles are fused together in the corporate identification with Christ, without having to identify with the nationalistic legal tags of Israel. Though the Gentiles formerly were separated from Israel's "promise" (Eph 2:12), they "now" are fellow-sharers in that same "promise" (Eph 3:6), including the promise of the long-awaited temple (Eph 2:19-22). Is 56:6 even says that Gentiles will "minister" to the Lord in the temple as priests, to which Is 66:18-21 also attests. It is difficult to know how Old Testament readers could have conceived of this happening, since Israel's law affirmed that only those from the tribe of Levi could serve as priests in the temple. Possibly, the thought may have been that some Gentiles could have been conceived of as converting to Israel's faith and law and joining the tribe of Levi. For more on Is 66:18-21, see G. K. Beale, *A New Testament Biblical Theology: The Unfolding of the Old Testament in the New* (Grand Rapids, MI: Baker, 2011), 660-63.

ancient world, stones were not "joined together" with mortar, but were shaved down to fit perfectly together. Just as each stone was chipped away and refined to fit into something far more glorious, so God shapes and forms each believer (sometimes painfully) to be "joined together" into something far more glorious, the "dwelling place for God" (Eph 2:22; see also 1 Pet 2:4-5). In the early church, this process of shaving down differences to fit together as a dwelling place of God was particularly painful (see Rom 14). However, we persevere through this painful process because of the glorious hope that we "are being built together into a dwelling place for God by the Spirit" (Eph 2:22). Similarly, we should not be surprised when relational breakdown hinders our mission. Such breakdown is seen as far back as Eden, when Adam blamed Eve for their sin and they hid from each other in shame (Gen 3:7, 12). God often uses such relational struggles to refine and develop us so that "being joined together" we might grow "into a holy temple in the Lord" (Eph 2:21). Such breakdown can only be reconciled by the peace from God's presence through Christ (Eph 2:13-14, 17).

While Ephesians 2 shows the power of reconciliation possible in the church as the temple of God, 2 Corinthians 6:16-18 reminds us that the church must walk in the purity and holiness that the temple demands. Paul declares in 2 Corinthians 6:16, "We are the temple of the living God." This explicit identification of the church with the temple is supported in 2 Corinthians 6:16 by two Old Testament quotations from Leviticus 26:11-12 and Ezekiel 37:26-27 (see table 7.1).

Table 7.1

LEVITICUS 26:11-12 AND EZEKIEL 37:26-27	2 CORINTHIANS 6:16b
Lev 26:11-12: "*I will* make my dwelling among you. . . . *I will* walk among you and *will be* your God, and *you shall be* my people."	"*I will dwell in* them *and walk among* them; and *I will be* their God, *and they shall be my people.*"
Ezek 37:26-27 "I . . . will set my sanctuary in their midst forevermore. *My dwelling* place shall be *with them, and I will be their God, and they shall be my people.*"	
Cf. Ex 29:45.	

Old Testament prophecies of a coming temple are fulfilled in the church, suggesting that Christians *are* the beginning fulfillment of the prophecy of the end-time temple, which focuses on God's special, revelatory presence commencing to dwell among his people. Both Leviticus 26:11-12 and Ezekiel 37:26-27 prophesy not an architectural temple but one whose essence was the end-time presence of God with his people.[4]

As a result, 2 Corinthians 6:17 continues with a call to purity and holiness:

Therefore go out from their midst,
   and be separate from them ...
and touch no unclean thing.

So often moral compromise undermines the mission that God has entrusted to us. Blatant moral failure by way of sexual immorality or financial indiscretion can disqualify people for ministry and discredit the God we serve. More subtle moral failures of pride, sloth, lust, or greed can sap our power and effectiveness in ministry. Our holy calling and mission as God's temple demands purity. We will discuss this call to purity in 2 Corinthians 6:17 in more detail in the next chapter.

Since our worship in God's temple as the church provides power for reconciliation (Eph 2:17-22) and reason for purity (2 Cor 6:16-18), we must understand this worship properly as worship in the "true" tabernacle and temple (Heb 8–9). Remember that believers are not merely like a temple in Christ but really are the beginning fulfillment of the Old Testament prophecies of the true end-time temple. Christ is a high priest and "minister in the holy places, in the true tent that the Lord set up, not man" (Heb 8:2).[5] The earthly tabernacle was patterned on this "true tabernacle" in heaven (Heb 8:2, 5;

---

[4]See also E. P. Clowney, "The Final Temple," *Westminster Theological Journal* 35 (1972): 185-86, who has made a similar point about 2 Cor 6:16. This focus on prophetic fulfillment is confirmed by the wider context of 2 Cor 1–7. This section is sandwiched between two statements of the fulfillment of the promises of God in 2 Cor 1:20 and 7:1. In this section of 2 Corinthians, a number of Old Testament promises find fulfillment, including a "new covenant" with Israel (2 Cor 3:1-18), resurrection (2 Cor 5:14-15), new creation (2 Cor 5:16-17), restoration from captivity (2 Cor 5:18–6:14), and the restored temple of God (2 Cor 6:16-18). All of these Old Testament "promises of God find their Yes in [Christ]" (2 Cor 1:20; see 7:1).

[5]The "holy places" refers elsewhere to the earthly temple complex in general (e.g., Lev 21:23; Jer 51:51; Ezek 7:24) and the Holy of Holies (Heb 9:3; see 9:8; 10:19; 13:11) in particular.

see 9:24), and this "true tabernacle" is the genuine[6] and the prophetic typological[7] fulfillment of the old tabernacle. The earthly tabernacles were imperfect models of the coming eternal temple (Heb 8:5), which is "a greater and more perfect tent (not made with hands, that is, not of this creation)" (Heb 9:11).[8] The former architectural temple was only an imperfect anticipation of the genuine and "true tent" (Heb 8:2) in Christ, just as a photograph is an imperfect image of a genuine person. A photograph may be adequate when the person is absent, but it serves as no replacement when that person is present. During studies in Jerusalem, a picture of my (Mitch) girlfriend (now wife) became a well-worn reminder of her in her absence. However, when I returned to America and saw her again, I no longer gazed at that imperfect representation when the more glorious reality of her presence stood before me. In the same manner, since we now have the true tabernacle established in our midst through Christ's death and resurrection (Heb 8:1-2; 9:11-12), longing for the appearance of another earthly temple in Jerusalem in the future would be equivalent to desiring to gaze at a photograph of the one we love when we are holding the hand of our beloved.[9] Through Christ,

---

[6]Similarly, Rev 3:14 calls Christ "the faithful and true witness" in contrast to the false witness of the nations to their idols. Christ is the true witness after which all other faithful witnesses are modeled (see Rev 2:13). Similarly, the tabernacle in heaven is the true tabernacle, after which the earthly tabernacles are modeled.

[7]See our discussion on typology in chap. 10.

[8]Heb 9:11 probably alludes to Hag 2:9, "The latter glory of this house shall be greater than the former." The influence of Hag 2:9 may not only lie behind "the greater and more perfect tent" of Heb 9:11 but also later in Heb 12:26-27, where the author builds on Hag 2:6: "Yet once more, in a little while, I will shake the heavens and the earth and the sea and the dry land." This refers to the removal of "things that have been made—in order that the things that cannot be shaken may remain" (Heb 12:26-27). "Things that have been made" (Heb 12:27) are contrasted with the more perfect tabernacle "not made with hands" (Heb 9:11), suggesting a reference to the removal of the imperfect sacrifices and offerings of the earthly tabernacle in order to establish the newly inaugurated temple through Christ's once-for-all sacrifice (Heb 10:8-9). This new temple is "greater and more perfect" because it "cannot be shaken" (Heb 9:11; 12:27).

[9]Some, however, would insist that the Bible insists on precisely this reality. Second Thess 2:4 is seen by many as one of the clearest statements of this, when the antichrist "takes his seat in the temple of God, proclaiming himself to be God." Although this may refer to the appearance of the antichrist in a future rebuilt temple in Israel or the Roman emperor's defiling of Israel's temple in AD 70, these verses seem to picture a future apostasy throughout the worldwide church and the antichrist's influence in the church, the inaugurated end-time temple of God. Arguments against a physical temple in a geographical Israel include the following: (1) 2 Thess 2:3 appears to focus not on a geographically conceived Israel but alludes to a future massive apostasy in the

the church is granted access to God in the true tabernacle in the heavenlies, a true tabernacle of which the earthly tabernacle was simply an imperfect model. Such worship in the true tabernacle is the powerful force behind our reconciliation and purity.

In this section, we have explored three New Testament statements that the church is the beginning fulfillment of the eschatological temple prophesied in the Old Testament. As a result, reconciliation with God and with fellow humanity is possible, even as God painfully builds and joins us together into his dwelling place (Eph 2:20-22). Also, we are called to live in holiness and purity because of our identification with this temple (2 Cor 6:16-17). However, our mission since Eden is to see the temple grow and expand to fill the earth. How is this possible? Our next section will explore the means and context of our growth.

GROWTH THROUGH THE WORD OF GOD AND SUFFERING

The church "grows [*auxanō*] into a holy temple in the Lord" (Eph 2:21). Buildings are naturally static, but living organisms grow. So how can a building grow? The church as a temple fulfills God's intention for the expanding Garden-temple seen in Genesis 1:28 (in the context of Gen 2-3). In this section, we will explore how this Garden temple will grow by means of the word of God in a context of suffering. This temple must expand in this way and fill the earth through believers as Christ's witnesses to the ends of the earth (Acts 1:8).

Growth by the word. In the Greek translation of the Old Testament, "grow" (*auxanō*) is used in God's commission to Adam and Eve in Genesis 1:28, "Increase [*auxanō*] and multiply and fill the earth." In connection with subduing the animals, this task could only be fulfilled through obedience to God's word, and disobedience led to failure (i.e., Eve's twisting of God's word

---

church; (2) the phrase "temple of God" (2 Thess 2:4) almost always refers to the church in the New Testament (Mt 26:61; 1 Cor 3:16-17 [2x]; 2 Cor 6:16 [2x]; Rev 3:12; 7:15; 11:1, 19); and (3) the church is created by "God who gives his Holy Spirit to you" (1 Thess 4:8), just as "your body is a temple of the Holy Spirit within you, whom you have from God" (1 Cor 6:19). See further discussion in G. K. Beale, *The Temple and the Church's Mission*, NSBT (Downers Grove, IL: InterVarsity Press, 2004), 269-92.

in Gen 3:2-4 [see Gen 2:16-17]). Adam and Eve would defeat the evil serpent by remembering and trusting in God's word of command (Gen 2:16-17), and their children would be raised as glorious image bearers through spiritual instruction in God's word, so that they might think God's thoughts after him and might reflect the divine image.

The emphasis on obedience to the word of God in multiplying image bearers becomes more prominent in the New Testament. The New Testament uses Genesis 1:28 to describe the growth and expansion of the word of God to multiply the people of God. The growth of the church in the book of Acts is made possible as "the word of God continued to grow [*auxanō*], and the number of the disciples multiplied greatly in Jerusalem" (Acts 6:7, translation modified; see 12:24; 19:20; and discussion later). Similarly, Paul celebrates that "in the whole world it [the word of the gospel] is bearing fruit and growing [*auxanō*]—as it also does among you, since the day you heard it and understood the grace of God in truth" (Col 1:6, translation modified; see 1 Cor 1:10, 12). In these cases the word of God "grows [*auxanō*]" to multiply disciples who bear the image of Christ; the word of God multiplies disciples and causes the church to grow.

In Ephesians 4:15-16, we must speak the word of God to grow the body of Christ, which is the temple of God:

> Rather, speaking the truth in love, we are to grow up [*auxanō*] in every way into him who is the head, into Christ, from whom the whole body, joined and held together by every joint with which it is equipped, when each part is working properly, makes the body grow [*auxēsin*] so that it builds itself up in love.

We "grow up . . . into Christ" by "speaking the truth in love" (Eph 4:15). Our growth into maturity in Christ is only possible by constant and ongoing exposure to the word of God through one another. This growth into Christ is the growth and building up of the temple of God; "speaking the truth in love" (Eph 4:15) builds up Christ's body so "the whole structure . . . grows into a temple in the Lord" (Eph 2:21). The parallels between Ephesians 4:16 and 2:21 confirm that the former develops the latter (see table 7.2).

Table 7.2

EPHESIANS 2:21	EPHESIANS 4:16
In Christ "the whole [*pasa*] building [*oikodomē*] being fit together [*synarmologoumenē*] grows [*auxei*] into a temple in the Lord" (our translation).	In Christ "the whole [*pan*] body, being fit together [*synarmologoumenon*] and held together by every ligament of support, according to the measure of each part makes the body grow [*auxēsin*] unto the building up [*oikodomēn*] of itself in love" (our translation).

As a result, the temple of Christ's body and dwelling place of God grows by means of the word of God spoken by believers to one another.[10]

Similarly, 1 Peter 1:23–2:7 connects God's word with growth as a temple of God. Those who have been born again "through the living and abiding word of God" (1 Pet 1:23) now "long for the pure spiritual milk [of the word], that by it you may grow up [*auxanō*] into salvation" (2:2). As they long for and drink from the milk of the word of God, they "like living stones are being built up as a spiritual house, to be a holy priesthood, to offer spiritual sacrifices acceptable to God through Jesus Christ" (1 Pet 2:5). This "spiritual house" is the temple in which we serve as priests to offer our sacrifices, and we grow by the spiritual milk of the word of God. Again, the word of God is the key to the church's growth as a temple.

The growth of the church in Ephesians 2:21 and 1 Peter 2:5 is understood as the growth and expansion of God's temple. This notion of a temple gradually increasing in size is one we have previously observed. The borders of Eden and all subsequent temples were to be expanded until they circumscribed the globe with God's all-pervasive presence. Yet this purpose was never successfully pursued until it began to be accomplished in Christ. Here, the temple begins to expand as its boundaries include Gentiles from around the world. The temple will continue to expand to include more and more people until God's presence will pervade the entire earth at the end of the age (see Eph 4:13).

---

[10]This verbal parallel was observed in a 2007 paper by a former student at Wheaton College Graduate School, Brandon Levering. The translation here is original to highlight the lexical parallels. The repetition of four words ("whole," "building," "fit together," and "grow") within one verse suggests that Eph 4:16 expands on the "growing temple" in Eph 2:21.

Similarly, in 1 Corinthians 3, God's people as a temple (1 Cor 3:16) grow by means of the word of God. Paul "planted" the church, and Apollos "watered, but God gave the growth" (1 Cor 3:6; likewise 1 Cor 3:7). They grow not only as "God's cultivated field" but as "God's building" (1 Cor 3:9), which reflects the background of Eden as a cultivated garden-sanctuary and Israel's later temple as an architectural building.[11] God's special presence made Eden and Israel's temple his unique dwelling places, and now the Corinthians are the continuation of God's special tabernacling presence, his temple, in the new age. "God's building" must be established on the foundation of Jesus Christ (1 Cor 3:11), and we must build "upon the foundation with gold, silver, precious stones, wood," lest the fire of the day of judgment destroy the builder's work (1 Cor 3:12-13). We are to build with "gold, silver, precious stones, wood" like Solomon built the first temple with "gold . . . silver . . . wood . . . precious stones" (1 Chron 29:2; see 1 Chron 29:1-7; 1 Kings 5:17).[12] We build not by "words of [human] wisdom" (1 Cor 1:17-21; 2:1, 4-5; 3:18-23) but by God's word as fulfilled in Christ, instructing them in how the Scriptures are fulfilled in Christ for the new community of faith (Rom 15:4-13; 1 Cor 10:11). In this instruction, we do "not . . . go beyond what is written" in the Old Testament and its fulfillment in the new age (1 Cor 4:6). God's word is like "gold and silver" since God's wisdom surpasses even the most valuable of earth's commodities (Ps 119:72; Prov 3:14; 8:10; 16:16), and those who receive

---

[11]As we have seen earlier in chapters 1, 4, and 5. The closest parallel is the early Christian Odes of Solomon 38:17-21, which says the saint was "established" on "foundations [that] were laid" and that he was "planted" and "watered" by God and was God's "cultivation." This text is probably a development of the Old Testament or early Judaism rather than of 1 Cor 3. Later Judaism could also speak of Solomon's temple as a "field" (*Targum Pseudo-Jonathan Genesis* 27:27; *Pesiqta Rabbati*, piska 39). While Paul may not explicitly equate "God's field" with the portrayal of the church as a temple (though the abrupt juxtaposition strongly suggests this), the close association of "garden" and "temple" in the Old Testament and Judaism would plausibly have influenced a similar link in Paul's mind.

[12]Paul also calls himself a "*wise* [or skilled] *master builder*" in laying the foundation (1 Cor 3:10, translation altered), just as the tabernacle builders were "filled with a divine spirit of *wisdom* . . . to be a *master builder* in all works of a *master builder* in order to form gold and silver . . . and works in stone" (our translation from LXX of Ex 35:31-32). Furthermore, Solomon's temple, like the new Corinthian temple of believers, was also filled and decorated with garden imagery (1 Kings 6:18, 29, 32; 7:18-20, 22, 24-26, 42, 49-50), perhaps recalling the primeval sanctuary of the Garden of Eden. This combination of precious metals with botanical depictions in Israel's temple may have influenced Paul's shift in imagery from a "cultivated field/vineyard" image to "God's building" in 1 Cor 3:9.

this valuable word become part of the authentic temple. In this manner, the dwelling place of God grows and expands by building with the gold and silver of the word of God.

We must build carefully on the foundation of Jesus Christ. Only God's word in Christ can grow believers so solid that they can withstand the fire of the last judgment. However, those who try to build people on the foundation of Christ without preaching and teaching God's true word and gospel will find that such people are like "wood, hay, [and] straw," and that their "work is burned up" (1 Cor 3:12, 15). We have a sober obligation to build the congregation on the true gospel and word of God, lest we discover at judgment that our work has been in vain. Thus, 1 Corinthians 3 is about those who lead God's people in ministry and their responsibility to build them up in the right manner.

God's dwelling place grows by the ministry of the word of God. This obvious truth bears repeating, since the desire for quick results in the church often trumps the arduous demands of the faithful ministry of God's word. Myriads of books and conferences prescribe the latest method and program to bring people to church. However, such methods and programs are only effective insofar as they connect people to the riches of the word of God. Success in ministry cannot be measured by numbers alone, since the wheat and the chaff are inevitably mingled (Mt 13:24-30). True success in ministry will be revealed by fire on the Day of Judgment (1 Cor 3:13), when the quality of our workmanship in building the temple will be revealed.

Shoddy workmanship takes time to be seen. When my wife and I (Mitch) were first married, our first set of dining room chairs were pretty, comfortable, and cheap. When people would visit our home, they would comment on our dining chairs, and I would swell with pride, knowing how little money we had spent on them. However, within a few years, they began to break down. People would lean back, a loud crack would be heard, and they would fall backwards. One by one, we got rid of those chairs. The craftsmanship of the chairs could not bear the demands of use. Shoddy craftsmanship may be frustrating when making chairs, but shoddy craftsmanship is damning when making disciples. We must build people with the gold, silver, and precious stones of the word of God. Otherwise, persecution will make them wither like a dandelion in summer, and the worries of life will choke their growth like a plant among thorns (Mt 13:21-22).

However, when people feast on the word of God and regularly connect the brokenness of their lives to the riches of the gospel of Jesus Christ, then they will bear fruit, thirty, sixty, and one hundredfold (Mt 13:23). Quality craftsmanship in making disciples is critical, and we must build solidly. Time (especially the very end of time) is the best judge for the quality of our discipleship, and we must minister with the sobering realization that our work will one day be tested by fire. Solid growth is growth through the word of God.

Growth in a context of suffering. While the means of growth is the word of God, the context of our growth is often suffering. Although we already are "the temple of the living God" (2 Cor 6:16), the glory of this new temple grows as we persevere through suffering. As Christians trust God in the midst of trial and their own weaknesses, God shines his glory through us: "We have this treasure in jars of clay, to show that the surpassing power belongs to God and not to us" (2 Cor 4:7). Suffering is not an automatic lever to release the life of Christ in us, but suffering is the occasion that we look for Christ's life to flow in us (2 Cor 4:10-11). When we are comfortable, we too easily trust in the adequacy of our resources. When we are afflicted, we realize the inadequacy of our resources and look to Christ so that his life is released in us. This life flows not only in us but through us to bless others: "Death is at work in us, but life [is at work] in you" (2 Cor 4:12). This life comes from the Spirit who assures us that we will rise again with Jesus and come into his presence (2 Cor 4:13-14), guaranteeing the resurrection life to come (see 2 Cor 5:5).[13]

As we turn to Christ in faith through suffering, God's dwelling place grows in and through us. The life of Christ not only strengthens us in weakness but

---

[13]Just as the Spirit is linked to the origin of the resurrection life of faith in 2 Cor 4:12-13, so the Spirit is the "guarantee" for the future consummation of resurrection life (2 Cor 5:5). The Spirit himself is the beginning evidence of the new creation, abounding in resurrection "life" and constituting the abode of the cosmic temple. God, "who has prepared us for this very thing" of receiving resurrection life and becoming a part of the eternal temple, "has given us the Spirit as a guarantee" of these realities (2 Cor 5:5). The Spirit is the beginning evidence that the latter-day promises have begun to be realized in Christ and his people (Is 32:15; 42:1; 59:21; Ezek 36:26-27; 37:14; Joel 2:28). Indeed, the Spirit is "the firstfruits" of the future "redemption of our bodies" (Rom 8:23), and we are "sealed with the promised Holy Spirit who is the guarantee" of the full "inheritance" to come at the end of the age (Eph 1:13-14).

also renews us in glory through suffering (2 Cor 4:16). As a result, these afflictions bring an "eternal weight of glory" that will lead to a "glory beyond
all comparison" at the time of the final resurrection (2 Cor 4:17; see 2 Cor 5:1-4).
God's special revelatory glory dwelt in the Old Testament temple of Israel. In
the new covenant age, 2 Corinthians repeatedly affirms that God's glory is
revealed through faithfulness in weakness, and this glory will be more fully
and consummately seen in "a building from God, a house not made with
hands, eternal in the heavens" (2 Cor 5:1), which is the new eschatological
temple.[14] God prepares and grows us into this temple as "we groan, longing
to put on our heavenly dwelling" (2 Cor 5:2-5).

Today we neglect the critical role of suffering that is necessary for spiritual
growth. God often uses suffering to humble us so that the life of Christ might
flow through us and grow his dwelling place in our midst. When God expands
his work through suffering, we must not be surprised. J. Hudson Taylor
(1832–1905), founder of China Inland Mission, suffered much pressure
throughout his time in China, but he recognized, "It does not matter how
great the pressure is. What really matters is where the pressure lies—whether
it comes between you and God, or whether it presses you nearer His heart."[15]

This conviction was tested in the Boxer Rebellion of 1900, when some of
the Chinese rose up to burn churches and kill Christians throughout the
nation. As the countryside was ravaged, fifty-eight adult missionaries and
twenty-one of their children in the China Inland Mission were killed. These
brutal murders pressed Taylor closer to God's heart. Although their mission
suffered more than any other mission in China, Taylor refused payment for
loss of property and life after the Rebellion "to show the 'meekness and

---

[14]This "house not made with hands" is fully consummated at the future resurrection when we "put
on our heavenly dwelling" (2 Cor 5:1-2). Our future resurrection will ultimately connect us with
the consummate, eschatological temple of God, just as Christ's own resurrection established him
as the beginning of the true temple. "Not made with hands," "building," "house" (v. 1) and
"dwelling" (v. 2) are typically references to the temple. Elsewhere this phrase almost always refers
to the temple (e.g., Ex 15:17; Is 66:1-2; Dan 2:34, 35 [LXX]; Mk 14:58; Acts 7:48-49; 17:24; Heb 9:11,
24). Further discussion can be found in E. E. Ellis, "II Corinthians V.1-10 in Pauline Eschatology,"
New Testament Studies 6 (1959–1960): 217-18, who is a leading proponent of the view that Paul
has in mind the church as a temple here, though his notion that the temple is a present reality
in 2 Cor 5:1-4 is questionable.

[15]Howard Taylor, *Hudson Taylor's Spiritual Secret* (London: China Inland Mission, 1955), 107.

gentleness of Christ.'" He declared by faith, "It is a wonderful honour . . . to have among us so many counted worthy of a martyr's crown. Some who have been spared have perhaps suffered more than some of those taken, and our Lord will not forget."[16] Such a faith-filled declaration in the face of such brutal suffering gives pause. Can such faith grow in the comfortable West? Taylor was prepared to deal with this brutal persecution by seeing all pressure as an opportunity to press closer to his Father's heart.

After Taylor's death, the church continued to expand in China, strengthened with a robust theology of suffering. They understood that "the blood of the martyrs is the seed of the church," as Tertullian said in the third century. A recent house church leader in China testified,

> We have numerous testimonies of powerful revivals that have broken out in places where Christians have spilled their blood and endured many hardships for the gospel. In some areas where there is much opposition, it seems that God's children must suffer and bleed before demonic powers are broken and people can see the light of the gospel.[17]

The relative absence of such physical persecution in the West does not thereby shelter its leaders from suffering; indeed, genuine shepherding and care for the people of God inevitably leads to suffering as their brokenness breaks the back of our own self-sufficiency. Our sacrifice and suffering is needed to spread the glories of God's presence to the ends of the earth. No wonder that Paul can say: "Now I rejoice in my sufferings for your sake, and in my flesh I am filling up what is lacking in Christ's afflictions for the sake of his body, that is, the church" (Col 1:24). May we rejoice in our sufferings for the sake of Christ's body, the church.

In past decades, church growth has been carefully studied.[18] The influence of the church growth movement waned in the nineties, and the rise of

---

[16]OMF International is the name today for China Inland Mission, and they detail their history during the Boxer Rebellion at www.omf.org/us/death-to-the-foreigner/.

[17]Brother Yun, Peter Xu Yongze, Enoch Wang with Paul Hattaway, *Back to Jerusalem: Three Chinese House Church Leaders Share Their Vision to Complete the Great Commission* (Carlisle: Piquant, 2003), 19-20.

[18]The church growth movement grew as a philosophy of foreign missions through the seminal work of Donald McGavran (*The Bridges of God* [New York: Friendship Press, 1955]), and its

megachurches like Willow Creek and Saddleback shifted the focus to church health, since growing churches may not be healthy but healthy churches grow. Rick Warren said that "the key issue for churches in the twenty-first century will be church *health*, not church growth."[19] However, both the literature on church health and on church growth has largely grown out of a sociological description of the activities of growing churches instead of a theological exploration of the roots of proper growth. Such studies begin with a model church (such as Willow Creek) or model churches (as the case with Christian Schwarz's study in *Natural Church Development*) to explore the underlying reasons for their growth. While these studies are helpful, Tim Keller rightly recognizes that "implicitly or explicitly, they made near-absolutes out of techniques and models that had worked in a certain place at a certain time."[20] However, a biblical exploration of the characteristics of a healthy church should be the starting point for the evaluation of churches. Theology must undergird our concepts and frameworks of both church health and church growth. If our analysis is correct, then church growth must take into account a robust understanding of the role of the word and suffering in the growth of the church as an end-time temple. While the importance of the word of God is recognized by many church growth studies, the notion of the expansion of the temple-church through suffering is often neglected. By neglecting the role of faithfulness in the midst of suffering, church leaders may unwittingly assume that techniques alone will result in church health and growth and neglect the role of God's preparation in the life of the minister both to deepen and grow the church.

---

principles were popularized and applied to the American context by Peter Wagner and the Institute of Church Growth at Fuller Seminary (e.g., *Strategies for Church Growth: Tools for Effective Mission and Evangelism* [Ventura, CA: Regal Publishing, 1987]).

[19] *The Purpose Driven Church* (Grand Rapids, MI: Zondervan, 1995), 17. Tools to measure church health have sprung up, such as Christian Schwarz's analysis of eight principles for natural church growth distilled from a study of one thousand churches in thirty-two countries on five continents (*Natural Church Development: A Guide to Eight Essential Qualities of Healthy Churches* [Carol Stream, IL: ChurchSmart Resources, 1996]).

[20] Tim Keller, *Center Church: Doing Balanced, Gospel-Centered Ministry in Your City* (Grand Rapids, MI: Zondervan, 2012), 14. This section compares a number of recent church growth books with those on biblical churches and presses further to articulate the need for theological vision, a "faithful restatement of the gospel with rich implications for life, ministry, and mission in a type of culture at a moment in history" (p. 19).

CONCLUSION

In this chapter, we have explored the church as a continuation of the true temple of God that has begun to fulfill the Old Testament prophecies of the presence of God in the temple. These prophecies of the temple grow out of the first temple in Eden that was to expand and fill the earth. These prophecies begin their fulfillment in the church, so that reconciliation is possible and purity is demanded in this true temple. Also, the growth of this true temple is possible by means of the word of God in a context of suffering. Our growth as an end-time temple and dwelling place of God is possible in this manner. Since the church is the true temple, what does our ministry as priests look like? In the next chapter, we will explore our calling to serve as priests in holiness and images of God in this glorious temple.

Chapter Eight

EDEN'S MINISTRY

SERVING AS PRIESTS
IN THE NEW TEMPLE

IF THE CHURCH IS the true temple of God, then we are priests, and our ministry should grow out of the work of the Old Testament priests in the temple. Not surprisingly, Christians are called "a royal priesthood" (1 Pet 2:9) and "priests to his God and father" (Rev 1:6). As a holy temple and dwelling place for God, the temple was a place for holiness and priestly service. How do the requirements for holiness and priestly service in the Old Testament carry over in our priestly ministry in the church as a temple? Just as Adam was called as the first priest in the sanctuary of Eden, so Christians are called as priests in the sanctuary begun by Christ. Adam failed in his mission in Eden by failing in his work as a priest in the sanctuary of Eden, and we will accomplish our mission only as we are faithful in our calling as priests in the true sanctuary. In this chapter, we will explore the call to holiness and priestly service in the new temple, since such holiness and service are critical to fulfill our mission in expanding Eden to fill the earth.

HOLINESS IN THE NEW TEMPLE

As we saw in chapter seven, the church as a "temple of the living God" (2 Cor 6:16) begins to fulfill the prophecy of the end-time temple from Leviticus 26:12 and Ezekiel 37:26-27. On this basis, believers are called to holiness:

> Therefore go out from their midst,
>   and be separate from them, says the Lord,
> and touch no unclean thing;
>   then I will welcome you,
> and I will be a father to you,
>   and you shall be sons and daughters to me,
> says the Lord Almighty. (2 Cor 6:17-18)

Holiness is demanded for those who "are the temple of the living God" (2 Cor. 6:16), and they must "go out from their midst" (that is, the midst of the defiled world) and "touch no unclean thing" because they are priests in that temple. The call to holiness grows out of Isaiah 52:11 and Ezekiel 11:17 (see Ezekiel 20:34, 41), Old Testament promises of a rebuilt temple after the exile. Isaiah 52:11 is a command to priests to come back to Jerusalem to help restore the temple. God will "welcome" his people as priests in the temple (2 Cor 6:17), just as he promised to "welcome" Israel back from captivity at the restoration of God's presence in the temple (Ezek 11:17 LXX).[1] The fulfillment of God's promises for his presence among his people in 2 Corinthians 6:16-18 leads to another call to holiness in 2 Corinthians 7:1: "Since we have these promises [of a rebuilt temple], beloved, let us cleanse ourselves from every defilement of body and spirit, bringing holiness to completion in the fear of God." Since we minister in the temple of the living God, we are called to holiness. Participation

---

[1] During the exile, God was "a sanctuary to them for a while in the countries where they have gone" (Ezek 11:16), since "the glory of the LORD [had gone] out from the threshold of the house" in Jerusalem (Ezek 10:18; similarly Ezek 11:23). Although God's glorious presence remained with the remnant in captivity, his presence would return with the restored people and would once again take up residence in the eschatological temple. Ezek 20:40-41 (LXX) looks forward to this: "For on my holy mountain, the mountain height of Israel . . . I will welcome them, and there I will require your contributions and the choicest of your gifts, with all your sacred offerings. As a pleasing aroma I will welcome you, when I bring you out from the peoples and gather you out of the countries where you have been scattered" (ESV; translation altered). When God will "welcome" Israel back, she will bring offerings to the temple on Mount Zion. This prophecy of Israel's return began to be fulfilled when God's tabernacling presence expressed itself in the coming of Christ (Jn 1:14), so that God's people might minister in that temple as priests.

in this new temple provides the basis for purity and holiness, just as the priests' participation in the Old Testament temple provided the basis for purity.

Table 8.1

ISAIAH 52:11; EZEKIEL 11:17	2 CORINTHIANS 6:17
Is 52:11: "Depart, depart, *go out from* there; *touch no unclean thing;* *go out from* the *midst* of her; purify yourselves, you who bear the vessels of the LORD."	"Therefore *go out from* their *midst*, and be separate from them, says the Lord, and *touch no unclean thing*;
Ezek 11:17 (20:34, 41): "*I will welcome you.*" (LXX)	then *I will welcome you.*"

More specifically, our identification with the true temple not only calls for holiness but also for us to flee idolatry. In Acts 15:16-21, the rebuilding of David's tabernacle (i.e., temple) provides the basis for holiness and Gentile abstention from idolatry. Since God had "cleansed their hearts by faith" (Acts 15:9), not by Old Testament cultic legislation, this statement is explained by quoting from Amos 9:11-12:

> After this I will return,
>> and I will rebuild the tent [*skēnē*] of David that has fallen;
> I will rebuild its ruins,
>> and I will restore it,
> that the remnant of mankind may seek the Lord,
>> and all the Gentiles who are called by my name. (Acts 15:16-17)

This tent/tabernacle (*skēnē*) of David is rebuilt and restored,[2] so that the nations might "seek the Lord" (Acts 15:17).[3] This confirms Old Testament

---

[2] The use of "tent," *skēnē*, here looks back to Stephen's discussion of David, who "asked to find a dwelling place [*skēnōma*] for the God of Jacob" (Acts 7:46). In this context, we find the only other references to *skēnōma* in Acts, referring to Israel's tabernacle in the wilderness (Acts 7:44), the temple (*skēnōma*; 7:46), and idolatrous tabernacles of worship (7:43). Similarly, in Hebrews *skēnōma* alludes either to Israel's tabernacle (Heb 8:5; 9:2-3, 6, 8, 21) or the new heavenly tabernacle in Christ, of which the physical tabernacle was "a copy and shadow" (Heb 8:5; 9:11; 13:10). This request found an initial fulfillment in Solomon's temple, but ultimately Jesus erects a permanent temple at his resurrection from the dead (Mk 14:58; Jn 2:19).

[3] This quotation of Amos 9:11-12 in Acts 15:16-17 is not precise, raising a number of difficult issues ably handled by R. Bauckham, "James and the Jerusalem Church," in *The Book of Acts in Its Palestinian Setting*, ed. R. Bauckham (Grand Rapids, MI: Eerdmans, 1995), 452-62.

prophecies of Gentiles streaming into the temple during the messianic age (e.g., Is 2:2-3; Zech 14:16). Just as God's presence at the tabernacle demanded both Israelites and foreigners to abstain from idolatry (Lev 17–18), so God's presence in the rebuilt tabernacle of David demands Jews and Gentiles to "abstain from the things polluted by idols, and from sexual immorality, and from what has been strangled, and from blood" (Acts 15:20). Each of these prohibitions, in the context of Leviticus 17–18, is associated with idol worship in the Lord's presence at the tabernacle,[4] and Gentile worshipers in the true temple must avoid even the appearance of idolatry.

The early church embraced its role in fleeing idolatry to establish God's temple on the earth through faith. The early second century Epistle of Barnabas 16:7-10 says,

> I find, therefore, that there is in fact a temple. How, then, will it be built in the name of the Lord? Learn! Before we believed in God, our heart's dwelling place was corrupt and weak, truly a temple built by human hands, because it was full of idolatry and was the home of demons, for we did whatever was contrary to God. "But it will be built in the name of the Lord." So pay attention, in order that the Lord's temple may be built gloriously. How? Learn! By receiving the forgiveness of sins and setting our hope on the Name, we became new, created again from the beginning. Consequently God truly dwells in our dwelling place—that is, in us. How? The word of his faith, the call of his promise, the wisdom of his righteous requirements, the commandments of his teaching, he himself prophesying in us, he himself dwelling in us; opening to us who had been in bondage to death the door of the temple . . . and granting to us repentance, he leads us into the incorruptible temple. . . . This is the spiritual temple that is being built for the Lord.[5]

---

[4] The four prohibitions of Acts 15:20 are listed in the same order in Lev 17–18, all of which are related in close proximity to the tabernacle: "things sacrificed to idols" (Lev 17:8-9), "blood" (Lev 17:10, 12), "things strangled" (Lev 17:13-14 speaks of eating only animals whose blood was poured out, but strangled animals did not have their blood poured out), and "sexual immorality" (Lev 18:26, our translation). These individual prohibitions specify the more general prohibition on idolatry in Lev 17:7, as well as Lev 18:1-5, 24-30. The Israelites must abstain from idolatry because "I am the LORD your God" (Lev 18:2, 4-6), whose presence was manifest at the tabernacle (Lev 17:4-6, 9). For further elaboration of the Leviticus background in Acts 15:20, see G. K. Beale, *The Temple and the Church's Mission: A Biblical Theology of the Dwelling Place of God*, NSBT (Downers Grove, IL: InterVarsity Press, 2004), 239-41.

[5] *Apostolic Fathers: Greek Texts and English Translations*, ed. and rev. Michael Holmes (Grand Rapids, MI: Baker, 1999), 320.

Here we see the corruption of the "temple built by human hands . . . full of idolatry," but replaced by a temple that is built gloriously "in our dwelling place—that is, in us" through God's word, a "spiritual temple that is being built of the Lord." This temple is established through faith, "receiving the forgiveness of sins and setting our hope on the Name" of Jesus Christ so that "God truly dwells in our dwelling place—that is, in us."

As John Calvin recognized, the human heart continues to be "a perpetual factory of idols."[6] Though modern idolatry in the West may not be expressed in food sacrificed to idols or blood, we continue to set up and adore "symbols in which [we] believed God appeared before [our] bodily eyes . . . overwhelmed with admiration for them, as if something of divinity inhered there."[7] Such idolatrous symbols can be found in pop stars and pets, athletes and accomplishments, gadgets and business gurus, celebrity pastors and popular politicians. When the enjoyment of the gifts of God imperceptibly replaces the worship of the giver of these gifts, God loses his proper place, and our hearts become a dwelling place for idols that do not satisfy. C. S. Lewis rightly diagnoses the tragedy of such idolatry:

> The woman who makes a dog the centre of her life loses, in the end, not only her human usefulness and dignity but even the proper pleasure of dog-keeping.
>
> The man who makes alcohol his chief good loses not only his job but his palate and all power of enjoying the earlier (and only pleasurable) levels of intoxication.
>
> It is a glorious thing to feel for a moment or two that the whole meaning of the universe is summed up in one woman—glorious so long as other duties and pleasures keep tearing you away from her. But clear the decks and so arrange your life (it is sometimes feasible) that you will have nothing to do but contemplate her, and what happens?
>
> Of course this law has been discovered before, but it will stand rediscovery. It may be stated as follows: every preference of a small good to a

---

[6]John Calvin, *Institutes of the Christian Religion*, ed. John T. McNeill, trans. Ford Lewis Battles (London: SCM Press, 1960), 1.11.8, 108.

[7]Calvin, *Institutes*, 1.11.8-9, 108-9.

great, or partial good to a total good, involves the loss of the small or partial
good for which the sacrifice is made.

  Apparently the world is made that way. . . . You can't get second things
  by putting them first. You get second things only by putting first
  things first.[8]

Idolatry in all forms must be identified and rejected. The vast array of modern
forms of idolatry can be easily seen on the magazine racks of any bookstore.
Just as James properly identified the destructive forms of idolatry in the first
century, so the church must rightly identify the forms of idolatry in its own
day and age.[9] Such idolatry cannot be overcome by diatribes alone, but
idolatry must be replaced by worship; we must "seek the Lord" in the rebuilt
"tent of David" (Acts 15:16-17). Thomas Chalmers rightly reminds us, "The
only way to dispossess [the heart] of an old affection is by the expulsive power
of a new one." Verbal prohibition alone fails to neutralize the power of idolatrous addictions just as a slap on the wrist does little to keep an alcoholic
from drink. Our idolatrous addictions can only be overcome "by setting forth
another object, even God, as more worthy of its attachment, so that the heart
shall be prevailed upon not to resign an old affection . . . but to exchange an
old affection for a new one."[10]

THE END-TIME TEMPLE DESIGNED FOR SUFFERING
SAINTS IN ISAIAH 66:1-2 AND ACTS 7

In chapter five, we briefly discussed Isaiah 66:1-2, where God's heavenly
temple and throne were spoken of as extending down to the earthly realm.
We contended that Isaiah 66:1 looked to a coming new world and temple
that God would create, and in which he would dwell forever as an extension
of the present heavenly temple. Further analysis of Isaiah 66 points in this

---

[8]C. S. Lewis, "First and Second Things," in *God in the Dock: Essays on Theology and Ethics* (Grand
  Rapids, MI: Eerdmans, 1994), 280.
[9]For a penetrating exposition of modern idolatries, see Tim Keller, *Counterfeit Gods: The Empty
  Promises of Money, Sex, and Power, and the Only Hope That Matters* (New York: Dutton, 2009).
  For the biblical notion of idolatry, see G. K. Beale, *We Become What We Worship: A Biblical Theol-
  ogy of Idolatry* (Downers Grove, IL: InterVarsity Press, 2008).
[10]Thomas Chalmers, "The Expulsive Power of a New Affection," in *The Protestant Pulpit*, ed. A. W.
  Blackwood (Grand Rapids, MI: Baker, 1947), 50.

direction and also reveals that part of the purpose of the coming temple
is to house God's suffering people. Specifically, Isaiah 66:1-2 appears to
develop 57:15 (see table 8.2).

Table 8.2

ISAIAH 57:15	ISAIAH 66:1-2
For thus says the One who is high and lifted up, who inhabits eternity, whose name is Holy: "I will dwell in the high and holy place, and also with him who is of a contrite and lowly spirit, to revive the spirit of the lowly, and to revive the heart of the contrite."	Thus says the LORD: "Heaven is my throne, and the earth is my footstool; what is the house that you would build for me, and what is the place of my rest? All these things my hands have made, and so all these things came to be, declares the LORD. But this is the one to whom I will look: he who is humble and contrite in spirit and trembles at my word."

Isaiah 57 is part of an eschatological prophecy about the temple (developing
Is 56:3-8). The passage appears to affirm that God will come from his heavenly
sanctuary and extend it to encompass "fallen" and "crushed" saints. Thus,
Isaiah 66:1-2 is not a general theological statement detached from redemptive
history but is amplifying Isaiah 57:15. In the time to come, God will cause
his heavenly temple to descend and to include "the humble and contrite"
(Is 66:2).[11] Consequently, Isaiah 66:2 gives two answers to the preceding
question in Isaiah 66:1 (asked in two different ways) about how any human-
made structure or any part of the old creation could be an enduring dwelling
for the eternal God. The first response is: "All these things my hands have
made, and so all these things came to be." That is, since God is the Creator,
no particular part of his creation is big enough to contain his presence, and
certainly no part of the sin-tainted old creation.[12]

This disjunction between the old, idolatrous world and God's coming new
world and temple is underscored by contrasting his people who were "humble

---

[11]See F. F. Bruce, *The Epistle to the Hebrews*, New International Commentary on the New Testament
(Grand Rapids, MI: Eerdmans, 1990), 212-13, who has drawn this parallelism between the two
Isaiah texts in connection with Acts 7:48-50 and Heb 9:11, but not Acts 7:55-56. "Look" in Is 66:2
refers to God's favor of blessing the afflicted from his heavenly tabernacling presence (this Hebrew
word for "look" can refer elsewhere to God issuing blessings from his heavenly temple: Is 63:15;
64:9; Ps 33:13; 80:14; 102:19; see Is 18:4, where it refers to cursings from the heavenly temple).
[12]Note the interspersed disparagement of the old creation conditions throughout Is 65:16-23 and
the association of idolatry with the old world in Is 65:2-12; 66:3-5!

and contrite" (Is 66:2) with those who prefer to dwell with idols (Is 66:3-5). These idolaters profess faith but hate the true people of God, and they will be judged by God from his heavenly temple (Is 66:5-6). All idolatry must be removed before the new creation is ushered in. The old "heavens [will] vanish," "the earth will wear out like a garment" (Is 51:6), and "all the host of heaven shall rot away" (Is 34:4) because of sin (cf. Is 51:6-8, as well as Is 13:9-13; 34:1-6). In contrast, God's eternal saving presence will dwell openly again in the new "Garden of Eden" (Is 51:3; 51:6-8).[13] Only an *entire* new creation can adequately house the Creator's presence, which is why Isaiah 66:1-2 is sandwiched in between two of the most well-known new creation texts in all of the Old Testament: Isaiah 65:17; 66:22. In fact, verses 1 and 2 are a continuation in some manner of the new creation prophecy that began back in Isaiah 65:16.[14]

The second response to the question of Isaiah 66:1 must be seen in the light of the parallel to Isaiah 57:15: in the new creation God will enable "the afflicted and smitten" to become part of his new order by "making them alive" (the Aramaic interprets this as resurrected people in Isaiah 57:16). Accordingly, God also "will dwell" with them as he extends his heavenly temple to include the new creation and those humans living in it. Anticipating the events of the New Testament, one can see how suitable it is to see "the afflicted and smitten" Jesus as a good example of the beginning fulfillment of this prophecy at his resurrection, as well as his suffering servant Stephen (Acts 7:54-60) and all those who follow their suffering example.

That Isaiah 66:1-2 refers to an end-time temple is supported further by Stephen's speech in Acts 7. Not coincidentally, Stephen quotes Isaiah 66:1

---

[13]We are not interested in discussing whether the cosmic conflagration language is literal or not but are content to understand these texts as affirming, at least, a renovated and purified new world system in contrast to the old, sinful world epoch. Our ultimate judgment on the issue is that the Isaiah prophecies begin fulfillment in the New Testament age in a nonphysical manner and have consummate fulfillment physically as well. For further discussion of the nature of this language, see Beale, *Temple and the Church's Mission*, 211-16, and Beale, *The Book of Revelation*, NIGTC (Grand Rapids, MI: Eerdmans, 1999), 396-99 (on Rev 6:12-14) and 1039-43, 1048-51 (on Rev 21:1, 4).

[14]In this light it is hardly coincidental that Is 65:22 (LXX, Targum) refers to part of the "new" conditions being "like the days of the tree of life," recapitulating the image of latter-day Eden from Is 51:3.

(Acts 7:49) as part of his answer to the charge that he had spoken "against this holy place and the law" by saying that "Jesus of Nazareth will destroy this place and will change the customs that Moses delivered to us" (Acts 6:13-14). This charge parallels the charge against Jesus in Mark 14:58: "We heard him say, 'I will destroy this temple that is made with hands, and in three days I will build another, not made with hands.'" Hence, Stephen's comments relate to Jesus' building of the eschatological temple that began with his earthly ministry and especially his resurrection (so Jn 2:19-22), which in turn was an escalated inauguration of the restoration promises to Israel, which had begun only on a small scale with the return of a tiny remnant from Babylon.[15]

In connection with Isaiah 66:1-2 being a prophecy about God's latter-day temple being designed to house suffering saints, it is all the more appropriate that soon after Stephen quotes Isaiah 66:1 (Acts 7:49),[16] he suffers and dies as he beholds Christ in God's heavenly temple[17] and prepares to enter into that temple himself upon his death. As Stephen was being "afflicted and smitten," he was on the verge of beginning to experience the latter-day tabernacling presence of God expressed in Isaiah 57 and Isaiah 66 in his midst. Neither he nor Luke quotes the last part of Isaiah 66:2 because Stephen's experience in Acts 7:54-60 is the fulfillment of it!

We will see in the next section that this suffering of saints in the temple is part of a priestly task of offering oneself as a sacrifice to God.

---

[15]On which see further, e.g., the various works of N. T. Wright (e.g., *The New Testament and the People of God* [London: SPCK, 1992]), as well as R. Watts, *Isaiah's New Exodus in Mark* (Grand Rapids, MI: Baker, 1997).

[16]Though the above-noted Is 57 passage is probably not alluded to in Acts 7:48 ("however, the Most High does not dwell in handmade things, as the prophet says" [authors' translation]), the passage may have served as the underlying transition to Stephen's quotation of Is 66 in verses 49-50. Is 57 has importance for how Stephen's quotation of Is 66:1-2 relates to his vision of "heavens [being] opened." It is part of an eschatological prophecy about the temple (developing Is 56:3-8). Apparently, God will come from his heavenly sanctuary and extend it to encompass humble and suffering saints. In the time to come, God will cause his heavenly temple to descend and will include "the afflicted and smitten."

[17]At this point, Acts 7:55-56 says that Stephen "gazed into heaven and saw the glory of God, and Jesus standing at the right hand of God, and he said, 'Behold, I see the heavens opened, and the Son of Man standing at the right hand of God.'" Elsewhere in the Bible, the expression "heavens were opened" together with the mention of the "glory" of God always introduces a vision of the heavenly temple where the "glory" of God abides (on which see further Beale, *Temple and the Church's Mission*, 220n39).

THE SACRIFICE OF WITNESS IN THE NEW TEMPLE IN HEBREWS AND 1 PETER

As priests in God's temple, we offer the sacrifice of witness. God builds believers up "as a spiritual house, to be a holy priesthood, to offer spiritual sacrifices acceptable to God through Jesus Christ" (1 Pet 2:5). If this "spiritual house" is built on the rejected cornerstone of Christ (1 Pet 2:6-8), what are the spiritual sacrifices that we offer to God? As "a chosen race, a royal priesthood, a holy nation, a people for his own possession," our calling is clear: "That you may proclaim the excellencies of him who called you out of darkness into his marvelous light" (1 Pet 2:9). As a royal priesthood living as "sojourners and exiles" (1 Pet 2:11), these spiritual sacrifices of praise would be offered as a witness among the Gentiles so that "when they speak against you as evildoers, they may see your good deeds and glorify God on the day of visitation" (1 Pet 2:12). Just as the Old Testament priests sacrificed on behalf of the people to bring them to God, so the New Testament priests sacrifice on behalf of the nations to bring them to God. This priestly ministry comes through their witness to Christ's redemptive work, the mediating priest par excellence.

Similarly in Hebrews, priestly sacrifice is expressed in witness. Christ is the "high priest . . . a minister in the holy places" (Heb 8:1-2; see Heb 9:11) in the "true tent" (Heb 8:2; see Heb 9:11). Just as Christ is the true high priest, we who identify with him are also priests. In response to their inclusion in God's unshakable kingdom and temple, Christians as priests are to "be grateful" and "offer to God acceptable worship, with reverence and awe" (Heb 12:28). Sacrificial living is appropriate for those who "have no lasting city" on this old earth but "seek the city that is to come" (Heb 13:14). This priestly sacrifice is expressed when we "offer up a sacrifice of praise to God, that is, the fruit of lips," and "do good . . . and share, for such sacrifices are pleasing to God" (Heb 13:15-16). These priestly sacrifices express their witness in both word and deed, both "the fruit of lips" and the acts of doing good. The work and words of the gospel are not split; both are inextricably linked as pleasing sacrifices to God as the expression of our priestly witness.[18]

---

[18]For a recent call back to a biblical balance between the words and work of the gospel, see Duane Litfin, *Word Versus Deed: Resetting the Scales to a Biblical Balance* (Wheaton, IL: Crossway, 2012).

Our mission as the true temple is to extend his dwelling place throughout the earth by our witness until that temple is completed. The new temple begins with Christ as the foundation "stone" and continues to be "built up as a spiritual house" (1 Pet 2:4-6) until it is consummated at the end of history.[19] Similarly, God's dwelling place grows because Christ is "the cornerstone, in whom the whole structure, being joined together, grows into a holy temple in the Lord . . . [and is] being built together into a dwelling place for God by the Spirit" (Eph 2:20-22). During the present age, the church as priests dwelling in the invisible temple witness to God's presence to others, either in blessing or judgment. All believers in Christ are priests whose service reflect God's presence to others through their life and words. This reflection of God's presence in the unseen sanctuary shines light into the darkness of the world and transforms those in the darkness to reflect God's presence and become reflective images of God in his temple. This is how the temple expands throughout the church age.

THE SACRIFICE OF WITNESS IN THE TEMPLE IN REVELATION 11

Revelation 11 presents the most compelling picture of the witness of the church as the temple of God, but the genre and imagery of this chapter demand careful attention. In this chapter, the church is a lampstand that stands before the presence of God in prophetic witness to the nations in the face of great persecution. The chapter begins with a measuring of the temple on earth:

> Then I was given a measuring rod like a staff, and I was told, "Rise and measure the temple of God and the altar and those who worship there, but do not measure the court outside the temple; leave that out, for it is given over to the nations, and they will trample the holy city for forty-two months." (Rev 11:1-2)

The "temple of God" probably refers to true believers who are secured in their spiritual relationship to God (= inner court) and yet whose physical existence

---

[19]See likewise Ignatius, *To the Ephesians* 9: "You are stones of a temple, prepared beforehand for the building of God the Father." Similarly, Epistle of Barnabas 4:11 says, "Let us become spiritual; let us become a perfect temple for God."

is not protected (= outer court). This temple endures throughout the church age.[20] God's presence previously revealed in Israel's physical temple is now present in the midst of God's people, the church, as the true temple.

Preliminary questions to understand Revelation 11. Before we can explore the significance of the church as a lampstand and witness to the nations in Revelation 11, we must answer a number of difficult questions raised by this passage: What is the temple of God here? What does it mean to measure the temple of God? What is the altar that is spoken of here? What is the court outside the temple? These questions emerge because, at first glance, Revelation 11:1-2 seems to refer to an earthly temple structure, but closer examination suggests that this temple refers to the people of God. In this section, we will explore how the temple is the people of God, measured and protected by God's presence, with an altar representing their suffering throughout time as the "outer court" of their body is trampled by the nations. Indeed, God does not protect their physical being since their lives are priestly sacrifices in the courtyard of the world.

First, what is the "temple (*naos*) of God" in Revelation 11? The temple in Revelation 11:1 likely refers to the new covenant community forming a spiritual temple where God's presence dwells, not an earthly temple structure. Outside of the Gospels and Acts, the New Testament usually uses temple (*naos*) to describe the church.[21] Different images from the temple describe the church in Revelation, such as "lampstands" (Rev 1:12-13, 20; 2:1, 5), doors/gates that cannot be shut (Rev 3:8; 21:25), and the city of God (Rev 3:12; 21:2),[22] because

---

[20]Other possible interpretations for this temple include a reference to the future temple structure at the end of time, a past temple structure destroyed in AD 70, or a nonstructural temple composed of believing (= inner court) and unbelieving (= outer court) ethnic Israelites that precede Christ's coming. See discussion and bibliography on each of these options in Beale, *Revelation*, 556-71, where especially arguments are found in favor of the temple being a nonstructural reality composed of authentic Christians whose saving relationship to God is secured (= inner court) but whose physical existence (= outer court) is not protected.

[21]The Gospels and Acts point to the inadequacy of the physical temple (*naos*), replaced by Christ or God's universal presence at Christ's resurrection (e.g., Mt 26:61; 27:5; Jn 2:20). Now, the church is the new spiritual temple (*naos*), as seen in the rest of the New Testament (e.g., 1 Cor 3:16-17; 6:19; 2 Cor 6:16; Eph 2:21-22; 1 Pet 2:5; see discussion in chapter 7).

[22]This temple is inaugurated in the earthly sphere to those who overcome compromise, as Christ has "set before [them] an open door, which no one is able to shut" (Rev 3:8), just as the dwelling place of God in the heavenly Jerusalem has "gates [that] will never be shut" (Rev 21:25). As a result, God promises those who overcome to be a "pillar in the temple of my God" and to write

Christians already participate in the new temple. The people of God are his "dwelling, that is, those who dwell in heaven" (Rev 13:6).[23] Throughout Revelation, "sanctuary" or "temple" (*naos*) always refer to some facet of the inaugurated or consummated end-time temple among God's people, focusing on its heavenly location.[24] As a result, if one insists on identifying the sanctuary in Revelation 11:1-2 as the earthly temple structure instead of the invisible and heavenly, then one must assume that this is a unique employment of that concept within Revelation,[25] as well as the rest of the New Testament outside the Gospels and Acts.

Second, what does it mean to "measure the temple of God and the altar" in Revelation 11:1, if the temple represents the people of God? In Revelation 21:15-17, the measuring of the walls of the new Jerusalem pictures the full inclusion and protection of the people of God throughout history. The city is 12,000 stadia (= about 1,500 miles) in its length, width, and height, with a wall 144 cubits thick (= 72 yards). Just as there were twelve tribes of Israel and twelve apostles, the predominance of twelve and multiples of twelve ($144 = 12 \times 12$) shows the emphasis on the inclusion of the people of God throughout history (e.g., 144,000 [Rev 7:4-8; 14:1-3]).[26] Like

---

on them "the name of my God, and the name of the city of my God, the new Jerusalem, which comes down from my God out of heaven" (Rev 3:12), alluding to the "holy city, new Jerusalem, coming down out of heaven from God" (Rev 21:2). The name is written on believers because they already participate in this dwelling place of God in Rev 3. Similarly, those who overcome in tribulation "serve him [God] day and night in his [heavenly] temple; and he who sits on the throne will shelter them with his presence" (Rev 7:15), a reality that is inaugurated for deceased but exalted saints, which also leads up to the very end of time (see Rev 3:22).

[23]God's people are called "his dwelling" (or tabernacle), "that is, those who dwell in heaven" (Rev 13:6), and they become "the dwelling place of God" (Rev 21:3) in the new Jerusalem when God's presence on earth is consummated without a physical temple because "its temple is the Lord God the Almighty and the Lamb" (Rev 21:22). They dwell in heaven spiritually even as they physically live on earth and face the full fury of the beast making war on the saints (Rev 13:7). On Rev 13:6 see Beale, *Revelation*, 696-98.

[24]On these uses see Beale, *Revelation*, 562.

[25]See further in M. Bachmann, "Himmlisch: der 'Tempel Gottes' von Apk 11.1," *New Testament Studies* 40 (1994): 478.

[26]Translating these dimensions to yards and miles makes the picture of the city almost comical. What type of wall is almost as thick as a football field (72 yards; 144 cubits)? What type of city is 1,500 miles (12,000 stadia) long, wide, and high? The translation of these numbers into miles and yards loses the intended effect, since the numbers in Revelation, like in much of apocalyptic literature, are metaphorical. Rev 21:17 itself hints that these measurements are not to be understood literally: "144 cubits by human measurement, which is also an angel's measurement"

a large family numbering off so that nobody is lost during a trip, this measuring connoted how God includes and protects his people. Similarly in Revelation 11, the "measuring" connotes God's holy and saving presence among his people on earth before the consummation of history without contamination. Just as the sealing of God's people in Revelation 7:3-8 connotes how God secures their salvation for all time,[27] so the measuring of the temple shows the secure establishment of God's saving presence with his people for all time.[28] Revelation 11 therefore pictures how God's end-time presence secures his people's ultimate destiny. This securing begins with the establishment of the Christian community in the first century and continues throughout the age of the church.

Third, what is the "altar" (*thysiastērion*) in Revelation 11:1, if not an altar in the earthly temple, as some think? Literally, "the altar" in Revelation 11:1 can be translated as "the place of sacrifice,"[29] which here would be the suffering covenant community. The "altar" refers to the way God's people now worship in the community. In Revelation 6:9, John sees "under the altar the souls of those who had been slain for the word of God and for the witness they had borne." This sacrificial calling shows that they have paid the ultimate price "for the witness they had borne," not only as worshipers but also as priests (see Rev 5:10) who have brought themselves to be sacrificed on the altar of the gospel to which they have been called to testify. Similarly in Revelation 11:7-10, the altar is connected with the price of witness in terms

---

(see further Richard Bauckham, *The Climax of Prophecy: Studies on the Book of Revelation* [London: T&T Clark, 1993], 398). The measuring of the people of God pictures the security of its inhabitants against harm and contamination of unclean and deceptive people (Rev 21:27), protecting God's latter-day community of Jews and Gentiles (so, e.g., Rev 3:12; 21:12-14, 24-26; 22:2). This measuring of the temple has its Old Testament roots in Ezek 40–48 as a metaphorical picture of the sure establishment and subsequent protection of worshipers in the temple from contamination of impurity or idolatry (J. W. Wevers, *Ezekiel*, New Century Bible [Camden, NJ: Thomas Nelson, 1969], 295-96). God's future presence is infallibly promised here, so that God's people will dwell forever in the midst of "a purified cult and purified community."

[27] See Beale, *Revelation*, 408-26, on Rev 7:3.

[28] The metaphors of "measuring" and "sealing" are synonymous theological concepts. Likewise E. Lohmeyer, *Die Offenbarung des Johannes* (Tübingen: Mohr Siebeck, 1970), 89; J. Ernst, *Die eschatologischen Gegenspieler in den Schriften des Neuen Testaments* (Regensburg: Pustet, 1967), 130.

[29] See W. Bauer, W. F. Arndt, F. W. Gingrich, and F. W. Danker, *Greek-English Lexicon of the New Testament and Other Early Christian Literature*, 2nd ed. (Chicago: 1979), 366.

of sacrificial martyrdom.[30] If the "temple of God" refers to the people among whom God makes his dwelling (Rev 11:1), then the altar is the place of their sacrificial service that occurs in the "outer court" of the world, as detailed in Revelation 11:7-10.

Fourth, who are the ones that are worshiping at the temple of God in Revelation 11:1? This refers to believers worshiping together in the temple community in the midst of God's tabernacling presence. While it is possible that these worshipers are the elders in heaven (Rev 4:10; 5:14; 7:11; 11:16; 19:4),[31] an earthly location of the "worshipers" is favored by the immediate context of Revelation 11:1-2 and the focus on the community of faith on earth in verses 3-10. More specifically, the measuring of the "worshipers" guarantees their membership in the heavenly spiritual temple, despite what happens to them on earth.[32]

Finally, what is "the court outside the temple" that is not to be measured but "given over to the nations" (Rev 11:2)? If the inner court stands for the true, spiritual temple protected by God's presence, then the outer court represents the physical bodies of God's true people, which are susceptible to harm. This is consistent with the notion that the outer court of the Old Testament temple represented the physical aspect of creation. This view of

---

[30]The connection between the altar and sacrificial service is also seen in Heb 13, since "we have an altar from which those who serve the tent have no right to eat" (Heb 13:10), an altar where they offer sacrifices as we "go to him outside the camp and bear the reproach he endured" (Heb 13:13-16). The offering of sacrifices on the altar is connected with bearing the reproach of Christ, presumably in persecution. The above analysis of the "altar" corresponds to early Christian interpretation. In Ignatius's epistle to the Ephesians (5:2), "the place of the altar" is the authoritative unity of "the whole church" (so also Ignatius, *To the Trallians* 7:2; see Ignatius, *To the Philadelphians* 4). The exhortation to maintain such unity is based on "the one temple [*naos*], even God . . . [and] the one altar . . . the one Jesus Christ" to whom all should come (Ignatius, *To the Magnesians* 7:2).This altar is later equated with believers being "stones of a temple [*naos*]," which is a "temple shrine [*naophoroi*]" carried by all in the church (so Ignatius, *To the Ephesians* 9; likewise, 15). See also Rom 12:1, where believers are exhorted to offer their bodies "as a living, holy sacrifice, acceptable to God, [which is] their reasonable service of worship" (our translation). See Beale, *Revelation*, 391, on Rev 6:9 with regard to whether the altar in Rev 11:1 refers specifically to the altar of incense or the altar of burnt offering.

[31]C. H. Giblin, "Revelation 11.1-13: Its Form, Function, and Contextual Integration," *New Testament Studies* 30 (1984): 455.

[32]Likewise, the Qumran saints were identified with the heavenly community in their worship: e.g., IQS 11, 7ff.; 1QH 3, 21ff.; 6, 12ff. (so R. J. McKelvey, *The New Temple: The Church in the New Testament* [London: Oxford University Press, 1969], 37-38).

Revelation 11:1-2 is linguistically allowable because the language of "casting outside" ("leave out" [ESV]) can also have the nuance of God's true people who are rejected and persecuted by the unbelieving world.[33] The measuring demonstrates that their salvation is secured, despite physical harm. This is a further development of the "sealing" of Revelation 7:2-8 and is consistent with 1 Enoch 61:1-5, where the angelic "measuring" of the righteous elect ensures that their faith will be strengthened and not demolished, despite the fact that their bodies will be destroyed. In the Old Testament generally, "measuring" was metaphorical for a decree of protection.[34]

Understanding witness from the lampstand of God in Revelation 11.
Returning to our original concern, the church witnesses as a lampstand in the face of opposition in Revelation 11. The measuring of the temple of God and altar and trampling of the holy city in Revelation 11:1-2 are amplified with the persecution and protection of the people of God in the face of their witness in Revelation 11:3-13. Revelation 11:3-4 asserts: "'And I will grant authority to my two witnesses, and they will prophesy for 1,260 days, clothed in sackcloth.' These are the two olive trees and the two lampstands that stand before the Lord of the earth." The centrality of witness in this temple context is explicit, and the two witnesses are two olive trees and lampstands. While Revelation 11:1-2 affirms that believers presently dwell in the true temple by offering themselves as priestly sacrifices, Revelation 11:3-4 explains further how they exercise their priestly service as lampstands in the unseen temple of God's presence, as they shine the light of God's presence to the outer court of the world. The two lampstands refer not to individual people but the faithful church of God (see Rev 1:20), who are identified as a part of the temple, since the lampstands were in the Holy Place of Israel's temple. This imagery draws from the two olive trees and lampstand with seven lamps in Zechariah 4, which calls for the rebuilding of the temple of the Lord despite opposition and inauspicious beginnings, "not by might, nor by power, but by my Spirit" (Zech 4:6). Similarly, the new Israel, the church, as God's lampstands (and

---

[33]See Mt 21:39; Mk 12:8; Lk 4:29; 20:15; Jn 9:34-35; Acts 7:58; see 1 Macc 7:16-17; Josephus, *Jewish War* 4.316-17; Heb 13:11-12.

[34]E.g., with reference to protection, see 2 Sam 8:2; Is 28:16-17; Jer 31:38-40; Zech 1:16, though sometimes "measuring" refers to judgment (e.g., 2 Sam 8:2; 2 Kings 21:13; Lam 2:8; Amos 7:7-9).

thus part of the spiritual temple on earth) must draw its power from the Spirit, standing before God's throne in order to stand against the resistance of the world. God's presence among his people ensures the effectiveness of their prophetic witness.

Both Revelation 11:1-2 and Zechariah 4:14 are focused on the establishment of the temple despite opposition. Just as the Spirit used the two anointed ones (= priest and king) to build the temple in the face of opposition in Zechariah 4:14, so the two witnesses are empowered by the Spirit to witness in the face of opposition in Revelation 11:5-6, 11. Just as the temple in Zechariah seemed small to the visible eye (Zech 4:10), so the spiritual temple of God appears insignificant and subject to defeat by the power of the beast (Rev 11:7-9). Despite resistance, the Christian community's successful establishment as God's temple throughout the church age is assured by means of the Spirit's empowerment of the church's faithful, prophetic witness (Rev 1:13-15; 19:10).

Revelation 2:5 anticipates the witness of the church as a lampstand in Revelation 11:4, where the church's faithful witness (Rev 2:5) leads to an invitation "to eat of the tree of life" (Rev 2:7). Both "the tree of life" and the lampstand represent God's presence. In particular, Israel as a lampstand was to shine the light of God's presence to the world,[35] just as the church as "lampstands . . . stand *before* the Lord of the earth" (Rev 11:4, emphasis added). Earlier, we explored how the lampstand in the temple represented the tree of life in Eden, since the lampstand's "stylized tree shape and vocabulary of botanical terms that describe it suggest that the cultic lampstand symbolized the fructifying powers of the eternal, unseen God."[36] Intriguingly,

---

[35]See also Beale, *Revelation*, 206-8, on Rev 1:12.

[36]C. Meyers, "The Tree of Life," in *Harper's Bible Dictionary*, ed. P. J. Achtemeier (San Francisco: Harper and Row, 1985), 1094; see also Meyers, "Lampstand," in *Harper's Bible Dictionary*, 546. For the botanical descriptions, see especially Ex 25:31-40; 37:17-24. This tree of life in Eden is described in the Dead Sea Scrolls as a "well-spring of light" with "brilliant flames" directly linked to the "testimony" (1QH 6, 14-19), and the seven lamps on the lampstand shone "with a *seven-fold li[ght]* in the E[den which] Thou has [m]ade for Thy glory" (1QH 7, 24). (For including "Eden" in this translation, see further Beale, *Temple and the Church's Mission*, 79n125). Furthermore, just as the lampstand was composed of gold (see Ex 25), so Judaism conceived of Eden's tree of life as gold (2 Enoch 8:3-4 [J]). And just as the seven lamps of Zech 4 were fed oil by olive trees, so 2 Enoch thinks of the tree of life in the same way (8:5 [A]). Philo also appears to have associated the tree of life and the lampstand of the later temple, since he compared both with the planetary lights (see *Questions and Answers on Genesis* 1.10 with, e.g., *Questions and Answers on*

in this connection, the Old Testament "tree of life" was associated with witnessing (Prov 11:30). The connection between the lampstand and the tree of life in Eden confirm further that humanity's original purpose in the first Garden sanctuary was to expand outward and spread the light of God's presence throughout the earth. After the fall, the commission to spread this presence entailed "witnessing" to those in darkness and in need of light from God's glorious presence through his priest-king image bearers (e.g., Ex 19:6). Therefore, the church's role as an arboreal lampstand of witness begins at the commencement of the church age and is consummated when Christ returns.[37]

The church symbolized as a "lampstand" in Revelation 11 represents God's temple-presence that is given power by "the seven lamps" (= the Spirit, as in Rev 1:4; 4:5) on it. This power to witness shines light uncompromisingly to the world so that the gates of hell (see Rev 2:9-11, 13) might not prevail against the building of God's temple.[38] This reiterates the mission of true Israel, as expressed by the use of Exodus 19:6 (Israel "shall be to me a kingdom of priests") in Revelation 1:6 ("he has made us [the church] a kingdom, priests to his God and Father"; so also Rev 5:10), both of which have their ultimate roots in the first "Great Commission" in Genesis 1:26-28. Revelation 11:1-13 confirms that the lampstands represent the church as the true temple and the totality of the people of God witnessing between the period of Christ's resurrection and his final coming. In light of Revelation 1:5-6, Christ's death and resurrection have laid the foundation for the new temple, which he will build through the Spirit (the lamps on the lampstand).

Exodus 2.73-81). For these references to Judaism with respect to the tree of life, see Margaret Barker, *The Gate of Heaven: The History and Symbolism of the Temple in Jerusalem* (London: SPCK, 1991), 90-95.

[37]For the church's beginning identification with the "tree of life" see the following: the Epistle of Barnabas 11:10-11, where the image of eating from the trees of the new creation (so Ezek 47:1-12; see Rev 22:2) is used to describe the *present* experience of baptism; Odes of Solomon 11:16-24, which refers to those who are presently identified with the blessing of the trees of paradise (so likewise 20:7); Psalms of Solomon 14:2, which affirms that "the Lord's paradise, the trees of life, *are* his devout ones," and yet this is also seen as a future hope in 14:10. Also see J. Daniélou, *Primitive Christian Symbols* (London: Burns and Oates 1964), 30-35, who shows that the earliest Fathers predominantly understood the symbols of the tree of life and paradise as referring to inaugurated realities of which Christians already partook.

[38]See Beale, *Revelation*, 206-8, 210-12, on 1:12, 16.

GOD'S PRESENCE IN ISRAEL'S TEMPLE AND THE NEW TEMPLE IN REVELATION

In this connection, we must ask another question: What is the relationship of God's presence in the Holy of Holies of Israel's temple to his presence in the new temple? While God's common grace presence filled the entire creation in the time before Christ (i.e., God was omnipresent), his special revelatory presence was focused more in the Holy of Holies than anywhere else on earth. In this place, God's heavenly throne extended down to the inner sanctum. God sat on his heavenly throne with his "feet" resting on the sacred "footstool" of the ark of the covenant. The Holy of Holies was open only to the high priest once a year. God moved out of the Holy of Holies at the inception of the Babylonian exile (Ezek 10:18; 11:22-23), and does not appear to have dwelt in the second temple that was rebuilt after the return from Babylon. God's presence returned at the coming of Christ to earth again as "the Word became flesh and dwelt [tabernacled] among us" (Jn 1:14; see Jn 1:51). After his resurrection and ascension, God's tabernacling presence descended in the form of the Spirit, so that those identified with Christ are included as part of the temple. The Father and Son, however, still reside in the heavenly temple and not on earth. Therefore, the temple's center of gravity during the church age is located in the heavenly realm, but it has begun to invade the earthly through the Spirit in the church. This is why the book of Revelation usually portrays the "temple" (*naos*) in heaven (eleven of fifteen times[39]), though it is related to believers on earth (e.g., Rev 1:13; 11:1-4) through their identification with the Spirit existentially (see Rev 1:4 and Rev 4:5 with Rev 1:13; 2:2; and Rev 11:4) and with Christ (see Rev 3:12 with Rev 21:22) and their angels positionally (see Rev 1:13 and Rev 1:16; 2:1).[40]

Though the three parts of Israel's old temple no longer exist in the new covenant era, the three dimensions of the new temple remain until the end

---

[39]Three of the four remaining uses (Rev 3:12; 11:1-2) refer to the church on earth, though Rev 3:12 is likely already and not yet, including the church's being on earth and its future existence in the new creation (see Rev 21:1–22:5). The fourth use refers to God and the Lamb as the temple in the new creation. The synonym "tabernacle" (*skēnos*) occurs three times, twice referring to the heavenly sphere (Rev 13:6; 15:5) and once with respect to the new creation. "Tabernacling" (*skēnoō*) is used twice of those who dwell in heaven (Rev 12:12; 13:6) and twice of God who dwells in the new creation (Rev 7:15; 21:3), though Rev 7:15 could be already and not yet.

[40]On all of these passages see further Beale, *Revelation*, in loc., including the additional Rev 13:6.

of the age. First, the Holy of Holies remains in heaven, the place of the temple's center of gravity for God's presence. Second, the Holy Place is the spiritual dimension that extends to earth, where God's people function as a "kingdom of priests" (Rev 1:6; 5:10; see Ex 19:6) and as "lampstands" shining God's revelation to the world (Rev 1:13, 20; 2:2; 11:1, 4). The Spirit is the lamp on these lampstands that enables the church to shine (see Rev 1:4 with Rev 4:6). Third, the "outer court" represents the world where the church also physically exists (Rev 11:1-2), especially in its suffering on earth.[41] Just as animals were slain to be sacrificed in the outer courtyard, so believers sacrifice themselves in the courtyard of the world in their willingness to suffer for their faith (see Rev 6:9-11; Heb 13:10-13).[42] As in the old temple, so in the new inaugurated one there is an increasing gradation in holiness, beginning in the outer court and proceeding through the Holy Place into the Holy of Holies.

Priests in the old epoch had to be ritually clean in order to enter and minister in the Holy Place. If they tried to minister while unclean, they would be put to death (e.g., Lev 10:1-2). Believers as priests minister in the spiritual "Holy Place," even though they are unclean because of sin. Though believers may be existentially imperfect, they are not destroyed because of their "blamelessness" in God's sight because of their corporate identification with Christ, the perfect Last Adam and great high priest. As a priest, he suffered the penalty of their sin through death on their behalf and imputes his righteousness to them. He has "once for all" performed the priestly task that had originally been given to the first Adam. Thus, they have been "washed . . . and made white . . . in the blood of the Lamb" (Rev 7:14), which allows them to be "before the throne of God" when they die (Rev 7:15).

Therefore, believers on earth still do not yet *personally* enter into the heavenly Holy of Holies, but do so through their representative high priest, Jesus Christ. He has entered in on their behalf (just as Israel's high priest entered in as a representative of the rest of the nation, and as a typological foreshadowing of Christ) and secured "an eternal redemption" (Heb 9:11-12,

---

[41]A. Spatafora, *From the "Temple of God" to God as the Temple* (Rome: Gregorian University Press, 1997), 168-73, believes that the outer court in Rev 11:2 continues as an image for the church as the temple but that it refers to the sinful aspect of the church.

[42]See also Rom 12:1; Phil 2:17; 2 Tim 4:6.

24-28; see Heb 3:17). On the basis of Christ's priestly work of entering that heavenly sanctuary, believers "have confidence to enter the" Holy Place (Heb 10:19-21).[43] Believers have a "hope" that "enters within the veil, where Jesus has entered as a forerunner for us, having become a high priest" (Heb 6:19-20, our translation).[44]

The temple curtain tore at Christ's death, and at his resurrection "he entered through the veil" of the heavenly temple (Heb 10:20, our translation). The removing of the veil of the heavenly temple will occur for believers when the church (the body of Christ) suffers death and resurrection at the end of the age, according to the principle that the church "follow[s] the Lamb wherever he goes" (Rev 14:4). As a result, after the church's suffering, demise, and vindication according to the model of Christ's career, "then God's temple in heaven was opened, and the ark of his covenant [symbolic of the divine presence] was seen within his temple"[45] (Rev 11:19; so similarly Rev 21:1–22:5). Perhaps this is what Isaiah 25:7-8 refers to:

> And he will swallow up on this mountain
>> the covering that is cast over all peoples,
>> the veil that is spread over all nations.
> He will swallow up death forever.[46]

Until that final day of unveiling, God's people "draw near" to the heavenly Holy of Holies by entering the outer court and Holy Place of the celestial temple (Heb 10:22). They have *begun* to "come to Mount Zion and to the city of the living God, the heavenly Jerusalem" (Heb 12:22), a mountain and city

---

[43]Some contend that believers have progressed into the celestial Holy of Holies not merely in a redemptive-historical manner (positionally in Christ), but in some way existentially. If so, the existential link with the Holy of Holies would be through the Spirit that bridges the two. Nevertheless, it is preferable to see the Spirit as having brought the church into the initial phase of the end-time temple, where their physical existence in the world is the outer court and their spiritual existence is in the heavenly dimension of the Holy Place that invisibly extends to earth.

[44]From one perspective, saints are like the Old Testament high priest who could enter in and partially experience the Holy of Holies because he could not see the divine luminous presence, since the incense cloud shielded it. Otherwise, the priest would have been struck dead, since he was a sinful human. Likewise, Christians have partially entered the heavenly Holy of Holies: positionally in Jesus but not personally, otherwise they would be annihilated because they are still sinful.

[45]On which see Beale, *Revelation*, 567-68.

[46]Note the explicit reference to the final resurrection also in Is 26:19.

that suggest the eternal temple. Our arrival in this "heavenly Jerusalem" is not yet consummate, for we are still "receiving a kingdom that cannot be shaken" (Heb 12:28) and continue to "seek the city that is to come" (Heb 13:14). During this present era, therefore, the three sections of the temple continue into the new temple, though invisibly, until their purpose and fulfillment are completed at the destruction of the old order and establishment of the new. The consummate form of the new temple will appear at the end of time in the new creation, when the heavenly dimension of God's Holy of Holies fully breaks in and replaces the old earth that has been destroyed (Rev 21:1-3).[47] At this time only one section of the temple will remain, which is the Holy of Holies covering the whole cosmos. Heaven will come down and fill every part of the new creation. The church will no longer serve as a lampstand, since their role of witnessing to God's light will be finished. They will no longer need to shine God's light in a dark world, since that world will be gone; instead, in the new creation "the glory of God" will have "illumined it, and its lamp [will be] the Lamb" (Rev 21:23, translation altered; so also Rev 22:5). The shining function will have shifted to God and the Lamb, and the saints merely will reflect that glorious light. In chapter eleven, we will unpack the practical implications of this call for the church today more fully.

PRACTICAL IMPLICATIONS

The power of God's word empowers our witness. Our sacrifice is expressed in witness, as we offer up "the sacrifice of praise to God, that is, the fruit of lips that acknowledge his name" (Heb 13:15) and "proclaim the excellencies of him who called you out of darkness into his marvelous light" (1 Pet 2:9). Our witness must be empowered by the promises of God in our heart. Bold witness must be empowered; Jesus promised, "But you will receive power when the Holy Spirit has come upon you, and you will be my witnesses" (Acts 1:8). The powerful witnessing church pours out fire from its mouth to

---

[47]Spatafora, From the "Temple of God" to God as the Temple, 214, gives partial confirmation of this idea: although the "open [heavenly] temple" in Revelation signifies God's greater revelation to and his presence within the church, "the full vision of divine glory is denied until this age is over." The church as a "temple . . . in the world" belongs to the heavenly sphere, but because it "is still in the world . . . union with God is not total" (300).

consume their enemies (Rev 11:5), just as a sword goes out from Christ's mouth to defeat his enemies (Rev 1:16; 19:15). Christ's sword from his mouth is the word of God, just like the fire from the witnessing church is the power of God's word in our heart. More specifically, this fire brings down God's judgment upon their enemies through the word of God (see Rev 2:16; 19:15, 21).[48] When the word of God fills our hearts, then our mouths are emboldened to witness.

Also, sacrificial witness must be expressed from a heart of repentance and worship. The powerful witnessing church in Revelation 11 is "clothed in sack-cloth" (Rev 11:3). Sackcloth throughout Scripture is a picture of repentance, both in repentant mourning and judgment. Both Elijah and John the Baptist are attired in sackcloth (2 Kings 1:8; Mk 1:6), and the church has the same prophetic calling as they mourn over sin and the judgment of others.[49] Witness does not flow from superiority over the world but brokenness over our hearts and our world. When sinful thoughts and inclinations rise up within our hearts, we repent before God. When we see the effects of sin in the world around us, we repent and cry out with broken hearts, standing in the gap in prayerful intercession. We must "pray and not lose heart," trusting in God's promise to bring justice when we "cry to him day and night" (Lk 18:1, 7). As the church clothes itself in the sackcloth of brokenness and repentance over the sin in the world, then its witness grows stronger.

Also, the powerful witnessing church is "the two lampstands that stand before the Lord of the earth" (Rev 11:4) empowered by the fiery lamps of God resting upon them (see Rev 4:5); our witness must flow from our worship. The church too often takes sin lightly because it takes God lightly. Lives of repentance flow out of lives of worship. The brightness and intensity of our witness grows as "the two lampstands . . . stand before the Lord of the earth"— before his very tabernacling presence (Rev 11:4). As we stand before the Lord of the earth in worship and under his word, then our sin is exposed and hearts of repentance grow. The effectiveness and power of our witness does not come because of biblical, theological, or apologetic knowledge alone, but powerful witness comes because we "stand before the Lord of the earth" in

---

[48]See further discussion with numerous references in Beale, *Revelation*, 580-81.
[49]See further Beale, *Revelation*, 576.

whom we trust. The early apostles were powerful in word and deed because "they had been with Jesus" (Acts 4:13).

However, in the busyness of our modern lives, we spend little time with Jesus and wonder why we have so little power. We wonder why the church lacks power to heal broken marriages, lives wrecked by depression and alcoholism, and hearts addicted to pornography. Our lives are frantic, busy, and powerless because we do not take time to "stand before the Lord of the earth." As we stand "beholding the glory of the Lord," then we who are in the temple are "being transformed into the same image from one degree of glory to another" (2 Cor 3:18). This "image" is the image (*eikōn*) of God originally given to Adam and Eve (Gen 1:26-27), which God is restoring in the lives of believers becoming "conformed to the image of his son" (Rom 8:29) in the context of worship in the temple (2 Cor 3:18). Powerful witness comes from ongoing and sustained time in the presence of God, and as we spend time beholding him in his glory, then the power of our witness grows exponentially.

CONCLUSION

In this chapter, we have explored the priestly witness of the church in relation to the church as the inaugurated temple of God. Until the church as a dwelling place of God grows to fill the whole earth, those in the temple who offer priestly service and sacrifice must continue to persevere in this task. The scope of this growth is the entire earth, and the means of this growth is the word of God. Indeed, Adam and Eve as the first priestly couple were to know God's word in order to experience God's presence and protect the first sanctuary from corruption, but they failed in rightly keeping his word, resulting in the Edenic temple becoming unclean. On the other hand, Christ, the Last Adam and true Israel, perfectly kept God's word, and so defeated the serpent (see Mt 4:1-11). All believers truly in union with Christ as their High Priest will progress as priests in knowing God's word and protecting the temple of their families and churches. This temple is inaugurated but not yet consummated, and we are to serve as priests in holiness and images of God in this temple. God paradoxically shines his glorious life through our weakness in sacrifice, thus rendering our priestly, mediatorial witness effective. In this way, his glory is reflected in us as images in his temple. The temple was to be a locus of prayer (e.g., 1 Kings 8:30), and "a house of prayer for all the nations" (Is 56:7, translation altered; Mk 11:17), so the church must be a locus of prayer for all the nations. May God give us grace to realize that we dwell as priests in his temple—in his very presence—wherever we are in this world. May this reality that we are priests who always dwell in the midst of God's tabernacling presence color everything we think, say, and do. As the church serves as priests in God's temple, then his temple will expand to fill the entire cosmos. In the next chapter, we shall explore a picture of that climactic reality.

Chapter Nine

EDEN COMPLETELY
EXPANDED

THE NEW HEAVENS AND NEW EARTH
IN REVELATION 21:1-4

IN REVELATION 21-22, we see a picture of our mission accomplished. God fulfills his original purposes for the cosmos as spelled out in Genesis 1-2, since the dwelling place of God, originally limited to Eden, has expanded to fill the entire new heavens and earth. As one early Christian writer puts it, "He made a second creation at the last; and the Lord says, 'Behold I make the last things as the first'" (Epistle of Barnabas 6:13). To this point, we have traced God's intentions to expand the sanctuary of Eden until it filled the whole earth. Adam and Eve were in the first temple in Eden, but they were cast out of that temple and excluded from God's presence because of sin. After God's repeated appearance to the patriarchs in Genesis, his commitment to his people is seen in the building of the tabernacle and temple. However, even Solomon recognized the inadequacy of this temple at its completion (1 Kings 8:27), and Jesus' death and resurrection are a destruction and raising

up of the temple (Jn 2:19-21). Jesus therefore becomes the cornerstone of the
new temple, and Christians are like living stones being built into the dwelling
place of God (Eph 2:22; 1 Pet 2:5), which "grows into a holy temple in the Lord"
(Eph 2:21) through the proclamation of the word of God during the church
age. Through faithful witness, even in the midst of suffering, the church
expands with power, eventually to fill the entire earth. In this chapter, we
will explore how Revelation 21–22 provides the consummate picture of this
vision, a vision first seen in the sanctuary of Eden and completed in the new
heavens and the new earth.

THE CONSUMMATE ESCHATOLOGICAL STAGE OF
THE WORLD-ENCOMPASSING TEMPLE IN
REVELATION 21:1-22:5

Why is "a new heaven and a new earth" in Revelation 21:1 followed by the
description of a Garden-like city in the shape of a temple (Rev 21:2, 10-21)?
Instead of describing contours and details of the wide expanse of the new
creation, John portrays an arboreal city-temple. The dimensions of Revelation 21:16 ("its length and width and height are equal") are based on the
dimensions of the Holy of Holies in the temple, where the "length . . . and the
breadth . . . and the height" were equal in measurement (1 Kings 6:20 LXX).
The precious stones forming the foundation in Revelation 21:18-21 allude to
the description of Solomon's temple overlaid with gold and filled with precious
stones.[1] Other architectural features of this city are drawn from the prophecy
of the future temple in Ezekiel 40–48 (e.g., Rev 21:2, 10-12; 21:27–22:2).[2] The
entire city is laid out as a temple because "its temple is the Lord God the
Almighty and the Lamb" (Rev 21:22); the temple is not an isolated building
within the city, but the entire city is the temple and dwelling place of God.

Why does he see a new heaven and earth in Revelation 21:1 and then focus
only on a Garden-like city structured like a temple in the remainder of the
vision? While John may see the new creation in verse 1 and then focus on a

---

[1]See, respectively, 1 Kings 6:20-22 (and 1 Kings 5:17) and 1 Kings 7:9-10.
[2]See G. K. Beale, *The Temple and the Church's Mission: A Biblical Theology of the Dwelling Place of
God*, NSBT (Downers Grove, IL: InterVarsity Press, 2004), 346-54, for a fuller description and
discussion of the use of Ezek 40–48 in Rev 21:1–22:5.

Garden-city-temple *in* that world in the following verses, he seems rather to equate the new heavens and earth with the following description of the city-temple. This equation is plausible for three reasons. First, uncleanness is excluded not only from the new Jerusalem but the entire new creation. Revelation 21:27 says, "Nothing unclean will ever enter it" (the city-temple). In the Old Testament, uncleanness was to be kept out of the tabernacle or temple precincts (e.g., Num 19:13, 20; 2 Chron 23:19; 29:16). If the new heavens and earth were distinct from the new Jerusalem, then this verse would suggest that uncleanness may enter the new heavens and new earth but not the city-temple. Rather, it seems more likely that the perimeters of the new city-temple finally encompass the whole of the new creation, so that uncleanness is prohibited from both the new creation and the temple, because both refer to the same thing. Furthermore, the unclean are excluded from the city, just as they are excluded from dwelling in the new creation and thrown into the lake of fire (Rev 22:15; see Rev 21:8, 27; 22:15).

Second, the seeing-hearing pattern of Revelation suggests the equation of the new cosmos with the city-temple. Elsewhere in Revelation, John's vision is interpreted by what he hears (or vice versa). For example, when John hears about a "Lion of the tribe of Judah" who "conquered," he turns to see a Lamb that was slain (Rev 5:5-6). These images mutually interpret one another, as the power of the Lion who conquers is ironically accomplished by dying as the "Lamb who was slain." Similarly, John sees a "a new heaven and a new earth" (Rev 21:1) as the "new Jerusalem, coming down out of heaven" (Rev 21:2), and then he hears that "the dwelling place of God is with man" (Rev 21:3). If what John hears interprets what he sees, then the new heavens and new earth and the new Jerusalem are understood as "the dwelling place of God."

Third, "heaven and earth" in the Old Testament sometimes refer to Jerusalem or its temple,[3] so it is likely that the new heaven and new earth of Revelation 21:1 would refer to the new Jerusalem of 21:2 and 21:9–22:5. Isaiah 65:17-18 illustrates this connection:

---

[3] Jon Levenson, *Creation and the Persistence of Evil: The Jewish Drama of Divine Omnipotence* (San Francisco: Harper & Row, 1988), 89-90; Levenson, "The Temple and the World," *Journal of Religion* 64 (1984): 294-95.

> For behold, I create new heavens
>   and a new earth,
> and the former things shall not be remembered
>   or come into mind.
> But be glad and rejoice forever
>   in that which I create;
> for behold, I create Jerusalem to be a joy,
>   and her people to be a gladness.

Here, the creation of the "new heavens and . . . new earth" *appears* to be interpreted as the creation of "Jerusalem to be a joy." Revelation 21:1-2 follows the pattern of Isaiah 65:17-18. Since the "new heaven and . . . new earth" (Rev 21:1) alludes to the "new heavens and . . . new earth" of Isaiah 65:17, it is natural that the "new Jerusalem" (Rev 21:2) would allude to the recreated Jerusalem of Isaiah 65:18. As a result, the use of Isaiah 65:17-18 in Revelation 21:1-2 suggests that the new heaven and new earth are interpreted as the new Jerusalem.

The new creation and Jerusalem are interpreted then in Revelation 21:3 to be God's tabernacle, the true temple of God's special presence, which is portrayed throughout Revelation 21. God's presence was formerly limited to Israel's temple but began to expand through the church, and will eventually fill the entire new heavens and earth. At that time, the eschatological goal of the sanctuary of Eden filling the entire creation will be fulfilled (so Rev 22:1-3). God's purposes from the beginning are fulfilled at the end of time.[4]

Why does John equate the new cosmos with the arboreal city-temple? God's original purpose was to expand the boundaries of the temple to fill the earth. Adam's call in the sanctuary of Eden was to expand its boundaries until it encompassed the earth, so that the earth would be completely filled with the glorious presence of God (Gen 1:28). Adam's failure eventually led to Israel's tabernacle and temple, patterned after the model of Eden and constructed to symbolize the entire cosmos. Since God intended throughout

---

[4]In other words, eschatology (study of the last things) not only recapitulates the protology (study of the first things) of Eden but escalates it; on which see further Beale, "The Eschatological Conception of New Testament Theology," in *"The Reader Must Understand": Eschatology in the Bible and Theology*, ed. K. E. Brower and M. W. Elliott (Leicester: Apollos, 1997), 11-52.

history to fill the earth with his presence, it should not be surprising that Revelation 21:1–22:5 presents the entire new cosmos as a temple that fills the heavens and earth. These chapters form the consummation of the prophetic hope of an end-time universal temple, which began to be fulfilled through Christ and the church (Eph 2:19-22; 1 Pet 2:4-10; Rev 3:12; 11:1-2).

Therefore, God's purpose and design for his dwelling place from the beginning of creation was to fill the entire heavens and earth (Rev 21:1-3). In Revelation 21:1–22:5, God finally fills all of the heavens and earth with his glorious presence and establishes his dwelling place throughout all of the cosmos. In the temple, as we have seen in chapter four, the Holy of Holies stood for the invisible heavenly dimension of the cosmos where God dwelt, the Holy Place represented the visible heavens, and the outer court symbolized the visible earth (land, sea, the place of human habitation). This cosmic symbolism of the temple pointed to the future when God's presence in the Holy of Holies would break out and fill the visible heavens and the visible earth. This eruption began through Christ and has continued through the church (Christ's body), and will at last completely encompass the whole new earth and heaven because of the work of Christ. At the very end of time, the true temple will come down from heaven and fill the whole creation (Rev 21:1-3, 10; 21:22).

In Revelation 21, the place of God's presence in the Holy of Holies has expanded to fill the whole earth. The city is paved with gold (Rev 21:18) just like the Holy of Holies of Israel's temple (1 Kings 6:20-22; 2 Chron 3:4-8), and the whole city is a cube (Rev 21:16), just as the Holy of Holies was a cube (1 Kings 6:20), since the Holy of Holies has now expanded to fill the entire new creation. As a result, the three sections of Israel's old temple (Holy of Holies, the Holy Place, and the outer courtyard) are no longer found in the temple in Revelation 21, because God's special revelatory presence has expanded out of the Holy of Holies to cover the heavens and the earth. Furthermore, the right of the high priest to wear God's name on his forehead is now extended to all people in the new creation, all of whom will be high priests with God's "name . . . on their foreheads" and standing, not one day a year, but forever in God's presence (Rev 22:4). They are high priests because they have become consummately identified and in union with Jesus, the High Priest.[5]

While God's throne was formerly limited to the heavenly temple,[6] this throne is now in the midst of God's people (see 22:1, 3) throughout the new creation. Furthermore, the ark of the covenant in Israel's Holy of Holies was viewed as Yahweh's "footstool," which was to be seen as an extension of his heavenly throne (see Is 66:1 with 2 Chron 9:18; 1 Chron 28:2; Ps 99:5; 110:1; 132:7; Acts 7:49),[7] where the high priest could enter once a year into the sacred space. In the new creation, all of God's people living throughout the new world will be high priests always in the presence of God, because the dimensions of the heavenly Holy of Holies and God's throne have broken in and expanded to include the entire new cosmos.

As a result, the two outer sections of the temple in the old covenant age of theocratic Israel (the Holy Place and outer court, representing, respectively, the visible sky and the earth)[8] have fallen away like a cocoon from which God's Holy of Holies presence has emerged to dominate all creation. This is why Hebrews 9:8 says "that the way into the holy places is not yet opened as long as the first section is still standing." The way was not blocked for Christ when he entered into the heavenly Holy of Holies, and it will not be blocked for his people when they consummately enter at the very end of the age. Nothing in the final new creation shall barricade the all-glorious presence of God from his people. To expect the restoration of a physical temple after the inaugurated new creation in Christ "would be to offer new reason for confidence in the flesh, to build again the wall of partition and to destroy the unity of the people of God."[9]

---

[5]Note that Rev 1:5-6 portrays believers beginning to be identified with Jesus' kingship and priesthood, and in Rev 22:4 this identification is seen as consummated (for the idea in Rev 1:5-6, see G. K. Beale, *The Book of Revelation*, NIGTC [Grand Rapids, MI: Eerdmans, 1999], 192-96).

[6]The word "throne" occurs approximately thirty-seven times in Revelation outside Rev 21:3, 5 and Rev 22:1-3 with reference either to God or Christ's throne *in heaven*.

[7]As observed earlier, "footstool" was also attached to Solomon's "throne" (2 Chron 9:18), which likely was modeled after the notion that the ark of the covenant was the footstool of God's heavenly throne.

[8]While the previous chapter distinguished the outer from the inner court in the end-time temple in the new age, the two outer sections of the temple here refer to the first temple in the old covenant age.

[9]E. P. Clowney, "The Final Temple," *Westminster Theological Journal* 35 (1972): 177.

PRACTICAL IMPLICATIONS

Refocused hope and prayer. We must reshape our stunted imaginations about the new heavens and earth. When we picture heaven as a place populated with angels on clouds with harps, little longing is evoked. As a result, C. S. Lewis says,

> Most of us find it very difficult to want "Heaven" at all. . . . One reason for this difficulty is that we have not been trained: our whole education tends to fix our minds on this world. Another reason is that when the real want for Heaven is present in us, we do not recognise it.[10]

Today, our desires are trained by multimillion-dollar marketing budgets designed to create an appetite for the latest gadget, article of clothing, or vacation. When we seek to satisfy our appetite for heaven by consuming more stuff, food, or relationships, we end up frustrated. However, Lewis rightly says, "There have been times when I think we do not desire heaven; but more often I find myself wondering whether, in our heart of hearts, we have ever desired anything else."[11]

Hope reshaped by the vision of "a new heaven and a new earth" (Rev 21:1) will form tear-soaked prayer. In this "new heaven and a new earth," God will "wipe away every tear from [our] eyes" (Rev 21:4). What tears will be wiped away? The tears of Revelation 21:4 are the tears of faithful witnesses who stand strong in the face of tribulation, suffering, and even death. Their witness caused them to pay a heavy price; they have sown in tears, but they will reap with shouts of joy in the harvest (see Ps 126:5). When the time of the harvest of the new creation (including resurrection) comes and the saints gather before the throne of God, then God "will wipe away every tear from their eyes" (Rev 7:17).

Similarly, we must sow in tears until the time of harvest. As our vision is reshaped for the temple of the new heaven and new earth, we declare war on the status quo of the brokenness of this world and labor in the place of prayer in the inaugurated form of the temple. As our hearts are broken by the reality of sin in the world and injustice in society, then we must cry

---

[10]Lewis, *Mere Christianity* (New York: HarperCollins, 1952), 135.
[11]C. S. Lewis, *The Problem of Pain* (New York: HarperCollins, 1944), 149.

out before the Lord and pray. This broken world is not the way it is supposed to be. The longing for a new heaven and new earth naturally rises
up from the hearts of those who are engaged in the battle in the midst of
their own suffering and death (Rev 11:7-13) to see "the kingdom of the
world . . . become the kingdom of our Lord and of his Christ" (Rev 11:15)
and to behold "God's temple in heaven . . . opened" (Rev 11:19). These suffering saints rest in their Savior's presence, transformed into high priests
who serve their Lord forever. Despite their unceasing tears in prayer to the
Lord over the brokenness in the world (see Lk 18:7-8), they cry out with
confidence in the promise that "God will wipe every tear from their eyes"
(Rev 7:17), as they "serve him day and night in his temple" forever (Rev 7:15).
Tears are not removed simply because sorrow is forgotten; tears will be
wiped away when sowing leads to the resurrection harvest, and all of the
saints enjoy the full unbroken presence of God in the worldwide tabernacle,
which is their eternal shelter.

Refocused witness. God renews creation through our witness. Even as
John sees "a new heaven and a new earth" (Rev 21:1) as God's dwelling place
filling the cosmos, this new eschatological reality is not only something that
will occur in the future. God declares, "Behold, I am making all things new"
(Rev 21:5). Though the clear focus in Revelation 21:6 is on God's consum-
mative work of new creation, other New Testament passages suggest that
God does not wait until the end of the world to renew all things but has already
begun his work of establishing his dwelling place in all the cosmos. Indeed,
the new creation prophecy in Revelation 21:6 (see Is 43:18-19 in Rev 21:5, and
Is 65:17; 66:22 in Rev 21:1) has already been inaugurated in the first coming
of Christ (e.g., see 2 Cor 5:17 and Rev 3:14[12]).

Isaiah's prophecies of the new creation begin to be fulfilled in Christ's
"faithful and true witness" to his resurrection as "the beginning of the [new]
creation of God" (Rev 3:14, translation altered, which develops Rev 1:5, "Christ
the faithful witness, the firstborn of the dead"). How has God's work of

---

[12]On the inaugurated new creation prophesied by Isaiah in these two passages, see, respectively,
G. K. Beale, "The Old Testament Background of Reconciliation in 2 Corinthians 5–7 and Its
Bearing on the Literary Problem of 2 Cor. 6:14–7:1," *New Testament Studies* 35 (1989): 550-81; and
Beale, "The Old Testament Background of Rev 3.14," *New Testament Studies* 42 (1996): 133-52.

establishing his dwelling place already begun in the new creation? Paul explains this connection in 2 Corinthians 5:17-20:

> Therefore, if anyone is in Christ, he is a new creation. The old has passed away; behold, the new has come. All this is from God, who through Christ reconciled us to himself and gave us the ministry of reconciliation; that is, in Christ God was reconciling the world to himself, not counting their trespasses against them, and entrusting to us the message of reconciliation. Therefore, we are ambassadors for Christ, God making his appeal through us. We implore you on behalf of Christ, be reconciled to God.

"If anyone is in Christ, he is a new creation," and this new creation will be consummated in our "building from God, a house not made with hands, eternal in the heavens" (2 Cor 5:1). The new creation is already made visible in those who are in Christ. This new creation "is from God, who through Christ reconciled us to himself " (2 Cor 5:18). However, God does not accomplish this work of new creation by himself, but he "gave us the ministry of reconciliation" (2 Cor 5:18). Therefore, in this work of new creation, God is "making all things new" through his people entrusted with the message of reconciliation: "Therefore, we are ambassadors for Christ, God making his appeal through us" (2 Cor 5:20). God speaks to the world through the church as his witnesses and reconciles the world to himself through these ambassadors. This work of reconciliation is understood by Paul as the work of new creation, as God is establishing his dwelling place in our midst.

As we witness faithfully despite suffering, we join in God's work in bringing about a "new creation" (2 Cor 5:17). "The one who conquers will have this heritage, and I will be his God and he will be my son" (Rev 21:7). We enter the new Jerusalem as we follow the Lamb wherever he goes (Rev 14:4), the Lion who conquers through his suffering as a slain Lamb (Rev 5:5-6). Conquering is the path of faithful witness in the face of suffering, as seen in the call to "the one who conquers" in the letter of each of the seven churches in Revelation 2–3 (Rev 2:7, 11, 17, 26-28; 3:5, 12, 21; especially in the letters to Smyrna and Philadelphia). The church does not idly watch God accomplish his purposes, but we join the work of establishing the dwelling place that

God is birthing within our midst. Those who conquer and faithfully witness with love and prayer will receive this inheritance.

The church at Philadelphia pictures such faithful witness and is rewarded with a place in God's eschatological temple. Though they had little power in the face of the "synagogue of Satan" (Rev 3:9), Christ calls them to endure patiently and promises "to make [them] a pillar in the temple of my God" (Rev 3:12) and "write on [them] the name of . . . the new Jerusalem," the new Jerusalem that is later described as "the dwelling place of God . . . with man" (Rev 21:3). Because the church faithfully witnesses at Philadelphia, it is included in the dwelling place of God in the new heavens and earth. Such inclusion in God's dwelling place is only possible because they "have kept my word and have not denied my name" (Rev 3:8). Similarly, we are included in God's dwelling place as we keep his word and do not deny his name.

CONCLUSION

In this chapter, we have explored the consummate picture of how the temple has expanded to fill the new heavens and earth. The mission of God's dwelling place is now completed, and God's purposes for Eden are accomplished in the new heavens and the new earth. God's purposes are not realized through passive observation but sacrificial prayer and bold witness. The vision of Revelation 21–22 reshapes our hope for God's purposes in the world as we see the dwelling place of God expanded to fill the entire cosmos. This vision fulfills the commission given in Genesis 1–2 to fill the earth with images and representatives of God.

Admittedly, this vision of Revelation 21–22 as fulfilling the commission of Genesis 1–2 may be surprising to readers otherwise well-acquainted with the Scriptures. In the next chapter, we will explore why some readers may have never seen these truths before.

Chapter Ten

"WHY HAVEN'T I SEEN THIS BEFORE?"

SEEING THE PURPOSE OF GOD'S DWELLING PLACE IN EDEN

WITHOUT 3D GLASSES, watching a 3D movie only reveals blurry images dancing across the screen. As a result, we may understand the basic story but miss many of its nuances, since those glasses help us see more clearly the full picture of the movie. Understanding the cultural and canonical context of the Bible is like putting on a pair of glasses to see the riches of Scripture more clearly. Throughout this book, we have suggested that God's presence fills the new heavens and earth as his temple at the consummation of history. However, some readers at times may have wondered, "Why didn't I ever see this before?" In this chapter, we will try to show that the context of the Bible provides lenses to help us see the richly textured interconnectedness of Scripture.

Already we have explored God's purpose from creation for his dwelling place to fill the entire heavens and earth. Despite sin, this cosmic purpose continues to be evident in a microcosmic manner with the tabernacle and temple, and it is fulfilled even more fully through Jesus and the church as the temple that expands to fill the entire earth. For some, though, the concept of creation as the first temple (and Eden as a smaller temple therein) in Genesis 1–3 and the entire cosmos as a temple in Revelation 21:1–22:5 in particular may seem surprising. Why is that? A number of blinders can obstruct our vision of this glorious reality in Scripture. Specifically, differences in cosmology, biblical unity, history/typology, and understanding "literal" fulfillment may prevent us from seeing things that are present in Scripture. In this chapter, we will explore each of these in turn.

COSMOLOGY

First, our cosmology and view of the world today is different than the biblical writers. The worldview of the Old Testament, especially Genesis 1–2, viewed the cosmos as a temple, and this worldview was common in the ancient Near East. The view of the cosmos as a temple in Genesis 1–2, however, is the pristine perspective of what was only dimly understood by Israel's ancient Near Eastern neighbors. Today, our cosmology is far more naturalistic, focusing on the physical composition of the universe and disconnecting the visible world from the world of the spirit and ideas. We inevitably disconnect the physics of cause and effect from the metaphysics of the nature and purpose of the universe. As a result, the view that the cosmos is created as a dwelling place for God is not empirically verifiable and therefore, in many minds, unreasonable. However, such a statement would be far more comprehensible to the original readers of the Bible.

BIBLICAL UNITY

Second, we often read the Bible in its immediate context without regard to its overarching canonical context. However, later revelation often fills out our understanding of previous revelation, especially if we assume the divine inspiration of all of Scripture (2 Tim 3:16). In focusing on the immediate context of Genesis 1–2, we sometimes neglect the wider understanding of Eden as a temple evident in other parts of the Bible. We have explored at length the parallels between the accounts of creation and the tabernacle and temple, and we suggest that the reason for these parallels is that creation itself is viewed as a temple. The temple is created in a manner similar to the cosmos, since God

> built his sanctuary like the high heavens,
> like the earth, which he has founded forever. (Ps 78:69)

Eden is called the "garden of God" and "the holy mountain of God" (Ezek 28:13-14) and was said to contain "sanctuaries" (Ezek 28:18), language that uniquely describes only the temple. The Lord says,

> Heaven is my throne,
> and the earth is my footstool;
> what is the house that you would build for me,
> and what is the place of my rest? (Is 66:1)

This implies that his house and temple is the entire cosmos and not just a physical temple on earth, which could never ultimately contain God's presence. These later comments in the Bible on the nature of Eden and the cosmos highlight elements of Eden that are easily neglected in our initial reading of these accounts.

Furthermore, the prophecies of a temple in the Old Testament should be understood in light of their New Testament fulfillment. The Old Testament writers not only prophesied future events but a radically different world inaugurated by Jesus. The Old Testament construction and future prophecies of Israel's temple are like a small balloon with a map of the world stamped on them. Without air in this balloon, the contour lines of this map are hardly discernible. As the balloon begins to fill with air, the details of this map become slightly clearer. However, only when the balloon is blown to full size will the details of that map become fully clear. The blown-up version is just as literal as the smaller one, but its details are more understandable.

In like manner, the fulfillment of the temple in the New Testament does not cause a shriveling up or fading away of the architectural temple complex. Rather, the revelation of the New Testament constitutes a material and spiritual expansion from the Old Testament temple that had the symbolic stamp of the future cosmos on it. As revelation progresses in the New Testament, revelatory air expands the balloon of the Old Testament temple with the presence of Christ and his people, and fully inflates at the very end of history with the entire new heavens and earth. Just as John the Baptist, the greatest prophet of the Old Testament era, said that he must decrease that Jesus might increase (Jn 3:30), so with Jesus' coming, Israel's old architectural temple must decrease so that Jesus as the greater temple might increase (Mt 12:6, "Something greater than the temple is here").

Although the Old Testament writers did not have a comprehensive understanding of how their prophecies would be fulfilled, their portrayals and prophecies of the temple became progressively unpacked until they reached a climax in Christ. These prophesied events were in a new world that Jesus inaugurated. These writers are comparable to people in a spaceship far away from the earth. From a distance the earth is only seen as a globe with different shades of color, representing clouds, seas, and land masses. As the spacecraft gets closer and closer to earth, then mountains, rivers, and forests become visible, and then cities, buildings, houses, and people come into focus. Both the distant and close-up views are literal. The close-up picture reveals details that someone with only a distant view could never have guessed were there. The close-up even looks like a different reality from the distance. Nevertheless, both are literal depictions of what is actually there. Similarly, the literal picture of Old Testament prophecy is magnified by the lens of New Testament progressive revelation, which enlarges the details of fulfillment in the beginning new world that will be completed when Christ returns.

Consequently, Christ not only begins to fulfill all that the Old Testament temple and its prophecies of the future temple represent, but Christ is the unpacked meaning for which the temple existed all along.[1] His establishment of the temple (of his body) at his first coming is an initial magnified view of the new creational temple, and Revelation 21:1–22:5 is the clearest and most highly magnified picture we will have this side of the consummated new cosmos. Like the distant and close-up photographs, such a New Testament view of the temple should not be misconceived as diminishing a literal

---

[1]To paraphrase E. P. Clowney, "The Final Temple," *Westminster Theological Journal* 35 (1972): 177.

fulfillment of the Old Testament temple prophecies. Instead, this picture magnifies elements that were only a blur in the Old Testament.

HISTORY AND TYPOLOGY

Third, we must properly understand history and typology. Typology relates "the past to the present in terms of a historical correspondence and escalation in which the divinely ordered prefigurement finds a complement in the subsequent and greater event."[2] In other words, a type might be an event that provides a pattern for a later event. Such types are not limited to events (e.g., the flood as a type of Christian baptism [1 Pet 3:20-22]), but also include persons (e.g., Adam as a type of Jesus Christ [Rom 5:12-14]) and institutions (e.g., the sacrificial system as a type of the sacrifice of Christ [Heb 10:1-18]). When we understand typology in this manner, then it is not as surprising to see the temple as a type that is fulfilled in Christ.

Typological fulfillment of Old Testament historical events in Christ may seem surprising but help us gain a deeper picture of the work that Christ has accomplished. Christ sometimes fulfills Old Testament promises in surprising ways, but careful attention to how those promises are developed and reissued in the Old Testament usually helps us understand their fulfillment.[3] Christ not only fulfills the prophecies but also the people, institutions, and events of the Old Testament, and this fulfillment also comes at times in surprising ways, though always developing (sometimes creatively) something from the original meaning of the Old Testament context.[4]

---

[2]E. Earle Ellis, *The Old Testament in Early Christianity: Canon and Interpretation in the Light of Modern Research*, Wissenschaftliche Untersuchungen zum Alten und Neuen Testament 54 (Tübingen: Mohr Siebeck, 1991), 106. For a succinct introduction to typology, see Daniel J. Treier, "Typology," in *Dictionary for the Theological Interpretation of Scripture*, ed. K. J. Vanhoozer, et al. (Grand Rapids, MI: Baker Academic, 2005), 823-27. A fuller and classic discussion of typology can be found in Leonhard Goppelt, *Typos: The Typological Interpretation of the Old Testament in the New* (Grand Rapids, MI: Eerdmans, 1982). See also G. K. Beale, *Handbook on the New Testament Use of the Old Testament* (Grand Rapids, MI: Baker Academic, 2012), 13-25.

[3]Here we are qualifying the perspective of G. Goldsworthy, *According to Plan* (Leicester: InterVarsity Press, 1991), 87, who seems to see a dichotomy between Old Testament promises and their fulfillment in Christ.

[4]On which see G. K. Beale, "Did Jesus and His Followers Preach the Right Doctrine from the Wrong Texts? An Examination of the Presuppositions of Jesus and the Apostles' Exegetical Method," in *The Right Doctrine from the Wrong Texts?*, ed. G. K. Beale (Grand Rapids, MI: Baker, 1994), 391-98.

For example, the earthly tabernacle was constructed on the pattern/type of the heavenly sanctuary shown to Moses and ultimately fulfilled in Christ. Moses was instructed to "make everything according to the pattern (Greek *typos*; "type") that was shown you on the mountain" (Heb 8:5). The earthly tabernacle is only a "copy and shadow" of the "true" tabernacle to come (Heb 8:5). Christ comes as a new and perfect high priest in heaven, "a minister in the holy places, in the true tabernacle that the Lord set up, not man" (Heb 8:2, translation altered). Clearly, Christ is seated in the true, heavenly tabernacle. Thus, the first tabernacle that Moses constructed was only a small earthly model of the eschatological sanctuary that began with Christ on earth and continued on in his ascent into heaven.[5] The reality is the eschatological, cosmic temple; the shadow is the earthly tabernacle. The author of Hebrews employs the category of typology to help us see how the temple institution foreshadows and anticipates the greater temple that is established in Christ.

Just as the Passover sacrifice was a type for the sacrifice of Christ's body, so the earthly temple is a type that is fulfilled in the cosmic temple beginning with Christ and the church. When we understand this concept of typology, we will not hope for a return of the earthly temple among the glories of the eschatological temple, just as we do not hope in the bare bones of the Passover lamb amidst the riches of the glory of Christ crucified, the ultimate Passover lamb. If we do not understand how types work in Scripture, then we will be surprised at their presence. Typology, however, brings a far greater awareness of the rich interconnectedness of Scripture.

LITERAL FULFILLMENT

Finally, we need to explore the meaning of literal as opposed to figurative prophetic fulfillment. Some would criticize our view of the temple in this book as an overly spiritual and figurative interpretation of the Bible. However, it is simplistic to equate *literal* with physical and *figurative* with spiritual realities. The book of Hebrews suggests the opposite. The earthly sanctuary is figurative (a "copy and shadow"; Heb 8:5), while the heavenly sanctuary

---

[5]The first tabernacle was also a small earthly model or reflection of God's then-existing heavenly tabernacle, which Heb 8:1-5 says Christ entered at his exaltation and which would eventually descend and expand over the whole earth (cf. Rev 21:2).

is the literal sanctuary, "the greater and more perfect tent [tabernacle]" (Heb 9:11), and the "true tent [tabernacle]" (Heb 8:2; 9:24). The reference to the tabernacle as "true" in Hebrews 8:2 and 9:24 connotes both (1) that which is "genuine" or represents "the real state of affairs"[6] and (2) prophetic fulfillment. Just as the "faithful and *true* [*alēthinos*] witness" (Christ, Rev 3:14) is the perfect witness toward which all Old Testament witnesses look forward, so the heavenly tabernacle is the perfect model toward which the Old Testament tabernacle and temple looked forward.[7] All of these physical temples were only intended to be small architectural models and copies of the coming true, eternal temple (see again Heb 8:5). That consummate temple cannot be changed, nor can it ever pass away, because it is not made by human hands but by God's hand as a new creation. Thus, the eschatological temple is true not only in the sense of fulfillment but in that it will remain forever.

Since the heavenly sanctuary is true and the place of God's unfettered presence, it would be bizarre to suggest that another physical temple would be built to bring a return to the shadowy stage of the temple's existence. Since the eschatological temple has been inaugurated, we should not look forward to a return to the imperfect stage of the physical temple's existence. This view is neither an allegorical spiritualization of the Old Testament temple nor of prophecies of an eschatological temple, but an identification of the temple's real meaning. Christ not only fulfills what the temple represents but also is "the meaning for which the temple existed."[8] Jesus himself expressed this when he said, "Something greater than the temple is here" (Mt 12:6).

This new temple is both spiritual and physical. Jesus himself inaugurates this new temple in his (physical) resurrection. Believers are first spiritually part of the temple through spiritual resurrection, and they later become an actual physical part of the temple at the time of the final physical resurrection (e.g., Rev 3:12; 21:1–22:5). Indeed, resurrection is the beginning of the

---

[6]On which see R. Bultmann, "ἀλήθεια κτλ.," in *Theological Dictionary of the New Testament*, ed. G. Kittel et al. (Grand Rapids, MI: Eerdmans, 1964), 1:238-51.

[7]The word *true* in the Old Testament refers to that which really exists and corresponds to reality (1 Sam 9:6; 1 Kings 10:6; 2 Chron 9:5), and *false* describes the opposite. Typically, a false witness or prophet does not speak that which corresponds to reality, whereas the true witness and prophet does (e.g., Num 11:23; Deut 13:2, 14; 17:4; 18:22).

[8]Clowney, "Final Temple," 177.

rebuilding of the eschatological temple (Jn 2:20-22; likewise Mk 14:58; similarly, Heb 9:11, 24; 1 Pet 2:4-7; Rev 21:22). Therefore, the beginning form of the temple is not only composed of God's spiritual presence, but also composed of the spiritually resurrected saints with the physically resurrected Christ as its cornerstone.

Old Testament prophecies of an apparently future architectural temple should be understood in terms of predictions of a nonarchitectural structure.[9] While indefinite prophecies of a future temple may refer to a physical temple like Solomon's, their contexts speak of a temple far more glorious or greater than the prior ones (e.g., Ezek 40–48; Hag 2:1-9; Zech 6:12-13). While this increase in glory may involve a larger building complex, these more indefinite prophecies should be understood in light of the more explicit prophecies of an immaterial nonarchitectural structure,[10] extending over all of Jerusalem (Is 4:5-6; Jer 3:16-17) or even over all of the land of Israel (Ezek 37:26-28; similarly Lev 26:10-13). We have seen elsewhere that even Ezekiel 40–48 is not best interpreted as a prophecy of the building of an architectural temple.[11] Furthermore, Christ and his church have clearly inaugurated the latter-day temple, so the subsequent construction of another physical temple to fulfill these same Old Testament prophecies would seem like a redemptive-historical hiccup and reversal. Indeed, at the destruction of the old world at the end of the age and the advent of the new creation, such an antiquated architectural structure as a localized physical temple seems to have no place.

Our interpretation is not mystical spiritualizing, since the end-time temple is physical, but on a grander scale than former temples. Indeed, as

---

[9]Some of these include prophecies where no establishment of a temple is mentioned but the existence of a latter-day apparently physical temple is assumed and noted (e.g., Dan 8:11-13; 11:31).

[10]See Is 8:13-14 (see the use in 1 Pet 2:8 and 1 Pet 3:14-15); Is 57:15 in relation to Is 66:2; Ps 114:2 ("Judah became his sanctuary"); Ezek 11:16, which refers to an immaterial temple for Israelite exiles.

[11]See Beale, *The Temple and the Church's Mission: A Biblical Theology of the Dwelling Place of God*, NSBT (Downers Grove, IL: InterVarsity Press, 2004), 335-64. If the detailed prophecy of Ezek 40–48 is jettisoned as such a prediction, then other much less descriptive prophecies usually placed in such a category wane in significance. However, see C. L. Feinberg, "The Rebuilding of the Temple," in *Prophecy in the Making*, ed. C. F. H. Henry (Carol Stream, IL: Creation House, 1971), 109, who sees Ezek 40–48 as a reference to a physical structure and, because of its detail, as determinative in defining the other briefer prophecies about the temple as also foreseeing physical structures.

we have tried to demonstrate earlier, the entire new creation is what the localized temple pointed to and symbolized all along. Rather than a little structure, the new cosmos is the physical abode for God's eternal glorious presence. This approach does not employ allegorical methods of interpretation or the uncontrolled reading in of symbols. Rather, the controlling paradigm throughout this study has been Genesis 1:28 in relation to the nonarchitectural sanctuary in the Garden of Eden in Genesis 2. We have seen that later temples and prophecies of the end-time temple often allude to one or both of these Genesis passages, so that the progressive revelation of Old and New Testaments has provided the interpretive "controls" for understanding the biblical theology of the temple.[12] In fact, the image of God's glorious presence in a Garden-like temple has formed an inclusio or kind of "bookend" structure around the entire canon (Gen 2 and Rev 21:1–22:3), providing an interpretive key for understanding the passages about the temple throughout Scripture. Another interpretive key has been the temple's cosmic symbolism, which pointed to the goal of its own extension to become coequal with the cosmos itself.

CONCLUSION

In this chapter, we suggested that perhaps some contemporary readers may not have seen the cosmos as a dwelling place of God for a variety of reasons. Although this view sounds foreign to our naturalistic cosmology, the cosmology of the Old Testament frequently viewed the cosmos as a temple, and so this view would be understandable to some original readers of the Genesis account. When we recognize the unity of the Bible, we see how later revelation shows more clearly how the original creation is like a temple. Also, the New Testament helps us see how the earthly tabernacle was the pattern and type of the end-time tabernacle, a tabernacle that was inaugurated by Jesus' death and resurrection. Finally, this view is not a spiritualizing of the text, but a literal understanding of the texts that are under discussion.

We have observed that God's unique presence in the structural temple in the Old Testament is focused in the new covenant age on the God-man, Christ,

---

[12]The potential criticism of allegorizing noted in this paragraph has been lodged by Feinberg, "Rebuilding of the Temple," 108-9.

the true temple. As a result of Christ's resurrection, the Spirit continued building the end-time temple with the living stones of God's people and extended the temple into the new age. This building process will culminate in the eternal new heavens and earth as a paradisal city-temple. Or, more briefly, the temple of God has been transformed into God, his people, and the rest of the eternal new creation as the temple.[13] How should this reality affect our lives? We will conclude in the next chapter by exploring a few practical applications.

---

[13]This is a paraphrase of the book title of A. Spatafora's *From the "Temple of God" to God as the Temple* (Rome: Gregorian University Press, 1997).

Chapter Eleven

CONCLUDING PRACTICAL REFLECTIONS

FOUNDATIONAL CONVICTIONS FOR SACRIFICIAL MISSION IN THE TEMPLE

MISSION DEMANDS SACRIFICE, and sacrifice grows from conviction. We began this book with a brief look at missionary Adoniram Judson, who spent thirty-eight years in Burma, lost two wives, seven of thirteen children, and eventually died at sea in terrible pain. Deep conviction formed the bedrock of his sacrificial labor, and today Burma (known today as Myanmar) has over four million Christians because of that sacrifice. Almost 250 million people in over three thousand unreached and unengaged people groups remain around the world, many in closed countries where the gospel can penetrate only with great sacrifice and cost.[1] However, if our faith simply revolves around "subjective well-being,"[2] then nobody will make the painful

---

[1]"Global Status of Evangelical Christianity: Listing of Unreached and Unengaged People Groups," International Mission Board of the Southern Baptist Convention, accessed August 13, 2012, www.imb.org/research/reports. Of these, almost 1,189 people groups do not have a written Scripture in their language.

[2]See detailed discussion in Christian Smith with Melinda Lundquist Denton, *Soul Searching: The Religious and Spiritual Lives of American Teenagers* (Oxford: Oxford University Press, 2005), 163-64.

sacrifices that such mission demands. In this concluding chapter, we will share a few convictions that we hope will ignite a greater flame of passion for God's worldwide mission.

SACRIFICE

Conviction brings sacrifice of our lips and our lives, and the spread of the gospel demands sacrifice. As priests in the worldwide temple of God, our essential sacrifice is our body, "a living and holy sacrifice, acceptable to God," which is our "spiritual worship" (Rom 12:1, translation altered). In so doing we follow our Savior's example, who "gave himself up for us, a fragrant offering and sacrifice to God" (Eph 5:2).

Sadly, today the church too often fails in its calling to offer "spiritual sacrifices acceptable to God" (1 Pet 2:5). Our lives often fail to reflect the faith that we profess.[3] A groundbreaking study of the beliefs of American teenagers termed their outlook as "moralistic, therapeutic deism":

> This is not a religion of repentance from sin, of keeping the Sabbath, of living as a servant of sovereign divinity, of steadfastly saying one's prayers, of faithfully observing high holy days, of building character through suffering, of basking in God's love and grace, of spending oneself in gratitude and love for the cause of social justice, et cetera. Rather, what appears to be the actual dominant religion among U.S. teenagers is centrally about feeling good, happy, secure, at peace. It is about attaining subjective well-being, being able to resolve problems, and getting along amiably with other people.[4]

Such a therapeutic deism is a far cry from the God who calls us to "present [our] bodies as a living sacrifice, holy and acceptable to God" (Rom 12:1), which is usually not a comfortable and easy thing to do.

What are the roots of such feel-good, therapeutic deism? Why does the biblical call for sacrifice and holiness fall on deaf ears? The call to holiness

---

[3]In a 2009 LifeWay Research survey of US young adults born between 1980 and 1991 who call themselves Christian, 65 percent said they rarely or never attended worship services, 67 percent did not read the Bible, and 65 percent rarely or never prayed with others. See Cathy Lynn Grossman, "Survey: 72% of Millennials 'More Spiritual Than Religious,'" *USA Today*, October 14, 2010.

[4]Smith and Denton, *Soul Searching*, 163-64.

in the Bible is always an imperative based on the indicative reality of what God has already done for us in Christ. God establishes us "as a spiritual house" so that we might "offer spiritual sacrifices acceptable to God through Jesus Christ" (1 Pet 2:5). Ignorance of the realities of what God has already done for us render the imperatives of the gospel frustrating and impossible. However, it is "since we have these promises," the multifaceted and rich promises of the Old Testament, that we have the power and thus motivation to "cleanse ourselves from every defilement of body and spirit, bringing holiness to completion in the fear of God" (2 Cor 7:1). Without the power to obey, the motivation to obey lags considerably; you cannot motivate a lame man to train for a marathon! But power to obey elicits motivation to carry out the task. Too many churches and youth groups, however, have busied themselves in entertaining and not teaching young people, and a powerless morality flows out of such anemic theology. We must restore a rich understanding of the promises of God fulfilled in Christ in order to access the power and have the motivation to bring "holiness to completion in the fear of God" (2 Cor 7:1).

THE POWER OF THE WORD

The power of our witness grows from the power of God's word burning in our hearts. Adam's failure as a priest in the sanctuary of Eden grew out of his failure to keep God's word. God places Adam and Eve into the Garden "to work it [cultivate] and keep it" (Gen 2:15). Though this task was to be accomplished by obeying God's word (Gen 2:16-17), Eve disobeyed God's word (see discussion in chapter 2). Adam and Eve did not remember God's word, and they "fell" and failed to extend the boundaries of God's Edenic temple.

If God's dwelling place is to fill the earth, then faithfulness and obedience must prevail in the place of Adam's disobedience. The building of the tabernacle raises hopes for Israel's obedience in the face of Adam's failure, but the sin of the golden calf during that time precipitates Israel's persistent idolatry throughout her history. However, Jesus, the Last Adam and true Israel, is faithful where the first Adam and first Israel were faithless. When Jesus, "the son of Adam, the son of God" (Lk 3:38), is tempted in the wilderness like

Adam and Israel before him, Jesus prevails by quoting accurately from God's word and thus being fully faithful to that word (Lk 4:4, 8, 12). Specifically, Jesus quotes passages from Deuteronomy where Moses called Israel to obey God's word faithfully in the face of their own failure in the wilderness (Deut 8:3 in Lk 4:4; Deut 6:13 in Lk 4:8; Deut 6:16 in Lk 4:12). Christ succeeded where Adam and Israel failed because he remembered God's word, was faithful to it, and obeyed it.

If Jesus, the Word made flesh and tabernacle of God's presence (Jn 1:14), quoted God's Word and remained faithful to it in order to resist temptation and deception from Satan, should we not also follow him in doing the same thing? If we are to expand God's presence to the ends of the earth, then God's Word must burn in our hearts. However, much of the church is ignorant of even basic facts in the Bible.[5] Without knowledge of even such basic facts of the Bible, Christians stand no chance against the wily and subtle distortions of God's Word that the evil one has used throughout history.

We must return to the solid foundations of the Word of God. Pastors must carefully study to teach and preach God's Word. Congregations must embrace expository preaching corporately, while individuals must exult in God's Word through careful, personal study. If slight though significant changes to God's word deceived Eve, then detailed study and knowledge of God's Word is needed to protect us from deception and sin. We must store up the ammunition of God's Word to fight sin like the psalmist:

> I have stored up your word in my heart,
> that I might not sin against you. (Ps 119:11)

The tragedy of the ubiquitous presence of God's Word in our homes and our phones is that we have failed to hide it in our hearts. When temptation strikes, only the Word of God in our heart can protect us; the proximity of God's

---

[5]From a random survey of two thousand Americans in 2012 by the American Bible Society. While 79% saw themselves as knowledgeable about the Bible and 68% believed that the Bible contains everything they need to live a meaningful life, 54% could not properly identify the first five books of the Bible, and 50% thought that "Abraham [instead of Moses] lifted his staff and parted the Red Sea" (Barna Research, "The State of the Bible 2012" [New York: American Bible Society, 2012], 5, 25-27).

Word in a book or on our phone is not enough. By our priestly task of keeping and guarding God's Word in our heart, a priestly task in which Adam failed, we can be faithful in the face of temptation and fulfill our priestly ministry in the temple. Through such priestly ministry, we convey God's presence to those outside that temple in unbelief. As they trust Christ, they also become a part of the temple in Christ, expanding the size of the present temple.

THE POWER OF PRAYER

If we do not pray, then God's presence will never penetrate the darkest places of the earth. Our status as God's dwelling place must not lull us into complacency because of our privileged position. At the end of time, the temple was to "be called a house of prayer for all peoples" (Is 56:7), who would be priests "to minister" to God, and one of the ways they were to minister was to be through prayer (Is 56:6-7). However, those in charge of Israel's temple failed to pray for the nations and were judged and rejected by Jesus (on which, see the discussion of Mt 21:13; Mk 11:17; Lk 19:46 in chapter 6). Today, we must beware lest our status as God's dwelling place lull us into spiritual complacency instead of spurring us to sacrificial prayer.

What do we pray for? Jesus teaches us to pray, "Give us this day our daily bread" (Mt 6:11). Prayer for daily needs provides the training wheels for prayer; God's provision in these areas helps us expect God to work in greater needs. As we are priests of God in his temple, God promises to provide for his priests (Is 61:6). Early in my (Mitch's) marriage, I remember looking at our bank statement and realizing that we had only a hundred dollars to our name. The problem was that our taxes were due very soon, and we would owe over a thousand dollars. That night, my wife and I prayed, "Give us this day our daily bread." Specifically, we asked that God would provide a fish with a coin in its mouth to pay the taxes like he did for Peter (Mt 17:27). The next day we had fish for dinner and fished out a gold coin worth two thousand dollars to pay our taxes. Actually, that did not happen. However, the next day in the mail, the dreaded letter from the IRS was on top of the pile, requesting money for our taxes. I hid that in my pocket to keep my wife from stress. At the bottom of the pile was an envelope with a check for more than two thousand dollars—refund money for a deposit that my wife had made as an international student at college almost five years earlier. God provided more than enough for our daily needs.

As our faith grows through the training wheels of prayer, we begin to pray with greater faith and expectancy. Jesus commanded:

> Have faith in God. Truly, I say to you, whoever says to this mountain, "Be taken up and thrown into the sea," and does not doubt in his heart, but believes that what he says will come to pass, it will be done for him. Therefore I tell you, whatever you ask in prayer, believe that you have received it, and it will be yours. (Mk 11:22-24)

When Jesus spoke of "this mountain," he probably looked at the Temple Mount in Jerusalem. In the wider context of this passage, Jesus curses the fig tree, cleanses the temple because of its failure to be "a house of prayer for all the nations" (Mk 11:12-17), and exposes the ignorance of the temple authorities (Mk 11:27-33; see further discussion in chapter 6). Praying to move a mountain is a prayer for transformation into a new temple. Just as the fig tree withered under Jesus' curse because it bore no fruit (Mk 11:21), so ethnic Israel and her flawed temple would wither because they did not bear the fruit of its witness to the nations. However, Jesus' curse is not only a message of judgment but hope, because when God's people would pray, then the mountains would move and the nations would be saved. Jesus himself becomes the cornerstone of a new temple (Mk 12:1-11) that would expand to fill the entire earth (see discussion in chapters 6 and 7).

Therefore we should pray. We should pray not only for our daily needs, but we should pray for the nations. Jesus drove out the people in the old temple because of their failure to make it "a house of prayer for all the nations" (Mk 11:17). Jesus took over the role of the old temple in becoming the *true* temple. When we believe in Jesus, we become identified with him as the new, true temple. Our status as priests in the temple and dwelling place of God should ignite a greater passion for prayer in our lives. God gives us authority as participants in the end-time temple so that we might pray and break down barriers for his glorious presence to spread throughout the whole earth. Jesus not only commands us to "make disciples of all nations" but also promises us, "Behold, I am with you always, to the end of the age," since "all authority in heaven and earth has been given to me" (Mt 28:18-20). In chapter six, we explored the "making of disciples" as a temple-building process. The power of mission is found in the authority of Christ. As discussed in chapter six, the authority of Christ grows out of the authority of the son of man/Adam in Daniel 7, who completes what Adam failed to accomplish in ruling over the animals in Genesis 1–3. As our hearts embrace God's worldwide call to mission, we pray with the full authority of Christ in heaven and on earth to overcome every challenge to enlarging God's temple by drawing many in through faith in Christ, the true temple.

Sometimes we know of our authority in theory but fail to practice that authority in reality. As a pastor, I (Mitch) am often called into challenging situations. One time, a woman called me because her drunk husband was verbally berating her son. After listening to the situation, I prayed over the phone in the name of Jesus and commanded the father to go to sleep. To this day, I don't know where I got the idea to pray him to sleep; I've never done that before and I have never done that since. But at that time, this prayer came out with a sense of urgency within me. We closed our prayer, and I hung up the phone. The next day I saw them. A bit embarrassed at my unorthodox prayer the night before, I hesitatingly asked, "How did it go last night?" The son replied, "Yeah, it was really weird. Around the time that my mom called you, he went out for a smoke. Then he came back in the room and just went back to sleep!"

We have great authority as children of God and members of God's temple. As we embrace our calling to spread the dwelling place of God to fill the entire earth, we will encounter many obstacles: discouragement, financial setbacks, depression, persecution, recalcitrant hearts, and broken families. However, we must pray. God has given us authority to spread his glorious tabernacling presence to the ends of the earth, and we access that authority through prayer.

Even as Adoniram Judson's sacrificial commitment to the Burmese people grew out of conviction, this conviction was sustained and tended in the secret place of prayer:

> Without this the others [self-denying sacrifice and doing good to others] have no strength.... Consider secret prayer as one of the three great works of thy life. Arrange thy affairs, if possible, so that thou canst leisurely devote

two or three hours every day, not merely to devotional exercises, but to the very act of secret prayer and communion with God.[6]

Judson decries the "defective" opinion of those who only pray morning and night and calls people to "endeavor, seven times a day, to withdraw from business and company, and lift up thy soul to God." Such prayer, indeed, sustained his soul in the face of tremendous sacrifice, and such prayer can sustain our souls as well.

As Christians, we now are identified with Jesus through the Spirit as part of the end-time temple. Until Christ returns, we pray as new covenant priests and exiled new Israelites as we live as pilgrims in exile on the old, fallen earth. In both cases, our prayer is directed toward God in his heavenly Holy of Holies until it descends to fill and encompass the new earth. Prayer as an activity inextricably linked to the temple is what is behind Jesus' words in Matthew 18:19-20:[7] "Again I say to you, if two of you agree on earth about anything they ask, it will be done for them by my Father in heaven. For where two or three have gathered together in my name, there I am among them." Our ongoing task is to serve God as praying priests in his temple in which we always dwell and of which we are a part. The prayers of saints are now the "incense" offerings given to God (Rev 5:8; 8:3-5) that replace the old incense offerings made at the altar of burnt offering and the altar of incense in the Holy Place (e.g., 1 Chron 6:49). Our prayers fulfill the Old Testament prophecy when incense offerings would be made to God "in every place" (Mal 1:11).

CONCLUSION

Just as plants cannot flourish without adequate sunlight, so the church will not flourish without remaining in the light of God's tabernacling presence. The church will not bear fruit and fill the earth unless it stays out of the shadows of the world and remains in the light of God's presence. The mark of the true church is an expanding witness to the presence of God in the invisible temple: to our families, the church, our neighborhood, city, country,

---

[6]Edward Judson, *The Life of Adoniram Judson* (Philadelphia: American Baptist Publication Society, 1883), 572.

[7]Judson, *Life of Adoniram Judson*, 165, who makes almost the identical application to the Christian community; likewise I. H. Marshall, "Church and Temple in the New Testament," *Tyndale Bulletin* 40 (1989): 211.

and ultimately the whole earth. But the church will only expand its witness as it stands in the presence of God, submitted to the power of his Word and praying in brokenness for the nations.

As God's people exult in and manifest his presence to the world, then we expand the boundaries of his new Garden-temple to fill the earth. May the church, the true Adam, true Israel (and corporate Adam), and true temple, experience the priestly blessing pronounced on Israel from the tabernacle as it extends God's tabernacling presence:

> The LORD bless you and keep you;
> the LORD make his face to shine upon you and be gracious to you;
> the LORD lift up his countenance upon you and give you peace.
>   (Num 6:24-26)[8]

The psalmist understands this very blessing from the book of Numbers to have a worldwide goal:

> May God be gracious to us and bless us
>   and make his face to shine upon us, *Selah*
> that your way may be known on earth,
>   your saving power among all nations.
> Let the peoples praise you, O God;
>   let all the peoples praise you!
> Let the nations be glad and sing for joy,
>   for you judge the peoples with equity
>   and guide the nations upon earth. *Selah*
> Let the peoples praise you, O God;
>   let all the peoples praise you!
> The earth has yielded its increase;
>   God, our God, shall bless us.
> God shall bless us;
>   let all the ends of the earth fear him! (Ps 67:1-7)

May God release his grace and blessing upon his church, his temple, that his saving power may be seen upon all nations.

---

[8]Not coincidentally, this blessing was apparently first pronounced "on the day when Moses had finished setting up the tabernacle" (Num 7:1), which further suggests that the blessing at that time was God's glorious presence that dwelt in the tabernacle. This presence now blesses those who are a part of "the temple of God" in Christ and the Spirit.

DISCUSSION QUESTIONS

1. What evidence do we see in Genesis 1–2 that the Garden of Eden is a temple and place of God's presence? How can that affect the way we live in creation? (chap. 1)

2. How does Adam's commission to multiply and fill the earth with image bearers connect to our calling to make disciples? How does this calling work out in your own life? (chap. 2)

3. God's presence guarantees the fulfillment of the commission to Adam even in the face of sin, as seen with Isaac (Gen 26:24), Jacob (Gen 28:15), and Moses (Ex 3:12). How can the promise of God's presence encourage you to fulfill God's commission in the face of your own weakness and sin? (chap. 3)

4. The tabernacle is Eden remixed, setting the dwelling place of God in the midst of sin in the world. How does the tabernacle deal with the problem of sin? (chap. 4)

5. Even as Israel sinned and faced exile, the prophets reiterated God's purpose for his presence to fill the earth as seen in Eden (Is 54:2-3; 66:1-2; Ezek 37:26-28; Dan 2; Jer 3:16-17). Consider one of these

passages. What new insight does it offer on how the presence of God will fill the earth? (chap. 5)

6. Why did Jesus turn over tables in the temple (Jn 2:13-17)? How might the church today similarly miss the point of its witness to the nations? (chap. 6)

7. Which passages help you see most clearly that Jesus himself is the locus of the new temple? What insight does this knowledge about Jesus bring? (chap. 6)

8. As Jesus' death and resurrection inaugurates a new creation (Mt 27:50-54), how does Jesus succeed where Adam and Israel failed? (chap. 6)

9. The church as the dwelling place of God makes reconciliation possible (Eph 2:14-22) and calls for purity (2 Cor 6:16-17). What implications might this have for you? (chap. 7)

10. How does God use his Word and suffering to grow the church? How do you see that in Scripture, in history, or in your own life? (chap. 7)

11. As priests in God's temple, we offer our witness as our sacrifice before God. Powerful witness comes in sackcloth and repentance (Rev 11:3), standing before the Lord in worship (Rev 11:4). Does this posture of repentance and worship characterize your witness? Why or why not? (chap. 8)

12. Revelation 21 pictures God's presence filling every corner of heaven and earth. How can the glorious vision of God's presence in Revelation 21 refocus your sense of hope and witness? (chap. 9)

13. In chapter ten we consider a number of reasons we may not have seen the interconnectedness of God's purpose in Scripture: differences in our understandings of cosmology, biblical unity, history/typology, and "literal fulfillment." Which of these concepts is most helpful for you in understanding the overarching themes of Scripture that we see in this book?

14. We conclude this book on a note of prayer in chapter eleven, praying with Numbers 6:24-26 and Psalm 67. Take some time to pray that God's own presence might shine on his people and propel us forward in witness to the nations.

BIBLIOGRAPHY

Allison, D. C. *The New Moses*. Minneapolis: Fortress, 1993.

Anderson, Courtney. *To the Golden Shore: The Life of Adoniram Judson*. Valley Forge, PA: Judson Press, 1987.

Arnett, Jeffrey. *Emerging Adulthood: The Winding Road from the Late Teens Through the Twenties*. Oxford: Oxford University Press, 2004.

Augustine. *Confessions*. Translated by J. G. Pilkington. New York: Liveright Publishing, 1943.

Bachmann, M. "Himmlisch: der 'Tempel Gottes' von Apk 11.1." *New Testament Studies* 40 (1994): 474-80.

Barna Research. "The State of the Bible 2012." New York: American Bible Society, 2012.

Barrois, G. A. *Jesus Christ and the Temple*. Crestwood, NY: St. Vladimir's Seminary Press, 1980.

Barth, Karl. *Church Dogmatics*. Edited and translated by G. W. Bromiley and T. F. Torrance. London: T&T Clark, 1995.

Bauckham, Richard. *The Climax of Prophecy: Studies on the Book of Revelation*. London: T&T Clark, 1993.

———. "James and the Jerusalem Church." In *The Book of Acts in Its Palestinian Setting*, edited by Richard Bauckham, 452-62. Grand Rapids, MI: Eerdmans, 1995.

Beale, G. K. *The Book of Revelation*. New International Greek Testament Commentary. Grand Rapids, MI: Eerdmans, 1999.

———. "Colossians." In *Commentary on the New Testament Use of the Old Testament*, edited by G. K. Beale and D. A. Carson, 842-46. Grand Rapids, MI: Baker Academic, 2007.

———. "Did Jesus and His Followers Preach the Right Doctrine from the Wrong Texts? An Examination of the Presuppositions of Jesus and the Apostles' Exegetical Method." In *The Right Doctrine from the Wrong Texts?* edited by G. K. Beale, 387-404. Grand Rapids, MI: Baker, 1994.

———. "The Eschatological Conception of New Testament Theology." In *"The Reader Must Understand": Eschatology in the Bible and Theology*, edited by K. E. Brower and M. W. Elliott, 11-52. Leicester: Apollos, 1997.

———. *Handbook on the New Testament Use of the Old Testament*. Grand Rapids, MI: Baker Academic, 2012.

———. *A New Testament Biblical Theology: The Unfolding of the Old Testament in the New*. Grand Rapids, MI: Baker Academic, 2011.

———. "The Old Testament Background of Reconciliation in 2 Corinthians 5–7 and Its Bearing on the Literary Problem of 2 Cor. 6:14–7:1." *New Testament Studies* 35 (1989): 550-81.

———. "The Old Testament Background of Rev 3.14." *New Testament Studies* 42 (1996): 133-52.

———. *The Temple and the Church's Mission*. New Studies in Biblical Theology 17. Downers Grove, IL: InterVarsity Press, 2004.

———. *We Become What We Worship: A Biblical Theology of Idolatry*. Downers Grove, IL: InterVarsity Press, 2008.

Blenkinsopp, Joseph. "Structure of P." *Catholic Biblical Quarterly* 38 (1976): 275-92.

Block, Daniel I. *The Book of Ezekiel*. New International Commentary on the Old Testament. Grand Rapids, MI: Eerdmans, 1998.

———. "The Privilege of Calling: The Mosaic Paradigm for Missions." *BibSac* 162 (2005): 387-405.

Blomberg, Craig. *Contagious Holiness: Jesus' Meals with Sinners*. New Studies in Biblical Theology 19. Downers Grove, IL: InterVarsity Press, 2005.

Bock, D. L. *Luke 9:51–24:53*. Baker Exegetical Commentary on the New Testament. Grand Rapids, MI: Baker, 1996.

Callender, D. *Adam in Myth and History*. Harvard Semitic Museum Publications. Winona Lake, IN: Eisenbrauns, 2000.

Calvin, John. *Institutes of the Christian Religion*. Edited by John T. McNeill. Translated by Ford Lewis Battles. Library of Christian Classics 21. London: SCM Press, 1960.

Caragounis, C. C. *Peter and the Rock*. Beihefte zur Zeitschrift für die neutestamentliche Wissenschaft 58. Berlin: Walter de Gruyter, 1990.

Carson, D. A. "Matthew." Vol. 8 of the *Expositor's Bible Commentary*, edited by Frank E. Gaebelein, J. D. Douglas, and Walter Kaiser. Grand Rapids, MI: Zondervan, 1984.

Clowney, Edward P. "The Final Temple." *Westminster Theological Journal* 35 (1972): 156-89.

Cohen, Jeremy. *Be Fertile and Increase, Fill the Earth and Master It*. Ithaca, NY: Cornell University Press, 1989.

Cole, A. *The New Temple*. London: Tyndale Press, 1950.

Daniélou, J. *Primitive Christian Symbols*. London: Burns and Oates, 1964.

Davidson, Richard M. *Flame of Yahweh*. Peabody, MA: Hendrickson, 2007.

Davies, W. D., and D. C. Allison. *The Gospel According to Saint Matthew*. International Critical Commentary. Edinburgh: T&T Clark, 1991.

Douglas, Mary. *Leviticus as Literature*. Oxford: Oxford University Press, 1999.

Edersheim, Alfred. *The Temple*. Peabody, MA: Hendrickson, 1994.

Ellis, E. Earle. *The Old Testament in Early Christianity: Canon and Interpretation in the Light of Modern Research*. Wissenschaftliche Untersuchungen zum Alten und Neuen Testament 54. Tübingen: Mohr Siebeck, 1991.

———. "II Corinthians V.1-10 in Pauline Eschatology." *New Testament Studies* 6 (1959–1960): 211-24.

Evans, Craig A. *Mark 8:27–16:20*. Word Biblical Commentary 34. Nashville: Thomas Nelson, 2001.

Feinberg, Charles. "The Rebuilding of the Temple." In *Prophecy in the Making*, edited by C. F. H. Henry, 89-112. Carol Stream, IL: Creation House, 1971.

Fitzmyer, Joseph. *The Gospel According to Luke X–XXIV*. Anchor Bible Commentary 28A. New York: Doubleday, 1985.

France, R. T. *Jesus and the Old Testament*. Grand Rapids, MI: Baker, 1971.

Gage, W. Austin. *The Gospel of Genesis*. Winona Lake, IN: Eisenbrauns, 1984.

Giblin, C. H. "Revelation 11.1-13: Its Form, Function, and Contextual Integration." *New Testament Studies* 30 (1984): 433-59.

Glickman, S. C. *Knowing Christ*. Chicago: Moody, 1980.

Goldsworthy, Graeme. *According to Plan*. Leicester: InterVarsity Press, 1991.

Goppelt, Leonhard. *Typos: The Typological Interpretation of the Old Testament in the New*. Grand Rapids, MI: Eerdmans, 1982.

Grossman, Cathy Lynn. "Survey: 72% of Millennials 'More Spiritual Than Religious.'" *USA Today*. October 14, 2010. https://usatoday30.usatoday.com/news/religion/2010-04-27 -1Amillfaith27_ST_N.htm.

Gunkel, Hermann. *Genesis*. Macon, GA: Mercer University Press, 1997.

Hagner, Donald A. *Matthew 14–28*. Word Biblical Commentary 33B. Dallas: Word, 1995.

Heath, Chip, and Dan Heath. *Made to Stick*. New York: Random House, 2007.

Holladay, William L. *Jeremiah*. Hermeneia. Philadelphia: Fortress, 1986.

Hooker, M. D. *The Gospel According to Mark*. Black's New Testament Commentary. Peabody, MA: Hendrickson, 1991.

Hutter, M. "Adam als Gärtner und König (Gen 2, 8, 15)." *Biblische Zeitschrift* 30 (1986): 258-62.

Judson, Edward. *The Life of Adoniram Judson*. Philadelphia: American Baptist Publication Society, 1883.

Juel, Donald. *Messiah and Temple*. Society of Biblical Literature Dissertation Series 32. Missoula, MT: Scholars Press, 1977.

Keller, Tim. *Center Church: Doing Balanced, Gospel-Centered Ministry in Your City*. Grand Rapids, MI: Zondervan, 2012.

———. *Counterfeit Gods: The Empty Promises of Money, Sex, and Power, and the Only Hope That Matters*. New York: Dutton, 2009.

Kilgallen, John. *The Stephen Speech*. Analecta Biblica 67. Rome: Biblical Institute Press, 1976.

Kim, Seyoon. "Jesus—The Son of God, the Stone, the Son of Man, and the Servant: The Role of Zechariah in the Self-Identification of Jesus." In *Tradition and Interpretation in the New Testament: Essays in Honor of E. E. Ellis*, edited by G. F. Hawthorne and O. Betz, 134-48. Grand Rapids, MI: Eerdmans, 1987.

Kissane, E. J. *The Book of Isaiah*. Dublin: Browne and Nolan Ltd., 1943.

Kline, Meredith G. *Glory in Our Midst*. Overland Park, KS: Two Age Press, 2001.

———. *Kingdom Prologue: Genesis Foundations for a Covenantal Worldview*. Eugene, OR: Wipf and Stock Publishers, 2006.

Koehler, L., and W. Baumgartner. *The Hebrew and Aramaic Lexicon of the Old Testament*. Revised by W. Baumgartner and J. J. Stamm. New York: Brill, 1994.

Lacocque, A. *The Book of Daniel*. London: SPCK, 1979.

Levenson, Jon D. *Creation and the Persistence of Evil: The Jewish Drama of Divine Omnipotence*. San Francisco: Harper & Row, 1988.

———. "The Temple and the World." *Journal of Religion* 64 (1984): 289-98.

Lewis, C. S. "First and Second Things." In *God in the Dock: Essays on Theology and Ethics*, 279-81. Grand Rapids, MI: Eerdmans, 1994.

———. *Mere Christianity*. New York: HarperCollins, 1952.

———. *The Problem of Pain*. New York: HarperCollins, 1944.

Lewis, T. J. "Beelzebul." In *Anchor Bible Dictionary*, edited by D. N. Freedman, 1:638-40. New York: Doubleday, 1992.

Litfin, Duane. *Word Versus Deed: Resetting the Scales to a Biblical Balance*. Wheaton, IL: Crossway, 2012.

Lohmeyer, E. *Die Offenbarung des Johannes*. Tübingen: Mohr Siebeck, 1970.

Longman, Tremper. *Immanuel in Our Place: Seeing Christ in the Old Testament*. Phillipsburg, NJ: P&R, 2001.

Marshall, Colin, and Tony Payne. *The Trellis and the Vine*. Kingsford, Australia: Matthias Media, 2009.

Marshall, I. H. "Church and Temple in the New Testament." *Tyndale Bulletin* 40 (1989): 203-22.

McCartney, D. J. "*Ecce Homo*: The Coming of the Kingdom as the Restoration of Human Vicegerency." *Westminster Theological Journal* 56 (1994): 1-21.

McGavran, Donald. *The Bridges of God*. New York: Friendship Press, 1955.

Meyers, Carol. "Lampstand." In *Anchor Bible Dictionary*, edited by D. N. Freedman, 4:141-43. New York: Doubleday, 1992.

———. "Lampstand." In *Harper's Bible Dictionary*, edited by P. J. Achtemeier, 546. San Francisco: Harper & Row, 1985.

———. *The Tabernacle Menorah: A Synthetic Study of a Symbol from the Biblical Cult*. Missoula, MT: Scholars Press, 1976.

———. "Temple, Jerusalem." In *Anchor Bible Dictionary*, edited by D. N. Freedman, 6:359-60. New York: Doubleday, 1992.

———. "Tree of Life, The." In *Harper's Bible Dictionary*, edited by P. J. Achtemeier, 1094. San Francisco: Harper & Row, 1985.

Millard, A. R., and P. Bordreuil. "A Statue from Assyria." *Biblical Archaeology* 45 (1982): 135-41.

Nolland, John. *Luke 18:35–24:53*. Word Biblical Commentary 35C. Dallas: Word, 1993.

Piper, John. *Let the Nations Be Glad*. 3rd edition. Grand Rapids, MI: Baker Academic, 2010.

Poythress, Vern. *The Shadow of Christ in the Law of Moses*. Brentwood, TN: Wolgemuth and Hyatt, 1991.

Sarna, Nahum. *Genesis*. JPS Torah Commentary. Philadelphia: Jewish Publication Society, 1989.

Schwarz, Christian. *Natural Church Development: A Guide to Eight Essential Qualities of Healthy Churches*. Carol Stream, IL: ChurchSmart Resources, 1996.

Smith, Christian. *Lost in Transition*. Oxford: Oxford University Press, 2011.

Smith, Christian, with Melinda Lundquist Denton. *Soul Searching: The Religious and Spiritual Lives of American Teenagers*. Oxford: Oxford University Press, 2005.

Spatafora, A. *From the "Temple of God" to God as the Temple*. Rome: Gregorian University Press, 1997.

Tolkien, J. R. R. *The Letters of J. R. R. Tolkien*, edited by H. Carpenter and C. Tolkien. Boston: Houghton Mifflin, 2000.

Towner, William S. *Genesis*. Louisville: Westminster John Knox, 2001.

Treier, Daniel J. "Typology." In *Dictionary for the Theological Interpretation of Scripture*, edited by K. J. Vanhoozer et al., 823-27. Grand Rapids, MI: Baker Academic, 2005.

Vance, A. B. "The Church as the New Temple in Matthew 16:17-19: A Biblical-Theological Consideration of Jesus' Response to Peter's Confession as Recorded by Matthew." ThM Thesis, Gordon-Conwell Theological Seminary, 1992.

Vawter, Bruce. *On Genesis.* Garden City, NY: Doubleday, 1977.

Von Rad, Gerhard. *Old Testament Theology.* Translated by D. M. G. Stalker. New York: Harper & Row, 1962.

Wagner, Peter. *Strategies for Church Growth: Tools for Effective Mission and Evangelism.* Ventura, CA: Regal Publishing, 1987.

Wallace, Howard N. "Tree of Knowledge and Tree of Life." In *Anchor Bible Dictionary,* edited by D. N. Freedman, 6:656-60. New York: Doubleday, 1992.

Walton, John. *Genesis.* New International Version Application Commentary. Grand Rapids, MI: Zondervan, 2001.

Warren, Rick. *The Purpose Driven Church.* Grand Rapids, MI: Zondervan, 1995.

Wenham, Gordon. *Genesis.* Word Biblical Commentary 1-2. Waco, TX: Word, 1987.

Wevers, J. W. *Ezekiel.* New Century Bible. Camden, NJ: Thomas Nelson, 1969.

Woudstra, M. H. "The Tabernacle in Biblical-Theological Perspective." In *New Perspectives on the Old Testament,* 88-103. Waco, TX: Word, 1970.

Wright, N. T. *Colossians and Philemon.* Tyndale New Testament Commentary 12. Grand Rapids, MI: Eerdmans, 1986.

———. *Jesus and the Victory of God.* Minneapolis: Fortress, 1992.

Yun, Brother, Peter Xu Yongze, Enoch Wang, with Paul Hattaway. *Back to Jerusalem: Three Chinese House Church Leaders Share Their Vision to Complete the Great Commission.* Carlisle: Piquant, 2003.

AUTHOR INDEX

SCRIPTURE INDEX

ANCIENT LITERATURE INDEX

ESSENTIAL STUDIES IN
BIBLICAL THEOLOGY

FROM ADAM AND ISRAEL
TO THE CHURCH
A Biblical Theology
of the People of God

BENJAMIN L. GLADD

EXODUS
OLD AND NEW
A Biblical Theology
of Redemption

L. MICHAEL MORALES

REBELS AND
EXILES
A Biblical Theology
of Sin and Restoration

MATTHEW S. HARMON

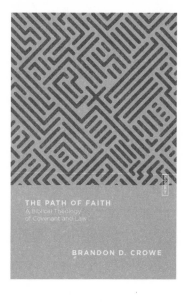

THE PATH OF FAITH
A Biblical Theology
of Covenant and Law

BRANDON D. CROWE